English Literary Criticism and Theory

An Introductory History

M S NAGARAJAN

Orient BlackSwan

All rights reserved. No part of this book may be (i) modified, reproduc
or utilised in any form, or by any means, electronic or mechanical,
including photocopying, recording or by any information storage and
retrieval system, in any form of binding or cover other than in which it
published, without permission in writing from the publisher; or (ii) used
or reproduced in any manner for the purpose of training, development
operation of artificial intelligence (AI) technologies and systems, includ
generative AI technologies, without permission in writing from the
copyright holder.

ENGLISH LITERARY CRITICISM AND THEORY

ORIENT BLACKSWAN PRIVATE LIMITED

Registered Office
3-6-752 Himayatnagar, Hyderabad 500 029, Telangana, India
email: centraloffice@orientblackswan.com

Other Offices
Bengaluru, Chennai, Guwahati, Hyderabad,
Kolkata, Mumbai, New Delhi, Noida, Patna

© Orient Blackswan Private Limited 2006
First Published 2006
Reprinted 2006, 2013, 2014, 2015, 2016, 2017, 2018, 2019 (twice), 202
2022, 2023, 2025, 2026

ISBN 978-81-250-3008-9

Typeset in Aldine 401 BT 10.5/12.5 by
Orient BlackSwan

Cover and book design
© Orient Blackswan Private Limited 2006

Printed in India at
B.B. Press, Tronica City, Ghaziabad, UP 201 103

Published by
Orient Blackswan Private Limited
3-6-752 Himayatnagar, Hyderabad 500 029, Telangana, India
E-mail: info@orientblackswan.com

In loving memory of my parents

The duty of criticism is neither to depreciate nor dignify by partial representations, but to hold out the light of reason, whatever it may discover, and to promulgate the determinations of truth, whatever she shall dictate.

Samuel Johnson, The Rambler

The world would be unimaginably poorer without literature and literature, in turn, needs the understanding, the sifting and judging provided by criticism.

Réné Wellek

Contents

Preface

'Why one more?' you might very well ask. Many learned histories of literary criticism exist, all written by historians of eminence. The best known are the ones by George Saintsbury, J.W. Atkins, Réné Wellek, Wimsatt and Brooks—names that conjure up visions of great and assiduous scholarship. To say the least, they are irreplaceable. Widely known for their deep erudition, their interpretations are at once acutely penetrating and illuminating. I shall not try to belong to this roster. This work has in mind, rather, the average Indian graduate student in English who needs a coherent history of criticism that will present to him some of the basic, seminal facts and influential ideas pertaining to literary creation and literary understanding. *English Literary Criticism and Theory: An Introductory History* is primarily designed to meet the requirements of such students and their teachers. We do not have in our market a handy and workmanlike type of history, a contour map of the critical scene over the ages. The existing ones are partial studies with commentaries on individual critics, an amalgam of critics and critical opinions. These do not fill the need of the English student for a coherent, systematically organised and synoptic view of the discipline of criticism. This book is the first of its kind: it addresses a specific need of undergraduate and graduate students of English in our universities.

Such a project demands a drastic principle of selection. A good number of critics have been omitted in this study. I had to make, regretfully, such acts of omission even as I made joyfully, a choice of inclusion. Such of those critics who have theorised about literature, and those who have applied their theory to specific works of literature, choose themselves automatically. They deserve their place in any history on account of their critical merit as well as their influence upon the critical temper of the succeeding ages. Alas, critics like Shelley, Keats, Addison, Lamb, Hazlitt, and de Quincey—to mention a few—have had to be left out! When we come to contemporary theories, the intention is to make a study of theoretical movements, rather than a study of individual critics. This is only an introductory history, and it does not purport to be a full-sized encyclopedia. This volume is far from being a specialised work in the subject. Received notions and ideas which are in wide circulation in the context of literary study, and ideas which an average Indian student is expected to equip himself with are given ample treatment with supporting textual evidences, wherever necessary. As such, the work is in the nature of a general introduction to the subject of literary criticism and theory.

The division into seven sections classifies the two-thousand-year-old history of Western critical thought into convenient units. The sections on classical and medieval criticism are meant to serve as the ground on which English criticism has grown. The middle section is devoted to a treatment, individually, of the critics who are prescribed for study in our undergraduate/graduate curriculum. The sections, starting from New Criticism going on to contemporary theories, take up movements as such. Several critics figure in these theoretical systems. While every effort is made to present their thought, they have not been given individual treatment. Given the scope of the book, it is well nigh impossible to subject everyone who has contributed to a theoretical movement to a close scrutiny. The audience for the book, as has been pointed out earlier, is not the advanced student of literary criticism, but an average graduate student.

I have received generous help from many in the writing of this book, all of whom I cannot thank individually. Dr N. Eakambaram, my colleague of many years, kept urging me to write a book on the subject I had taught for so long, and provided the enthusiasm for it. I shall always remain indebted to him. Professor S. Jagadisan read the initial drafts of this work and suggested improvements, besides a generous loan of his class notes. Professor S. Ramaswami, who has made me what I am today, has inspired all my academic writing; I owe him a heavy debt of gratitude. Our scriptures say, *guru sakshat para brahma*: he is. I am also grateful to my colleague of long-time ago, P.K. Sundara Rajan, for a meticulous reading of the manuscript, setting aside his own work on Richard Crashaw. My wife, children and grandchildren lent their support to me during the years I was working on my book: it was much too long in the making. Much of the work was done in the Alexander Library of Rutgers University, New Jersey. My occasional visits to the libraries of Harvard University, University of Connecticut, Dallas

Community College and Framingham State College too were helpful in gathering material. If this *Introductory History* is found useful by way of guidance to the understanding and judgment of literature to my Indian students, and enriches their knowledge of the strengths and weaknesses of the Western critical heritage, I shall feel more than amply rewarded for my efforts.

I extend my thanks to Mrs Usha Aroor of Orient BlackSwan: she has supported my efforts patiently right from the day I approached her with a vague idea of this book. My special thanks are reserved for the in-house editor Dr Madhavi Menon for her kindness and understanding all through the strenuous editing process. She has indeed been the better craftsperson! I am extremely honoured that this book is being published by Orient BlackSwan.

M.S. Nagarajan
Chennai

Background

iterary creation is almost as old as human history and literary criticism nearly as old as literature. But in a strict sense, the study of literature, as we understand it now, began as a serious pursuit only after the Renaissance. During the Renaissance, literary study meant different things to different people. It was history to those who studied it as a documentation of the events of the past. Those who looked for moral truths studied it as philosophy. And there were scholars who made a serious study of it with a view to establishing its authenticity as a literary text to be treasured and embalmed on purpose for a life beyond life. Some approached it as a piece of rhetoric while philologists studied it in order to gain knowledge of language. Literary criticism, meaning understanding and appreciating literature, evolved gradually out of these studies. Again, whereas most of these disciplines had developed methods of studying literature, literary criticism did not have any systematic method of enquiry into the artistic phenomenon.

The word 'criticism' is derived from the Greek root *krinei* which means 'to judge,' and the term *kritikos* means 'a judge of literature'. The Greek term originated as early as in the fourth century. The term *criticism,* as applied to the study and analysis of a body of literary writing, developed only in the seventeenth century in Europe, and later, became a term used in common parlance accepted as being authoritative. This wide and general use of the term 'criticism', meaning literary criticism, encompasses three distinguishable fields of inquiry—literary theory, literary history, and literary (or evaluative) criticism retaining the original Greek sense. Literary history, also called history of literature, treats the whole body of literary works as a process governed historically by time. It treats works as an integral part of a historical process. In the words of Robert Spiller, 'it is concerned with describing and explaining the expression *in literature* of a people during a period of time, in a place, and usually in a specific language' (55). Literary theory lays down principles of literature, its categories and criteria and describes the features and forms that make up a literary work. It is a systematic account of the nature of literature. Literary criticism deals with the understanding and appreciation of specific works and authors. It has generally been the practice to use this term to include all literary theory. In more recent times, however, scholars and aestheticians are uneasy with the use of this term, and its implications. This conventional use of the term restricts itself and does not allow for extension. It does not accommodate, for instance, considerations of the aesthetic, intellectual and political implications that are as important as the formal elements of a work. And so, the word *criticism* has come to be replaced by more comprehensive terms as *theory* (just theory and not literary theory), cultural studies, etc. In this sense, the term *theory* includes, in a very broad sense, the origins and history of literature: its nature and function, and its relationship to our life and society.

Each of the terms defined above is an independent form of enquiry in one sense. But in another sense, the knowledge gained in one is made use of in the other. A literary historian, for example, performs the task of textual analysis while discussing the relationships among texts, or while explaining how one movement led to another, historically speaking. A literary critic, while interpreting a work, discusses its relation to its period. Without an adequate knowledge of historical relationships, a critic is likely to go astray in his judgments, which may be no more than mere subjective pronouncements of what he likes and what he dislikes. Literary history and literary criticism enrich each other, and there can be no separation between the two.

In the discipline of literary criticism, we need to know about the earliest critics and their works that deal with literary criticism, however remotely they might be related. Ancient criticism has much to tell us. Historically speaking, ancient critics and their criticism are valuable to us; they were the earliest in point of time, and they represent the Graeco-Roman tradition in the arts on which the whole edifice of Western criticism rests. There is a great deal to be learnt from them. Intrinsically, they have a value of their own. They enquired into the nature and function of art.

They inspired, to a large extent, those who came later. This Graeco-Roman tradition is very different from our hoary Indian tradition that goes farther back in time. The origin of the Sanskrit critical tradition can be traced to the *Rig Vedas* and the Dravidian tradition to *Tholkappiam* of the fifth century BC. This Graeco-Roman tradition represents, even today, the orthodox critical tradition, which came under review and revision only in the nineteenth century. Whenever we take up any critic or critical work for discussion, we are in a position to recognise that some of the ideas that we talk about have been borrowed from the ancients. It will be futile to begin a study of modern criticism without at least a working knowledge of the ancients. They are the indispensable aid to a study of literary criticism as a unified discipline. In the words of J. W. H. Atkins: 'These ancient critics grasped firmly some of the main problems of art; they set forth for the first time many of the basic principles which underlie literary excellence. And many of the things said were said in final fashion; they could never again be put so simply and convincingly' (1: 10).

It is a commonplace that there are no beginnings in the history of criticism. Classical literary criticism takes its origin from classical philosophy. It was in the early fourth century, mostly from out of the views held by Plato and Aristotle who, for the first time, made a sustained and systematic inquiry into the nature of art and its modes of existence, Western literary criticism took its shape as an independent discipline. The whole of the Western critical tradition, as we know now, grew out of these two founding fathers. But if we allow ourselves to go farther back in time, we can trace some essential questions and problems relating to art and its forms in the works of Greek poets, scholars and rhetoricians. They must have talked, among other things, about literature and arts but much of what they talked about are no longer available to us. Yet it is possible to discern some general remarks and opinions about individual poets and their works. Unequipped with a developed vocabulary to articulate these issues, these poets and scholars did raise questions pertaining to art and did offer some opinions on how to judge works of art.

This early criticism—if we may use the term with reference to the critical writings of these poets—was by and large intuitive, though unsystematic; but we can put together the available scattered notions about art out of this early critical writing. The basic provisos of such early criticism have come to be called 'proto-criticism'. The earliest classical criticism extols the poet. He is thought to be the guiding star and the guardian angel of society. He is the lawgiver, moral teacher; he is inspired by the divine muse which grants him special powers to please his audience and bring them knowledge not available elsewhere. Hence he is the prophet as well as the priest. The Romans conferred the exalted title of 'vates' on the poet. The poet was on a par with the prophet. The divine oracles were delivered in verse. David's *Psalms* are nothing short of sheer poetry. Romantic theories that we have associated with the eighteenth century come close to such a belief about the poet's role in society. In Homer (circa 8th century BC) and Pindar (518–438 BC), among others, one notices this function assigned to the poet. Gods provide the poets the means by which they achieve excellence in speech in addition to the wisdom that they convey to people. They are also the mediating agents between the Gods and the people.

Aristophanes (circa 450–385 BC), the Greek poet, may be singled out as one who, for the first time, spoke of the rights and duties of the poet. He took upon himself the role of a social reformer and satirist. Deeply concerned with the integrity of his society, he exposed the political demagogues and the sophists. He echoed the view that the poet's function is to teach people to become responsible Greek citizens. He is generally thought to be one of the founding fathers of ancient literary criticism. His play *Frogs* is the earliest attempt at practical criticism in which the playwright weighs the merits of Aeschylus and Euripides as stylists. The conflicting views of both these poets are weighed and considered by Dionysus, patron and god of the theatre of festivals. In his literary judgments based on a commitment to moral values, Aristophanes displays his taste and deep insight into the phenomenon of artistic creation. He takes into consideration factors such as the choice of language in poetry and drama, and factors that constitute merit in art, with concrete examples. His selective and apt quotations from the works under examination, and his perceptive comments are similar to the analyses practised by present day critics. In the end when Aeschylus is declared the winner in the contest, the Greek Chorus concludes:

The entire population will gain
From a poet so sound and so sane,
He will tend us,
Defend us;
We'll all bless that bulging great brain. (1485–90)

Works Cited

Atkins, J.W.H. *Literary Criticism in Antiquity: A Sketch of its Development.* 1934. Vol.1. Gloucester, Mass.: Peter Smith, 1961.

Spiller, Robert. 'Literary History.' *The Aims and Methods of Scholarship.* Ed. James Thorpe. 2nd ed. Hyderabad: American Studies Research Centre, 1970.

1
Classical Criticism

Plato (circa 429–347 BC)

lato gathered the odds and ends of proto-criticism, and articulated them in a coherent manner. It is often said that the history of Western philosophy is a series of footnotes to Plato. We may substitute Western criticism for Western philosophy, and the remark would still hold good. He was the first to expound a theory of art in general terms, and his views have exerted a strong influence on every generation of thinkers who came after him. Any discussion on the general nature of literature must begin with Plato whose views are diverse and even contradictory. For instance, on the one hand, he is opposed to art as an end in itself, and, on the other hand, he glorifies and extols the artist and emphasises his role in human life. Sir Philip Sidney paid him the most extravagant tribute when he said, 'Of all philosophers, I have esteemed him most worthy of reverence and with great reason, since of all philosophers he is the most poetical.' He was a philosopher and a poet rolled into one. In his dialogue form, one finds the truth and science of philosophy coexisting with the beauty and art of poetry. One of his greatest admirers, Shelley says that Plato exhibits the rare union of close and subtle logic with the Pythian enthusiasm of poetry. Is it not, then, a paradox that Plato, the most poetic of philosophers is the avowed enemy of poetry? In Book 10 of the famous *Republic,* he banishes all poets from his ideal state. He exiles poets on two grounds. The first is the metaphysical and, the second, ethical. All art, being fiction, is untrue and necessarily twists and distorts truth, the attainment of which is the goal for man.

> This was the conclusion at which I was seeking to arrive when I said that painting or drawing, and imitation in general are engaged upon productions which are removed from truth, and are also the companions and friends and associates of a principle within us which is equally removed from reason, and that they have no true or healthy aim (35).

Art is an imperfect reflection of the real world, which, in turn, is a shadow, a pale reflection of the ideal world. Hence, Art, an imitation of an imitation, is thrice removed from reality. Arts are third-hand distortions of truth. This view goes by the name of the 'doctrine of ideas or forms.' The second objection is on the ground of ethics. Plato regarded the study of morals as basic, and wanted all arts to be guided by moral principles. Imitative art has a corrupting influence on man who should be governed by reason and not passion. A philosopher is the moral custodian of the welfare of his people; he has a right to stand in opposition to any form of artistic imitation that deviates from the norms of reason. Hence, he condemns poetic imitation on the ground that it 'fed and watered the passions instead of drying them up, and let them rule instead of ruling them as they ought to be ruled, with a view to the happiness and virtue of mankind' (37). He advocates strict censorship, and exhorts poets to inculcate in people the moral virtues of forbearance, tolerance and rectitude. Plato favours the narrative form more than the imitative (dramatic) form for the latter represents evil directly. For Aristotle, all forms of narration are imitative, and Plato's wish that virtue should be rewarded and vice punished would render Aristotle's notion of the tragedy non-viable. In Book 5 of *Republic*, Plato has a positive view of art in so far as it contributes to the spiritual growth of people. Imitation, which performs such a function, has a principal place in his view. Truth is the end in such imitation, and not pleasure.

Plato's didacticism seems unacceptable to many critics. However, some neoplatonists have modified it to mean that the poet directly imitates reality, and not merely copies images of physical nature. He is a seer, an inspired being who can see beyond the nature of things. Though much of modern criticism derives from Aristotle rather than Plato, whenever we discuss problems relating to value, truth, and social significance of literature, we find that there is a storehouse of knowledge available in Plato. It is with him that literary criticism truly begins! As a pathfinder, he inspired people and gave direction to criticism and stimulated it. He firmly established criticism, and placed it on a high pedestal. Poetry is not just a matter of words and technique, but is a lofty and mysterious creation of man. No wonder that Plato is regarded as 'the fountain of that which is most living in the orthodoxy of later ages.' In the words of Atkins, 'And his influence remains to the present day, that of one of the greatest of critics, in the truest sense a light-bringer, ever guiding men's steps to the spiritual side of art' (1: 70). It must be said to the credit of Plato that he did literature and literary study a great service. Have not his strong remarks directed against poets in his *Republic* generated equally strong defence, opening up fresh areas of dialogue?

ARISTOTLE (384–322 BC)

Also called the Stagyrite, Aristotle, the peripatetic philosopher established in 335 *the Lyceum*, a 'gymnasium' sacred to Apollo, and directed it for thirteen years. The Academy was devoted to all available forms of knowledge—mathematics, speculative and political philosophy, biological sciences, and the arts. On a modest estimate, his writings run to four hundred volumes. He spent some twenty invaluable years under the tutelage of Plato before establishing his own academy. Never again can there be such an instance of a brilliant student guided by an incomparable teacher! We (in India) know him as the tutor of Alexander the Great who almost conquered north-western India way back in 326 BC. Aristotle was an academic, a man of letters, a naturalist, and, in the words of Eliot, 'a perfect critic.' Aristotle owed his philosophical career to his great master Plato. He addresses many problems that Plato addressed, but in many cases, he shows his radical departure from Plato whose name is not even mentioned in his famous treatise *Poetics*, the most valuable document in the history of Western criticism. Interpreters of Aristotle used the term 'acromatic' with reference to his works by which is meant that each work of his cannot be completely understood without the aid of his other works. Knowledge of his *Ethics, Metaphysics,*

Rhetoric, for example, would throw greater light on *Poetics*. Aristotle dismisses Plato's view of the poet as an instructor when he says, 'correctness in poetry is not the same thing as correctness in morals, nor yet is it the same as correctness in any other act.'

Rhetoric and *Poetics* contain the literary criticism of Aristotle, and both works are his lecture notes. Many of his concepts are still being discussed and reinterpreted to suit the present day needs of literary critics. He seems to be more modern than most modern critics. His insights into the artistic phenomenon, the argument, and the sheer power of impeccable logic in which these are put forward, make the treatise a veritable delight in the art of sustained philosophical inquiry. Unfortunately, we are not in possession of the original text of *Poetics,* but there are a few manuscripts belonging to different centuries, which are available in translations. There is a eleventh century translation that is perhaps the earliest and the most important. This is the primary source for all later translations. There is a tenth century Arabic translation, and a few other thirteenth and fourteenth century translations of the Greek manuscript. Though there are differences of opinion with regard to some passages, we are not up against textual difficulties in our understanding of the basic concepts of Aristotle. There are some inescapable stylistic difficulties owing to the rather terse rendering of the text. The most plausible reason, of course, is that the works are only lecture notes gathered together by his students, and not a consciously developed, full-fledged treatise. Another view, not wholly acceptable, of course, is that his works are esoteric in nature, meant for a chosen and initiated few who may not need lengthy explanations. Apart from the *Bible*, no other work has appeared in more editions than *Poetics*. No other work of literary criticism, or theory has exerted as strong an impact as this short, and incomplete, treatise. *Poetics* raises many important and fundamental critical issues, constantly debated by scholars and critics. There are wide disagreements among them about the full meaning and implications of these terms and concepts. However, there is a close argument that rigorously controls the key concepts. Four of them deserve our special attention and these are 1. *mimesis* 2. *katharsis* 3. *hamartia* and 4. *spoudaios*.

***Mimesis*:** The most commonly accepted English equivalent of this Greek term is imitation. In a critical or literary context, the word imitation carries a special meaning. This term was peculiar to Greek thought. The term 'fine art' is a later coinage. The Greek phrases were 'imitative arts' and 'modes of imitation.' The concept of imitation is central to Aristotelian logic even as it is to the Platonic, but with an essential difference. The Platonic view (as we saw earlier) is that the world is an imperfect reflection of an ideal archetypal order. The world is a lower order of reality, and poetry, being an imitation of an imitation, is thrice removed from reality. Hence, Plato banished poets from his ideal commonwealth. Aristotle rejects Plato's doctrine of ideas. Whereas for Plato imitation implies copying, and hence, trivial and insignificant, it is creative and dynamic for Aristotle. The artist is the maker, and his creations are imitations of human action, human character, and human emotions. It is representation and not just copying that he has in mind, not a representation of men as they are. The artist imitates things as they ought to be, and so, art is a free and voluntary activity of the human consciousness, free from any utilitarian motives. Arts are different from crafts. Again, imitation bears relationship to learning and acquiring knowledge. We derive pleasure from the artistic representations of even the most repelling and disgusting of things. We see into the life of things. Imitation leads us from the particular to the universal, which is how the experience in learning takes place. It is a clarification of the particular representation which reveals to us universal laws of nature. Art is a source of insight into life. *Mimesis* also implies the active mode of constructing an art object according to the laws of probability and necessity (internal coherence) by which a universal form is imparted to the works. Aristotle gave a new dimension to the word 'imitation'. It does not mean photographic reproduction. It is often said that drama holds the mirror up to nature. The image of nature we see in drama is very different from the image of ourselves that we see in a mirror. The kings we come across in history books are different from the kings we see in Shakespeare's plays. Poetic imitation, for Aristotle, is an imitation of inner human action.

Katharsis: This is a key word in Aristotle, occurring only twice in *Poetics.* The meaning of the latter usage is what concerns us. It occurs in chapter 6 in which tragedy is defined as 'an imitation of an action that is serious, complete, and of a certain magnitude; in language embellished with each kind of artistic ornament, the several kinds being found in separate parts of the play; in the form of action, not of narrative; through pity and fear effecting the proper purgation (*katharsis*) of these emotions.' Aristotle's theory of *katharsis* may be considered to be his reply to Plato's charge against tragedy that it devitalises our emotions. The twin emotions of pity and fear (or terror) are dangerous and unhealthy according to Plato. Pity and terror constitute the two-fold audience reaction to the sight of tragic suffering. Pity is aroused by the magnitude of the suffering undergone by the protagonist, and terror by the knowledge that tragic suffering and fate overtake one similar to us. This is the awareness that is brought home to us when we witness a tragedy. Pity and fear (terror) describe a process of moral and imaginative identification with the agent. When we come out of this involvement, we find ourselves inwardly transformed, and feel a sense of release and serenity. *Katharsis* describes this process, or experience.

The meaning of the term has given room to a lot of discussion out of which at least four may be highlighted: 1. therapeutic, 2. moral, 3. structural and 4. intellectual. The therapeutic meaning, also called purgation, is akin to the homeopathic system of medicine that holds the view that the right cure for an illness is administering an agent similar to the disease. In this sense *katharsis* is translated as purgation. It means that by presenting the emotions of pity and fear to the audience, the audience is cured of the excesses of these emotions. The assumption is that all of us are subject to excesses of pity and fear, and tragedy is the panacea for such an illness. Tragedy effects *katharsis* by generating the very conditions that it seeks to cure. Aristotle cites the example of music. Those who are in a state of external agitation pass into a state of serenity on listening to exciting music. Similarly, spectators pass through purgation or emotional disturbance to emotional health or stability. But, many scholars cannot and do not accept this medical metaphor, the theory that Aristotle should have conceived of an art form merely as a system of cure.

The moral interpretation is closely analogous to the therapeutic; only it renders the term as 'purification'. The purpose of tragedy is to purify the emotions of the audience by disciplining it, and refining it by removing the excesses. Understood as a religious metaphor, *katharsis* suggests the sense of purification. We normally shrink from scenes of violence and crime in real life, or react to them with a feeling of horror and revulsion. It is paradoxical that we go to the theatre to experience delight from the spectacle of suffering. If we only see scenes of physical violence on the stage, such scenes would fill us with a sense of unrelieved horror. The element of external suffering on the stage is but one part, and perhaps the least important part, of the tragedy. True tragedy unfolds an inner process. It presents the protagonist in a state of clash at three levels—clash with oneself, with others, and with impersonal, inscrutable forces beyond one's control and knowledge. In this three-dimensional conflict, the protagonist displays a certain dignity and probity. We see this person survive the epic struggle in moral or spiritual terms though he/she may be physically or technically overpowered. The apparent destruction of virtue, goodness and innocence strikes terror. But, ultimately we realise that the good, virtuous, and innocent people may be destroyed, but the values of goodness, virtue, and innocence remain sound and secure. The moral foundation may be shaken, but it only becomes stronger and deeper. Our faith in the moral law suffers a temporary shock only to be restored and fortified. It is this awareness that produces a feeling of subtle, indefinable joy, or exaltation and serenity for an audience. We do not go to the theatre only to be purged of our emotions. F.L. Lucas is reported to have remarked, 'the theatre is not a hospital'. Tragedy goes much beyond a clinical or surgical function. It is productive of pleasure springing from spontaneous compassion for the protagonist who enters a larger, nobler world. Tragedy leads to an awakening. A new scale of value arises. In this sense tragedy is 'lustatory' in its influence, resulting in an enlargement of our spirit. The experience or end product of witnessing tragedy is similar to the joy and purification resulting from our participation in a ritual. Once again, many scholars find it hard to accept that Aristotle should have conceived of art as a moralising agent.

Structural interpreters put forth the view that it is a process by which the protagonist can absolve himself of the supposed evils he has perpetrated, so that the audience can respond with emotions of pity and fear appropriate for the occasion, and be willing to free the protagonist from pollution. The intellectual interpretation builds up further by rendering this term 'intellectual clarification'. *Katharsis* is a kind of 'insight experience'. It is an aesthetic experience that consists in the perception of coherence, a totality of significance underlying a series of incidents. This experience is 1. pleasurable and not painful as the events would be if seen in real life, 2. the pleasure is similar to that arising from the process of learning, 3. the learning process lies in the discovery of the relationship between the particulars of the plot and the universals they signify and it is these universals that impart coherence and totality to the particulars, 4. this experience leads to 'clarification,' an enlargement and deepening of awareness. According to Aristotle, the character of a wise, virtuous man is that he feels emotions—fear, anger, pity, pleasure, etc.—at the right time, with reference to the right people, the right object, with the right motive and in the right way. This is the principle of moderation. Nothing should be in excess! *Katharsis* obeys and conforms to this principle. Drama is a stimulus. It rouses our emotions from potentiality to activity. For the duration of the play, the potential emotions are stirred, and directed towards the right objects in the right way. When they return to potentiality after the play, 'it is a more trained' potentiality than before. Our responses are those of good, wise people. The result of *katharsis* is emotional balance, or equilibrium. It involves restoration of emotional health. Learning is a source of pleasure, and art is great for this very reason. That is why poetry is more philosophical than history. Whichever meaning one may support, Aristotle sees art not as being harmful as Plato does, but as being beneficial, either as therapy, or a moralising agent, or as a release from guilt, or as a supreme form of learning.

Hamartia: This term is usually rendered into English as 'tragic flaw'. It derives its meaning etymologically from archery. It means, 'to miss the mark,' 'to err or fail'. In the Gospel according to St John, the term means, 'sin'. The protagonist commits a moral error, and, for this, he receives his punishment. This religious connotation seems rather far-fetched. Hence, the view has been modified to relate the term to an intellectual rather than a moral error. For example, a character of conspicuous virtues and abilities who has distinguished himself through them in one sphere is thrown into a different sphere of action. Tragic flaw results in his exercise of his value system in the new sphere in which it does not hold good. Shakespeare's tragic heroes are an instance in point. Does not Brutus come to grief by imposing the ethical on the political? King Lear is a feudal lord. The tragic flaw occurs when he applies the laws that operate in the feudal world to the family by demanding a profession of love from his daughters. Feudal laws and relationships are at variance from familial ones. Affection is inexhaustible and a profession of it is a lie. Lear has sinned against love, demanding from it what it cannot give. His sufferings must be the atonement for this. There is no question of pity or fear if the protagonist receives a punishment that he deserves. Aristotle's view of tragedy is far more sophisticated than a melodramatic notion. Tragedy is an art form that does not accept perfect or divine justice. It is a refined form that poses and presents deeper philosophic questions about life in general.

***Spoudaios* (noble character):** For Aristotle, character is what determines moral choice. He even classifies genres using this principle. Tragedy imitates noble character, and comedy base character. Some critics, especially the neoclassical critics, mistake this as socially determined. Arthur Miller accuses Aristotle of social snobbishness and arrogance. He chooses Willy Loman, the common man as his protagonist in *Death of a Salesman*. Aristotle never even once said that someone of the common mould cannot be a tragic hero. Miller fails to grasp the basics in Aristotle's logic. Here is Miller:

> In terms of his (Willy Loman's) character, he has achieved a very powerful piece of knowledge, which is that he is loved by his son. In this he is given his existence, so to speak—his fatherhood, for which he has always striven and which until now he could not achieve. That he is unable to take this victory thoroughly to his heart, that it closes the circle for him and propels him to his death, is the wage of his sin, which was to have committed himself so completely to the counterfeits of dignity and the false coinage embodied in his idea of success that he can prove his existence only by bestowing 'power' on his posterity, a power deriving from the sale of his last asset, himself, for the price of his insurance policy (34).

It would be unfair to charge Aristotle with class-consciousness and arrogance. The nobility referred to in *Poetics* is morally determined, and not socially construed. The protagonist is important enough to claim the attention of the audience. The life of the protagonist is worth the sacrifice he is making, and we get deeply concerned with the enormity of the effect of his loss. In our days of democracy we may not be confronted with the lives of kings and nobles, but what makes the loss of life relevant to us is its value and loss to society. And this is precisely the situation reflected in *Death of a Salesman.* It is good for us to understand Aristotle in the right spirit, in keeping with the comprehensive nature of his philosophical inquiry.

Besides these, there are a few other concepts equally important, but perhaps less controversial. Aristotle devotes fourteen chapters for a full discussion of the tragic spirit. Greek tragedy being the most favoured art form of his time, such a full-length discussion is found necessary. He spells out the elements which are the different components of a tragedy. Hierarchically, they are plot, character, thought, diction, spectacle and song. Character is that which reveals moral purpose, and thought is the faculty of saying what is possible and pertinent in the given circumstances. In the representation of the action (tragedy is an imitation, not of men but of an action and of life), the poet should prefer 'probable impossibilities to improbable possibilities'. Aristotle holds that with respect to the requirements of art 'a probable impossibility is to be preferred to a thing improbable and yet possible'. These terms are loaded with meaning, and a complete understanding of these terms requires a related study of the other works that make up the Aristotle canon. Concepts such as *anagnorisis* (recognition), *peripeteia* (reversal), the parts of a tragedy, etc., and a few other ideas such as the function played by pity and fear in tragedy, the comparison of a work to an organism and the superiority of plot over other parts of a tragedy deserve our attention.

Aristotle discovered that pity and fear are the two emotions which arouse tragic feelings in humans. The tragic emotions unite the other concepts, and a wholesome theory of tragedy is built. Pity and fear demand the tragic hero to be noble; only then his fall from happiness to misery arouses in us these emotions. According to Aristotle, a work of art resembles a living organism, and the audience perceives the wholeness or the coherence of the work, if it is constructed in conformity with some laws of organisation, such as a beginning, middle and an end, possessing a proper magnitude. Then, it is capable of achieving the pleasure natural to an integrated and unified whole. Aristotle's most accommodative view of the plot has to be understood on the basis of his organic view of a work. Plot is the shaping cause that synthesises various elements in a concrete whole. To think that plot is the interrelated story of external events is to misread Aristotle. For him, plot is morally determinate action. Its excellence lies in its power of synthesising character, action and thought. The plot of *Romeo and Juliet* is different from the plot of the farce 'Pyramus and Thisbe', enacted by Bottom and his 'rude mechanicals', in *A Midsummer Night's Dream.* The external events are the same. The forlorn lovers die under similar circumstances. But the plot of the former is tragic, while that of the latter is farcical. Plot, which is the soul of tragedy, controls and shapes all the other elements that are subservient to it. It is the shaping principle that gives unity to a work. This definition of the plot frees him from far too narrow notions about the distinction between poetry and non-poetry. Poetry is not to be equated to writing in verse; rather it is the art of fiction-making, so to speak.

The history of *Poetics* since its publication has been an engaging study in itself. It exerted little, or no influence for more than 1800 years after it was transcribed for the first time. Is it not surprising that Longinus, Horace, Augustine or Aquinas or the others who had raised pertinent questions about the value and function of the arts hardly ever knew it? The scholars of the Renaissance in Europe were the first to recover it, and realise its greatness. Then it became a principal document for the neoclassical critics who complemented it with Horace's *Ars Poetica*. But then, they misinterpreted some of the doctrines and placed him in the Roman rhetorical tradition. This was a great disservice to Aristotle. He was never a dogmatic, prescriptive critic. He never laid down laws of poetic composition. A noteworthy example is the infamous misreading of his observations of his so-called theory of the dramatic unities by his Italian Renaissance commentators, Robertello and Castelvetro. There is no textual evidence in *Poetics* that suggests that the time of the play should be within twenty-four hours, or the place of action should be one locality. These were later Renaissance additions. Finally, it was given to the great cham Samuel Johnson to right the wrongs done by those commentators who missed the spirit of Aristotle's remarks. He only talks of the unity of action by which is meant that the action must be organic, a unified whole. All subservient parts must be organically related so as to form a unity. The unity of action alone is authentically Aristotelian. The Romantic period found no use for him for the Romantics believed that poetry was the outcome of imagination, and that it was not based on the materials with which it was made. They were reacting to the neoclassical version of Aristotle. Their expressive theory stood in opposition to imitation.

We must approach Aristotle with an open mind. He writes with the knowledge of Greek drama written before his time. His theory of drama is based on the practice of the founders of Greek drama, Aeschylus, Sophocles, Euripides, and Aristophanes. The subject matter of *Poetics* is limited to the forms of Greek literature. His knowledge is restricted to one language. He could not have had the historical understanding that we moderns possess. We cannot blame him for not doing things that none of his age could have ever done. The rebirth of *Poetics* took place in the twentieth century. Much of modern criticism derives from Aristotle. Without introducing Aristotelian concepts, it is well nigh impossible for modern critics to discuss literature, and in particular, drama. Though differing in principles and beliefs, Aristotle has inspired modern theoreticians and critics with his profundity of thought and discriminating powers of argument. Aristotle's empirical and deductive reasoning coupled with his tone of moderation keeps him flexible and undogmatic. He never saw literature as being cut off from life. That is why there is freshness and vitality in him all the time. The insights into the poetry he offers, and the wealth of principles one finds in him will ever be of perennial interest to us. Saintsbury sounds a little too generous in his enthusiasm for Aristotle when he says that we have not gone much beyond him. Nevertheless, Saintsbury puts Aristotle in the right place when he concludes, 'He is the very Alexander of criticism, and his conquests in this field, unlike those of his pupil in another, remain practically undestroyed, though not unextended, to the present day' (59).

When we consider the general plan and the contents of *Poetics*, we realise that it is unbelievably short. It has only twenty-six chapters, and it stands imperfect for all practical purposes. The second book in which, in all probability, Aristotle discussed the theory of comedy is irrecoverably lost. The work (*Poetics*) includes introductory remarks on the nature of poetry, some views on the theory of the epic, some on comedy, poetic diction, and the theory of tragedy which alone is more than half the treatise. By no means does it appear a coherent treatment of the subject. The first five are introductory chapters, the next fourteen are devoted to tragedy, the next eight, diction, and the next four are on the epic, and the very last one deals with problems in criticism. Lyric poetry is completely ignored, and the epic and the comedy are given only sketchy treatment. *Poetics* is composed in an esoteric style meant for the initiated ones. Read in isolation from his other writings, it cannot be easily understood. There are digressions, omissions, and inconsistencies in the use of terminology, and marks of haste in composition. From his lecture notes, it would seem that it was posthumously edited by one of his students. Casting aside all the methods of the previous philosophers as inadequate, Aristotle conducts a scientific, inductive and analytical enquiry into the nature of poetic art. It is a treatise on the 'productive' science. He was the first to raise essential questions. It is a veritable mine of suggestive ideas, and it is the first piece of systematic criticism to have come to us from the ancients. It is the earliest 'apology' for poetry. Aristotle says precious little about tragedy as an interpretation of life. He does not talk about destiny, fate and its intervention in man's life, and other Greek beliefs. He does not take into consideration the role of the imagination in poetic activity. The transforming power of the creative imagination is conspicuously absent in his valuable treatise. Of his views, some are so important in nature that they cannot be overlooked. Poetry is a concrete representation of the universal. It is not a copy of reality, and in judging art, the aesthetic should not be confused with moral standards. Atkins's summing up of Aristotle's contribution in his *Literary Criticism in Antiquity,* deserves to be quoted in full:

> Yet, when all is said, the *Poetics* is perhaps the most living of all Aristotelian works. Written in the severest of styles, devoid of all literary grace, it forms a treasury of ideas of lasting value, the full significance of which it has taken centuries to understand. In it we see Aristotle as the first of the systematic theorists, an early exponent of the historical and psychological methods, and incidentally a pioneer in the business of sane literary judgment; so

> that alike in the theory and the practice of criticism the work stands at the beginning of things, developing and extending the findings of Plato. Of late the small treatise has been subjected to some amount of depreciation, a reaction doubtless from the extravagant praise of former ages. Yet in the history of criticism its importance is unquestionable and fundamental. It is neither an infallible guide nor yet an antiquated textbook, but for breadth of outlook and sanity of judgment, for sheer penetrating power into the mysteries of art, the work is unrivalled; and all modern theorising has still to reckon with the contents of its 'discreet, unromantic' pages (1: 119).

Gilbert Murray, speaking of the permanent value of *Poetics,* remarks:

> But it is characteristic of the classical view that Aristotle lays his greatest stress, first, on the need for unity in the work of art, the need that each part should subserve the whole, while irrelevancies, however brilliant in themselves, should be cast away; and next, on the demand that great art must have for its subject the great way of living. These judgments have often been misunderstood, but the truth in them is profound and goes near to the heart of things (19).

We gather from history that even during the classical period Aristotle's *Poetics* did not have much of a noticeable impact. From the third century BC onwards, Greek culture became dispersed, and literary criticism came to be dominated by moralists and scholars who made a profession out of it. The Epicureans found poetry harmful and the Stoics always judged it strictly according to moralist and ethical norms. They always came up with allegorical interpretations of literary works. Heraclites, for example, draws allegoric meaning from the *Odyssey*. Many of the Hellenistic scholars were stylisticians, grammarians, connoisseurs of arts, and even editors of books. It was little wonder that they used textual analysis of works to arrive at judgments of these with very strong prescriptive, unprogressive, and inflexible predilections. They drew up elaborate schemata with which to classify works and found models for each from their own works of antiquity and renown.

HORACE (ALIAS QUINTUS HORATIUS FLACCUS) (65–68 BC)

Alexander, the greatest of the Greek emperors, Aristotle, the greatest of the philosophers, and Demosthenes, the greatest of the orators died within a short duration of twelve months of each other. And with the fading away of the grand and glorious Alexandrian empire, the focus shifted from the fourth century BC Athens to Rome in the first century BC. The greatest Roman poet-critic, Horace lived at a peaceful time conducive to discussion about art. He was a good friend of Augustus, the ruler of Rome, and his greatest contemporary was Virgil (70–19 BC). Virgil, Ovid, and Horace belonged to the age that is now called the Augustan Age. When Horace made his great contribution to literary thought, nearly three hundred years had passed since Aristotle wrote his *Poetics*. In the history of literary criticism his influence is next only to Aristotle's. Horace is more practically oriented though less philosophical than Aristotle, offering practical advice—himself being a practising poet—rather than making theoretical propositions. J.W.H. Atkins makes a point that there were three different attitudes prevalent, which served as models for Roman literature. One favoured the Greek authors as the right model to follow. These were the Atticists. The second was the Alexandrian school that favoured newer forms of writings with an emphasis on emotions and short forms. Virgil himself was influenced by this school. The third attitude was nationalistic which pleaded in favour of earlier Roman poets, raising objections to the borrowings from the Greeks. As a man of letters, Horace joined the controversies and conflicting discussions of his day. His major work of literary criticism, written towards the end of his life, is 'Epistle to the Pisos' which has come to be known as *Ars Poetica* or *Art of Poetry*. Ben Jonson was one of the translators of this text. The translation was published posthumously in 1640.

This treatise is in the form of a versified epistle addressed to a patron of the arts, L. Piso, advising aspiring poets as to what they ought and ought not to do if they wished to succeed in their poetic ambition. It is conjectured that the title by which it is known was given to it by Quintillion. It is a kind of a guide to the art of literary composition. Aristotle knew only the epic, tragedy, and comedy. Since his time more literary types—lyric, pastoral, ode, and satire—had developed. When *Ars Poetica* came to be written, Horace was well versed in these newer poetical forms. It has a three-fold structure: the content of poetry, style of poetry and a discussion on poets. Horace is somewhat of a practical poet-critic—perhaps the first one of the kind—whose aim was to improve the efforts and talents of his contemporaries. He always cites examples from ancient Greek poets whom he upholds as the true poetic model to be followed. His basic requirement is sensibility or taste, at once disciplined and flexible. Poetic decorum is primary for him, and this is the norm by which to judge all works. Poetry should conform to the principle of decorum, or what is congruous. Poetic license should not be stretched beyond limits. In achieving one quality, the poet may fall into an error. Brevity may lead to obscurity; grandeur may border on bombast; and smoothness may degenerate into lack of vitality. Parts must be interrelated so as to form a unified whole. A writer should exercise judgment in his choice of words, for words have personality, and are subject to the laws of change. Horace seems to favour verisimilitude as the poetic norm rather than probability (internal coherence) that Aristotle preferred. The difference between Aristotle and Horace is that while Aristotle is more philosophical, Horace is more practical. Thus, there is a shift to the rhetorical tradition in him. In the mode of narration he opts for *medias res* as is exemplified in the technique of *The Odyssey*. He takes up the question of poetic form. Excessively violent incidents ought not to be presented on stage; the appropriate practice of drama requires five acts; and the chorus should be the spokesman of what is morally right and just. Poets, for him, are born as well as made. He encourages aspiring poets to practise imitation by which is meant emulating and following in the footsteps of great models.

The ultimate goal of poetry is to instruct and afford pleasure. The ideal poet is one who combines these twin functions. Western criticism has accepted this Horatian dictum as an unwritten truth. In his *An Apologie for Poetry,* Sir Philip Sidney says, 'Poetry, therefore, is an art of imitation, for so Aristotle termeth it in the word *mimesis*, that is to say, a representing, counterfeiting, or figuring forth: to speak metaphorically, a speaking picture, with this end, to teach and delight.' Renaissance critics, in the manner of Sidney, used Horace to interpret Aristotle. The Romantic critics did not have much use for Horace. Humanists, such as Matthew Arnold, and later T.S. Eliot, did embody his spirit in their writings. Horace's treatise did not get lost, as it happened in the case of Aristotle. He was read and discussed during the Renaissance. It is said that Queen Elizabeth herself attempted a translation of the *Ars*. As we mentioned earlier, Aristotle too came to be interpreted in the light of Horace. Owing to its simplicity, his works have appealed to generations of students and scholars alike. Even Longinus, despite all his vitality and ebullience, did not dislodge him altogether. Horace will remain a source of inspiration, with all his maxims and lessons on poetry.

The importance and gravity of classical rhetoric as found in Horace is felt in three areas: motivation to compose, the moral issues that govern a work and the factors relating to the style of composition. Literary works were stylistically analysed, and the students of rhetoric were advised to learn as to how language could be used for purposes of communication and persuasion most effectively. Literature turned into a study in philology. Cicero provided the deep structures for rhetoric, which he classified into invention, arrangement, style, memory, and delivery. In terms of quantitative proportions, Horace classified rhetoric into exordium, statement of case, partition, proof, refutation and peroration. He divided style into high, middle and low. More than these, rhetoric was not just a technical discipline. It must be deeply grounded in moral principles, because it is related to law, philosophy and ethics. Aristotle, on the other hand, did not attach any moral value to rhetoric. He insisted on a clear distinction between rhetoric (aiming at persuasion) and poetics (aiming at imitation, and so an aesthetic experience). The works of Dionysius of Halicarnassus, and Quintillion (the leading teacher of rhetoric in Rome) have been constantly referred to in any discussion of the rhetorical studies of the period following Horace.

Horace's positive achievements cannot easily be ignored. He takes the literature of Greece as his standard when he discusses poetry. He asserts the supremacy of Greek literature, and this is an opening of a new phase in criticism. His conception of imitation meant a recreation, and not just copying as he came to be misinterpreted later in time. His pronouncements on the employment of proper diction; on the form of the verse; on ways by which unity can be achieved, and related matters about the form of the poem have a sound value in literary theory. He touches upon the essentials which are true for all time. For the attainment of the best results, he lays down a set of principles—in the form of scattered apothegms—which are true at any time. His influence began to be felt rather late during the Middle Ages, and his *Ars Poetica* attained the status of a textbook during the Renaissance. In many ways, it shaped the new doctrines, since it was close to the humanistic method of following the ancients. He was misunderstood time and again, and his advice came to be taken in a rigid manner which was not what he had intended. Brooks and Warren sound needlessly unforgiving and severe in their views: 'The *Ars Poetica* of Horace is a nice mélange of objective and critical rules with snatches of studio wisdom. . . . They are not strictly parts of criticism. They are, despite the random structure of the poem, not actually in great danger of being confused with criticism' (94). But the essential elements in Horace's teaching must be sought for, according to Atkins,

> in the new direction he gave to critical thought, in his grasp of fundamentals, and in his revelation of many of the secrets of his own poetic craft. In declaring for classicism, he may have missed something of the real classical spirit; but he rendered no slight service in establishing as literary standards the great masterpieces of classical Greece. And for the rest, much of his teaching has lasting validity; it is the fruit of the experience of one who, himself a great artist, had a clear conception of poetic principles, and who handed them on in exquisite and memorable phrase (2: 102–3).

Dryden, Pope, Johnson among others quite often invoke him to support their own views. Pope's 'Essay' opens with one such invocation. *Ars Poetica* has exerted tremendous authority over criticism and poetic creation in the western world.

LONGINUS (1 OR 3 CENTURY AD)

The third member of the 'Classical Triumvirate of Criticism', besides Aristotle and Horace, is Longinus. In the domain of

Greek thought, he is second only to Aristotle, the 'master of them that know' in the words of Dante. The authorship of the treatise *Peri Hupsous*, translated variously as 'Elevated Writing' by Wordsworth, 'On the Sovereign Perfection of Writing' by Arthur Quiller-Couch, 'Elevation of Language' by Allen Tate, but accepted by a large body of readers as 'On the Sublime' remains unsettled even today. The name of the author to whom the work is ascribed is just a conjecture, and even the date of composition (1 or 3 century AD) is uncertain. We may safely conclude that the treatise must have been written by a Greek, called Longinus, in the early Christian era. It was historically not a glorious period for Greece, since it had by now lost all its power and supremacy. He examines the Greek literature of the past even as we do Milton or Wordsworth today. Sublimity is that transcendent element that transmutes a work into more than a sum of its parts. For Longinus, sublimity is an inspiring outburst of revelatory illumination. It consists in

> a certain distinction and excellence in expression, and that it is from no other source than this that the greatest poets and writers have derived their eminence and gained an immortality of renown. The effect of elevated language upon an audience is not persuasion but transport. At every time and in every way imposing speech, with the spell it throws over us, prevails over that which aims at persuasion and gratification. Our persuasions we can usually control, but the influences of the sublime bring power and irresistible might to bear, and reign over every hearer. Similarly, we see skill in invention, and due order and arrangement of matter, emerging as the hard-won result not of one thing, not of two, but of the whole texture of the composition, whereas Sublimity flashing forth at the right moment scatters everything before it like a thunderbolt, and at once displays the power of the orator in all its plenitude (76).

The emphasis of Longinus is on the literature of power (as distinguished from the literature of knowledge whose purpose is to teach). The effect of this literature is achieved not by argument, but by revelation or illumination. Literature is not propaganda, not a sermon, not entertainment. It is vision. The effect of literature is the same as soul-stirring music or scriptural incantation. It makes us see with the eye of the spirit, and fills us with awareness. Its function is sacramental. The truly sublime has an uplifting effect. We are lifted out of ourselves and carried to a new realm of experience and perception, and filled with ecstasy as if we ourselves had created what we see and hear. It casts a permanent spell—not unlike the nightingale's song on Keats—and we return to it repeatedly to renew our experience. It bears examination without end, and it becomes an inalienable part of our whole being. Our reaction to the truly sublime is directed not by the power of discursive reason, but by intuition and insight. Immanuel Kant in his *Critique of Judgement* clarifies this Longinian Sublime thus:

> Bold, overhanging, and as it were threatening, rocks; clouds piled up in the sky, moving with lightning flashes and thunder peals; volcanoes in all their violence of destruction; hurricanes with their track of devastation; the boundless ocean in a state of tumult; the lofty waterfall of a mighty river, and such like; these exhibit our faculty of resistance as insignificantly small in comparison with their might. But the sight of them is the more attractive, the more fearful it is, provided only that we are in security; and we readily call these objects sublime because they raise the energies of the soul above their accustomed height, and discover in us a faculty of resistance of a quite different kind, which gives us courage to measure ourselves against the apparent almightiness of nature (102–3).

Building upon his theory of sublimity, Longinus classifies its characteristics. The five sources of sublimity are 1. capacity for great thought and a firm grasp of ideas, 2. inspired emotion and strong passion: these two characteristics, amplitude of mind and its passionate intensity are inherent and coextensive in the poet, 3. figures of speech and a proper construction of figures, 4. noble diction, and 5. the effect of dignity and elevation, the power to integrate and fuse the elements so as to give them a tone of sublimity. The three impediments to sublimity are 1. affectation 2. cold pedantry, and 3. sentimentality.

The treatise of Longinus deeply influenced the post-Renaissance critics. It was held to be complementary to *Ars.* Sublimity and decorum were the two concepts that balanced each other. Pope must have had Longinus in mind when he affirms the greatness of poets who can 'snatch a grace beyond the reach of art.' For Addison, Milton's *Paradise Lost* is a great poem on account of its sublimity. The Romantic concept of inspiration of the artist is surely an echo of Longinian sublimity. Longinus has come to be called the first Romantic critic. Some of his statements, 'Sublimity is the echo of the noble mind,' 'Literature is in the nature of revelation,' 'Poetry has the character of oracle,' find an echo in a long line of English critics. Sidney declares, 'Poetry was the first light-giver to ignorance and first nurse.' Wordsworth's oft-quoted remark runs, 'Poetry is the breath and finer spirit of all knowledge; it is the impassioned expression which is in the countenance of all Science.' Shelley almost restates Longinus when he proclaims, 'A poet is a nightingale who sits in darkness and sings to cheer its own solitude with sweet sounds; his auditors are as men entranced by the melody of an unseen musician, who feel that they are moved and softened but know not whence or why,' or again, 'Poetry is indeed divine. It is at once the centre and circumference of all knowledge.' Matthew Arnold's touchstone method is recognition of serious poetry by an insight rather than by a rational and objective analysis. Carl Jung's theory of racial consciousness is that during certain moments we feel an extraordinary release, a kind of transport, and at such moments, we are not individuals but members of a race. The voice of the whole of mankind seems to resound in us. Northrop Frye builds up a typology framed on the basis of Longinus' *ecstasies*. The New Critics too found a kindred soul in Longinus. Aristotle did not sufficiently theorise about the function of the non-structural elements in poetry; his interest was drama. The two elements, thought and diction, are primary in Longinus' sublimity. New criticism is based on this *res* and *verba* tradition. The transport of Longinus can be seen in relation to the concept of 'synaesthesia,' or an equilibrium or organisation of impulses suggested by I.A. Richards.

Longinus must be viewed as a continuation, or a part, of the critical tradition started by Aristotle himself. It is said that sublimity, being a natural endowment, will suffer when subjected to rules of art. Longinus, however, never subscribed to this view. On the other hand, he reinforces the view that freedom and restraint go together. In him, one finds a healthy compromise between Romantic exuberance and freedom, and Classical order and restraint. Divine frenzy should be tempered with the regulative principle of art. There is always a fresh appeal in him, and hence, he has withstood the test of time. He is always a force to reckon with in any theory of literature: what is literature for if it does not touch the very core of our inmost being! The originality of Longinus can be seen, not only in the truths he propounded, but also in his opening our eyes to new truths about the quality of great literature. Longinus was the first critic to talk extensively about the impact of poetry on the reader. This has led, in course of time, to 'reception aesthetics' and 'reader-response' theories. As one who defined the elements to be sought in literature, he is verily the forerunner of practical criticism and as one who took Latin and Hebrew works for critical enquiry besides his own Greek literature, the credit of being the earliest comparatist should go to him. There is hardly any moment of dullness in his enchanting style. He appealed to his audience to return to the ideals of Greek art. Others may have put forward the same suggestion, but he was most successful in capturing the spirit of the ancients. He remains the best exponent of the classical spirit, and he anticipates a good deal of modern criticism. His methods of analysis are inductive and analytical. In his suggestive and impassioned approach, he is the very opposite of the cold intellectualism of Aristotle. In spite of all his value, his influence fell short of what one would have expected. Later in time, he was rediscovered during the Renaissance, and from then on, he became one of the famous triumvirates. Commenting on the merits of *On the Sublime,* Atkins observes:

> Nowadays the supreme qualities of the work are no longer in question. Ranking in antiquity with the greatest critical achievements, it 'remains towering among all other works of its class'; and for sheer originality and power it has not been surpassed. . . . Yet its true meaning would seem to emerge only when viewed against its historical background; and in that same setting its manifold excellences are also most clearly seen. There are things in its pages that can never grow old; while its freshness and light will continue to charm all ages. All beautiful things, it has been said, belong to the same age; and the work of Longinus is in a sense contemporaneous with that of Plato, Aristotle and Coleridge. (2: 253)

Again, Atkins winds up his monumental work on ancient criticism with the following words that neatly summarise what the Age of Antiquity has to offer to the moderns in the field of criticism and theory.

> It suggests that art is a blend of both representation and expression; that its true ends are attained when there is a balance of free creation and control; and further, that its appeal is directed neither to an individual nor to an age but to something elemental and universal in man. And in these ideas and counsels are summed up not the least of the findings of antiquity. They are the considered judgements of sane and fastidious critics; and in art, as in life, it is the part of wisdom to let the ages instruct the years (2: 354).

It is well worth concluding our review of Longinus with Pope's tribute to him in his *An Essay on Criticism*.

> Thee, bold Longinus! All the Nine inspire,
> And bless their critic with a poet's fire:
> An ardent judge, who, zealous in his trust,
> With warmth gives sentence, yet is always just;
> Whose own example strengthens all his laws;
> And is himself that great sublime he draws. (675–80)

Brooks and Warren place him in the right perspective when they say, 'As Horace had subdued the theory of poetic words to a decorum of urbanity, conversation, idiom and satire, Longinus heightened it to a decorum of transport' (110).

We of the present age owe a great allegiance to the Classical Age that gave us three seminal texts: *Poetics, Ars Poetica, On Sublimity*: three texts which form the bedrock of Western critical thought. The critical terminology and vocabulary that we so freely use, we have learnt from the grammarians and philosophers of the Classical Age of Antiquity. In sum, the whole tradition of literary scholarship, textual exegesis and theory of interpretation traces its ancestry to that bygone age we call the Classical Age. There can be no better way of wrapping up our discussion of the ancient critics than by quoting Pope again from his *Essay*:

> But where's the man who counsel can bestow
> Still pleas'd to teach, and yet not proud to know?
> Unbiass'd or by favour or by spite'
> Not dully prepossess'd nor blindly right;
> Tho' learn'd, well-bred, and tho' well bred sincere;
> Modestly bold, and humanly severe;
> Who to a friend freely his faults can show.
> And gladly praise the merit of a foe;

Bless'd with a taste exact, yet unconfin'd,
A knowledge both of books and humankind;
Gen'rous converse; a soul exempt from pride;
And love to praise, with reason on his side?
And once were critics; such the happy few
Athens and Rome in better ages knew. (631–44)

Works Cited

Adams, Hazard, ed. *Literary Criticism since Plato*. 1971. Harcourt Brace Jovanovich College Publishers, 1992. Unless otherwise stated, all textual references are drawn from this volume.

Atkins, J.W.H. *Literary Criticism in Antiquity: A Sketch of its Development.* 1934. Vol.1. Gloucester, Mass.: Peter Smith, 1961.

———. *Literary Criticism in Antiquity: A Sketch of its Development.*Vol.2. Cambridge: Cambridge University Press, 1934.

Brooks, Cleanth and William Wimsatt. *Literary Criticism: A Short History.* New Delhi: Oxford & IBH Publishing Co., 1957.

Kant, Immanuel. *Critique of Judgement.* Trans. J.H. Bernard. 1931. Amherst, N.Y.: Prometheus Books, 2000.

Miller, Arthur. *Arthur Miller's Collected Plays.* 1957. New Delhi: Allied Publishers, 1973.

Murray, Gilbert. Preface to *Aristotle on the Art of Poetry.* 1920. Trans. Ingram Bywater. London: Oxford University Press, 1976.

Saintsbury, George. *A History of English Literary Criticism.* Edinburgh and London. William Blackwood & Sons Ltd., 1955.

Spiller, Robert. 'Literary History.' *The Aims and Methods of Scholarship.* Ed. James Thorpe. 2nd ed. Hyderabad: American Studies Research Centre, 1970.

Select Bibliography

Bloom, Allan, trans. *The Republic of Plato*. New York: Basic Books, 1968.

Butcher, S.H. *Aristotle's Theory of Poetry and Fine Art.* 1923. New York: Dover Publications, 1956.

Bywater, Ingram. *Aristotle on the Art of Poetry.* 1909. New York: Garland Publishers, 1980.

Cooper, L. *Aristotle on the Art of Poetry.* Boston: Ginn and Company, 1913.

Dalton, J.F. *Roman Literary Theory and Criticism: A Study in Tendencies.* New York: Russell & Russell, 1962.

Dorsch, T.S, trans. *Classical Literary Criticism.* London: Penguin Books, 1965.

Fergusson, Francis. *The Idea of a Theatre.* Princeton: Princeton University Press, 1949.

Henn, T.R. *Longinus and English Criticism.* Cambridge: The University Press, 1934.

Herrick, Marvin T. *The Fusion of Horatian and Aristotelian Literary Criticism.* Urbana: University of Illinois Press, 1946.

House, Humphrey, ed. *Aristotle's Poetics.* London: R. Hart-Davis, 1956.

Lodge, Rupert C. *Plato's Theory of Art.* London: Routledge & Kegan Paul, 1953.

Lucas, F.L. *Tragedy, Serious Drama in Relation to Aristotle's Poetics.* London: Hogarth Press, 1957.

McKeon, Richard. 'Literary Criticism and the Concept of Imitation in Antiquity.' *Critics and Criticism.* Ed. R.S. Crane. Chicago: University of Chicago Press, 1952.

Oates, Whitney J. *Plato's View of Art.* New York: Scribner, 1972.

Olson, Elder, ed. *Aristotle's Poetics and English Literature.* Chicago: University of Chicago Press, 1965.

Potts, L.J., trans. *Aristotle on the Art of Fiction.* 2nd ed Cambridge: Cambridge University Press, 1959.

Richards, I.A., ed. and trans. *Plato's Republic.* Cambridge: Cambridge University Press, 1966.

Russell, D.A., trans. *Longinus on the Sublime.* Oxford: Clarendon Press, 1969.

Showerman, Grant. *Horace and His Influence*: New York: Longmans, 1922.

Sterling Richard W. and William C. Scott, trans. *The Republic*. By Plato. New York: Norton, 1985.

Tate, Allen. 'Longinus and the New Criticism.' *Lectures in Criticism*. Ed. Elliott Coleman. New York: Harper, 1949.

2

Medieval and Renaissance Criticism

MEDIEVAL CRITICISM

The decline and fall of Rome took place around the 5th century AD. The greatness, and the invaluable contribution of the Classical Age were rediscovered during the Renaissance. The period in between the two major events in European history vaguely goes by the name of the Middle Age or the Medieval Age. As far as England is concerned, historians restrict it to a time span of eight centuries, from the year of composition of *Beowulf* in 725 AD to 1474 AD when Caxton published the first book ever printed in England. The one major development during this period of roughly eight hundred years is the adoption of Christianity as the religion of the Mediterranean region. Roman Catholicism was the religious faith that came to prevail in Western Europe.

The literary criticism of the medieval period has not been an area of much research and scholarship. There may be many reasons for it. It comprises wide and widely ranging texts belonging to different disciplines. They should have been written over a very long period of time. For one thing, medieval literature has now become a specialised area which is of interest to specialists and researchers alone. Again, the subject is not easy to identify and define. Medieval literature constitutes a very large area, extending far beyond national confines, and much of historical research in criticism restricts itself to self-defined territories with a recognisable culture. The only available standard work is *English Literary Criticism: The Medieval Phase by* J.W.H. Atkins published in 1952. Since the work treats the period along national lines, it does not take into account works, and the influences outside the national frontiers. Such a study becomes partial and fragmented in its nature. Those historians who have written about medieval times have thought it fit to choose other areas such as aesthetics and stylistics, branches that are not, strictly speaking, literary criticism. Another problem is one of chronology. There are no clear-cut dividing lines between the classical and the medieval. We can have no definite notions regarding the end of the classical phase and the commencement of the medieval. Classical elements were absorbed in the Medieval Age, or sometimes modified, and later made part of its own. We know from our own knowledge that a great deal of pagan literature got assimilated into the medieval ethos. The critical terms in vogue in the late Classical Age found favour with the writers of the Medieval Age, and they even followed the prescriptions on the art of composition as laid down by the rhetoricians of the bygone age.

By and large, medieval criticism followed the system of classifying literature under the heads of grammar, rhetoric, and logic. The Medieval Age developed a systematic poetic grammar. The term grammar meant for them the science of correct speaking, and a reading curriculum for poets. The curriculum suggested a list of required reading for poets in order that it could form the basis for literary creation and for developing eloquent speech. In fact this grammar curriculum provided for the humanising influence in the Middle Ages. Great works of antiquity of the Pagan Age, and critical commonplaces were made the objects of study and meditation. One type of treatise that was written to promote the reading of poets was the typical medieval glossary. These are like our modern annotated classics, supplying biographical information about the authors, giving meanings of difficult words and expressions, and explanations of allusions. These were intended to clarify the texts so as to help the readers develop their powers of speech, and to read and interpret the scriptures on their own.

Another form of criticism, close on hand with the previous type, was the study of versification and scansion of poetry, otherwise called prosody. This was meant to provide the basic training for the prospective poets in the basic poetic forms. Poetry is distinct from prose in that it has an inherent form of its own. It is not to be found in its content alone. The syllables, feet, metre, and numbers were given a full treatment. The tradition of drawing up a list of authors survives to the present day in our syllabus framing. In their glossaries, they took pains to follow an order such as the following: author, title, type of poem, intention of the writer, order, number of books, and explanation of the text. These formed the foundation for medieval humanism. The case of the medieval rhetorical criticism is not as clear as that of the grammatical criticism. In the Classical Age, these two were, in many cases, interrelated. The idea that these two must be kept as separate disciplines was not felt till the sixteenth century. Throughout the Middle Ages one witnesses a direct impingement of the one on the other.

Horace had a clear influence on the Middle Ages, but not Longinus. There was always a debate as to which of the two—logic or grammar—should gain precedence over the other. Philosophers such as Bacon, were to reconcile the two by maintaining that, as technique, poetry is part of logic, and, as an activity of the creative mind, it is a form of ethical teaching and a method of creating moral examples. This debate is endless and continues even today in many different ways. There are no documents which treat poetry in relation to music or arithmetic, but there are quite a few which deal with poetry in relation to theology or philosophy. Poetry was considered a prophecy or revelation, and was, therefore, equal to philosophy in the Old World. A considerable amount of medieval criticism dealt with biblical criticism and mysticism and allegorical readings of works. The poets were theologians and their poetry was the overflow of moments of inspiration. In the hands of Dante, poetry embodies deepest theological truths. Thus, we see that during the Middle Ages, poetry existed with and in grammar, rhetoric, logic, and philosophy. Some of these persisted and found expression in different versions in the succeeding ages, and some of these were assimilated into systems of thought at a later date. We may also divide medieval criticism into broad periods such as the following; but in some instances there is bound to be some overlapping. 1. Late Classical (1st century BC to 7th century AD), 2. Carolingian (8th century to 10th century), 3. High Medieval (11th century to 18th century), 4. Scholastic (13th century to 14th century), 5. Humanist (14th century to 16th century). Here is Saintsbury's evaluation of the contribution of the Middle Ages to literary criticism:

> In the Middle Ages proper this grasp has relaxed itself to such an extent that for the most part it hardly even attempts to touch its object. A few technical treatises exist, and we meet, now and then, a more or less banal expression of approval of a writer. Even the earliest dawn of the Renaissance in Italy and the renewed study (from at any rate textual and subject point of view) of the classical authors, give us little, if anything, of the kind; and from the year 1000 AD—the rather imaginary line between 'Dark' and 'Middle'—to the beginning of the sixteenth century, we meet practically nothing that can be called a critical treatise of substantive puzzling, but extraordinarily valuable, document of the *De Vulgari Eloquio* by Dante (21).

Most historians of criticism have turned a blind eye to this vast period. They make a sudden leap from the Classical Age to the Renaissance, from Longinus to Sir Philip Sidney. Consider, for example, the opinion of Wimsatt and Brooks in their *Short History of Criticism*: 'Middle Ages . . . were not in fact ages of literary theory or criticism . . . In short, it was an age of theological thinking in a theologically oriented and theocratic society. Such a society does not characteristically promote the essentially humanistic view of literary criticism. . . .' (154). Recent scholarship, however, contests such assumptions and a large-scale dismissal of a whole era. We need a reappraisal of medieval theory based on a framework of history and literary criticism. Recent poststructuralist theories ushered in by continental philosophers which are political and ideologically based (such as feminist criticism) have their antecedents in medieval beliefs. No criticism is objective and self-contained, and free from a world-view, or ideology. Medieval theory was based on a divine plan in which the function of literature was supposed to help an individual to become a better Christian.

The general view, uncontested in academic circles, is that literary criticism in England began only with the Renaissance in the sixteenth century. There is some truth to this assumption because only during the Renaissance did an accepted corpus of critical works come out for public inspection. It does not mean that the English began thinking about criticism only in the Elizabethan period. Though the Middle Ages were by and large a dark period, there are some works which will tell us that these were the ones that prepared the ground for Renaissance thought, and later, a continuous critical tradition. It would be far from the truth to conclude that the Middle Ages were wholly uncritical, and that it was an age of simple infancy, and nothing more. English itself attained the status of a literary medium only in the fourteenth century, replacing medieval Latin slowly. The dominance of studies in logic and queer notions about literature did permit a free exchange of ideas. Ignorance of the best in the classics and a self-imposed isolation were the other factors which led to the lack of assistance in matters of thought and guidance. There was an educational system following the Roman model, which encouraged cultivation of poetry. The use of the love theme in poetry, the recognition of the vernacular as the medium of literary art, the need for and methods of translation, attainment of good prose, and the nature of poetic composition occupied the minds of the people of medieval England. Some manuals from the age talk in general terms about specific works, and some others contain scattered remarks on them. Treatises on morals and discursive opinions on men and matters have also been found.

A critical climate developed slowly. In addition to these occasional *obiter dicta* found strewn about, there were a few works of note and significance. In the 7th century, Bede and Alcuin, educators of the clergy, expounded grammar, logic and Biblical and Christian poetry. In the 12th century, John Salisbury and a few classical theorists infused life into literary studies. In the 13th century Geoffrey of Vinsauf and John Garland taught techniques in poetic composition using manuals, which was a sort of theorising at its infancy. Roger Bacon and Richard of Bury kindled enthusiasm for poetry and literature. With the vernacular English occupying centre stage as medium for literature, literary discussions freely took place in English. *The Owl and the Nightingale* (circa 1210) written by an unknown author is a debate-poem. It is perhaps the earliest among the surviving English lyrics of the medieval period expressing a native and pure English sensibility. The poem is in the form of a dialogue between two birds, the nightingale and the owl. The two birds engage in a dispute which is finally settled by a mediator. The strength of the poem lies in its use of the vernacular. The employment of colloquial language as spoken by the common people, and the proverbs used in the dialogue carry the age-old wisdom of the English nation. This can be seen as a forerunner of the movement towards the use of the vernacular in English poetry.

Dante Alighieri (1265–1321) too defended the use of the native, or vernacular medium rather than the courtly Latin for literary composition. He set an example in composing *Divina Commedia* in Italian, thus establishing the spoken dialect for use in serious epic poetry. According to him, secular poetry too had its hierarchy of four levels of meaning corresponding to the four levels of scriptural exegesis. These were the literal, the allegorical, the moral, and spiritual (or anagogic). He maintained that it was essential for a practising critic to analyse and understand the literal sense first before he moved on to more appealing and edifying senses of higher levels of symbolic, or esoteric meaning. One can find a correspondence of thought in I.A. Richards's notion of the two uses of language, the referential and the emotive, and the four kinds of meaning defined by the terms, sense, feeling, tone, and intention. Several kinds and levels of meaning cohere in a poetic utterance. Chaucer, and later Wycliffe, contributed to the growth of the use of the vernacular in poetry and prose. In early 16th century attempts were made to evaluate the works of English poets. All teaching during the medieval period was based on doctrines drawn from the post-classical Christian tradition. Translating these ideas and doctrines into English cannot be construed as a critical achievement. Such shortcomings notwithstanding, for a student of literary criticism, the Medieval Age is, indubitably, an era of historical importance. Summing up the main features of critical activities in England during the medieval phase, Atkins remarks:

> Yet important questions had in the meantime been raised, some amount of theory established, and later problems anticipated; and in spite of shortcomings, expression had been given to a growing consciousness of literature, and to ideas of interest in critical history. To omit therefore such activities from a survey of English criticism is none other than to pass over the first phase in the critical development, and, incidentally, to ignore a chapter in the history of English thought which throws an interesting sidelight on medieval intellectual life (2: 199).

Works Cited

Atkins, J.W.H. *Literary Criticism: The Medieval Phase.* 1943. London: Methuen & Co. Ltd., 1952.

Saintsbury, George. *A History of English Literary Criticism.* London: William Blackwood & Sons Ltd., 1955.

Wimsatt, William K. and Cleanth Brooks. *Literary Criticism: A Short History.* New Delhi: Oxford & IBH Publishing Co., 1957.

LITERARY CRITICISM IN THE RENAISSANCE

The term 'Renaissance' is of Italian origin, meaning 'rebirth' or 'reawakening'. It stands for the historical rebirth of literary and cultural movements in the 14th, 15th and 16th centuries. Initially the movement started in Italy, and later spread gradually to France, Germany, England and other countries of Europe. There are two views regarding this movement. One view is that the Europeans believed that they had discovered the greatness and superiority of the ancient Greek and Roman culture after centuries of neglect and decline during the so-called dark Middle Ages. The other view, held by modern historians, is that the Renaissance was not an abrupt movement, but had its roots established even during the medieval times, and the movement was one of gradual progression. Whichever opinion one might hold, it is true that the Renaissance marks a clear departure from the earlier movement with its own characteristics to justify it as a separate movement in culture and the arts. This warrants an independent study and enquiry of the movement.

There was a revival in the study of arts and literature, sparked by an interest in Greek and Roman literature of the Classical Age. The basis for this study was the reinterpretation of the classics by Italian men of letters. The widening of the horizon of knowledge was accelerated by the discovery of what we now call printing technology. The focus of interest in study shifted from such abstract notions as God and nature to man. The inherent divinity in the human being and the dignity associated with him became a serious subject worthy of study. Did not Pope, later in time, proclaim, 'The proper study of Mankind is Man?' Literary criticism during the Renaissance was up against a major task of justifying imaginative literature. No doubt the Middle Ages were a glorious period of great literature. We cannot be blind to the wealth of its literature. But the basic belief was that literature was the by-product of theology or philosophy. Literature was not evaluated through literary criteria. The yardstick for judging poetry was neither literary nor critical. During the Renaissance, a huge body of literature of the past was recovered, and the real task was to establish justifiable considerations by which these writings on miscellaneous subjects could be justly estimated. The problem was one of establishing aesthetic criteria for the right understanding of works of great art. The scholastic and ecclesiastic authority of the medieval period gave room to an empirical approach based on reason and evidence.

One other task was to seek a just and proper answer to Plato's refutation and objections raised in his dialogues, and the *Republic*. Many Renaissance scholars successfully answered these charges by blaming the artist and not the art. Those who abuse art and betray the sacred office of art ought to be banished not only from Plato's, but also from any and every commonwealth. Renaissance criticism took upon itself the prime duty of uniting and reconciling the best elements in Aristotle and Horace, and establishing literary criticism as an independent field of study. Among Renaissance critics, the following stand out prominently for students of English literature: Petrarch, Scaliger, Minturno, Boccacio and the Italian commentators, Robertello and Castelvetro. J.E. Spingarn was the first historian of criticism to venture boldly to trace the lines of history and introduce to the world of scholarship the whole domain of Renaissance criticism. His pioneering work *Literary Criticism in the Renaissance* (1899) raises some fundamental questions. How did the Renaissance conception of poetry and the art of literature first develop in Italy, and then spread to France before finally emerging in England, forming the basis of English classicism? He is perhaps the earliest historian to discover a pan European tradition in Renaissance literary theory.

One must acknowledge that literary criticism during the Elizabethan age in England was not as rich and diversified as the criticism in Italy and France during the same period. The greatest and the most important work of this age is, of course, Sidney's

Apologie for Poetry. Elizabethan criticism exhibits two traits. First, there is in existence a complete body of critical works of the Renaissance, and secondly, it shares several characteristics with the works of other European countries associated with the Renaissance. Hence, it is wrong to discuss English Renaissance as though it were an isolated phenomenon, without touching upon the neighbouring countries of Europe. English Renaissance criticism exhibits a clear line of progression falling into the following demarcated divisions. There are mostly rhetorical studies of literature in the first stage of evolution. Thomas Wilson's *Art of Rhetoric* (1553) is probably the first work of criticism in the English language. Roger Ascham's *Schoolmaster* (1568) and Richard Tottel's *Tottel's Miscellany* (1559) are two other important works, the former, a treatise and the latter, an anthology of songs and sonnets. The English came to learn that form and style were important considerations in literary appreciation. It was during this period that English poetry was Italianised to a great extent.

The second phase was a period when attention was paid to the metrics and metrical patterns in poetical composition. *Art of English Poesie* (1589) by Richard Puttenham and *Discourse of English Poetry* (1586) by Mary Webb are the earliest works on classification of metre, and the introduction of classical metres into the English language. Thus, Italian verse forms came to be introduced into English. This meant that the Italian prosodists became the right models for the English poets. The third stage is the stage of philosophical criticism. Among the most prominent works of apologetic criticism of this period are Sir Philip Sidney's *Apologie for Poetry* (1583?), Thomas Campion's *Art of English Poesy* (1602) and Samuel Daniel's *Defence of Rhyme* (1605). Even as the titles signify, these works were in the nature of defences against the attack of the Puritans on poetry, and the classicists on versification. These defences are broad in their scope and treatment of the subject. They were not just defences to meet the charges, but works which raised some essential questions of poetic art and theme. As in versification, here too they borrowed from their Italian counterparts. The fourth stage belonged to the first half of the seventeenth century, and Ben Jonson, the Elizabethan dramatist, was the important figure during this period. Jonson was a classicist. If Sidney defended poetic art,

Jonson taught it. Here again, there is an unmistakable influence of Italian criticism. The fifth stage opens up a new dimension in English literary criticism when the French come on the scene. A patriotic spirit inspired this period. Some of its characteristic features were: a devotion to the national cause, commitment to classicism in a pure form, and the faith that art should imitate nature. John Dryden, the poet laureate, became the presiding genius of this period.

With its emphasis on humanism based on the idea that people are rational beings, and its faith in the dignity and worth of the individual, the Renaissance was a period of intellectual ferment that prepared the ground for later thinkers who arrived on the literary scene during the period of the Enlightenment. The Renaissance has left to the world what Yeats refers to in his poem, 'Sailing to Byzantium' as 'monuments of unageing intellect' which define much of what constitutes the Western world today.

Select Bibliography

Atkins, J.W.H. *English Literary Criticism: The Renascence.* London: Methuen & Co. Ltd. 1947.

Baldwin, C.S. *Renaissance Literary Theory and Practice.* Ed. Donald Lemen Clark. New York: Columbia University Press, 1939.

Hall, Vernon Jr. *Renaissance Literary Criticism: A Study of its Social Content.* Gloucester, Massachusetts: P. Smith, 1959.

Hardison, O.B. *English Literary Criticism: The Renaissance.* New York: Appleton Century-Crofts, 1963.

Hathaway, Baxter. *Marvels and Commonplaces: Renaissance Literary Criticism.* New York: Random House, 1968.

Spingarn, Joel E. *A History of Literary Criticism in the Renaissance.* New York: The Columbia University Press, 1908.

SIR PHILIP SIDNEY

After Longinus in the Christian era until Sir Philip Sidney in the English Renaissance, literary criticism, in the strictest sense of the term, was not practised. Such a statement is not meant to cast aside, much less eradicate out of memory, the accomplishments of a whole era. What are available during this vast span are some rhetorical treatises valuable for historical research. With Sidney this period of critical inactivity comes to a grinding halt. Sidney is the first critic—and a critic of lasting significance—representing all that is superlative in Renaissance criticism. Sidney's services to England are most memorable. Besides being a public servant, he was also a man of letters of great reputation. Spenser dedicated his *The Shepherd's Calendar* to him, and honoured him in his *Astrophel*. Sidney was the very model of excellence for many of his contemporaries. Many of his distinguished fellowmen dedicated their works to him as they considered him a 'rendezvous of learning.' His bountiful generosity is enshrined in his immortal phrase, 'thy necessity is yet greater than mine.' He is said to have addressed these words to a dying soldier, offering him his water bottle when he himself was wounded beyond recovery. It is said that his tutor at Christ Church wished that when he died his tomb should bear the inscription that he had been the 'preceptor of that most noble knight, Philip Sidney.' According to Ben Jonson, he was the 'one in whom all the Muses met.' Every succeeding generation has paid encomiums to his fond memory. Chaucer's description of the pilgrim to Canterbury may very well be applied to Sidney, 'He was a verray, parfit, gentil knight.'

Historically speaking, Sidney's work appeared at a time when such a treatise was a felt necessity. Elizabethan literature was still in its infancy. No great work had come out of England. In terms of quality, it was poorer than the writings from European countries. Chaucer was the only poet of whom the English could feel proud. Shakespeare was in his teens. No work of any standing was in existence in drama apart from *Gorboduc,* which in itself was no piece of dramatic art, but only a mediocre melodrama. In less than three decades after Sidney's work, England nearly became the cultural capital of Europe. In the words of Spingarn, he is 'the veritable epitome of the literary criticism of the Italian Renaissance' (170). What Spingarn implies is that Sidney drew from all the best that was available in Italian Renaissance thought. For example, it was from the Italians that Sidney borrowed the concept of the dramatic unities, the poet as second creator, and tragedy as evoking and winning our admiration. He drew from Horace the idea of the poet being the seer, and the notion of the twin function of poetry. He must have used the Latin translations of Aristotle and Plato rendered by the Italians. He must also have been touched by the spirit of nationalism that dominated French thinking. For these reasons, one may not consider him original in his theory. But what he has done with his eclectic borrowings is what matters to us. Critics like J.W.H. Atkins charge that he has not been able to absorb completely, and present a harmonious body of his eclectic borrowings.

We are not quite certain as to when Sidney's *Apologie* was composed. It was probably written in 1583 (according to external evidence), though it was published in 1595, posthumously. The treatise bears two titles. His work was published in two separate editions, *The Defence of Poesie* by William Ponsonby and *An Apology for Poetrie* by Henry Olney. The manuscript itself might have been without a title. Such uncertainties about the dates and titles of works were not an uncommon feature of the Renaissance. During the Renaissance, discussion on literature, and polemical pamphleteering maintaining a high level of debate were a common phenomenon. These constantly touched just four areas of literary culture: 1. the art of poetry in verse, 2. treatises on poetry and poetics, 3. treatises in the nature of answers to specific charges, and 4. apologetic essays in defence of the art of poetry. Obviously, Sidney's *Apologie* belongs to the fourth type. Defences, such as Sidney's, were quite popular during the Renaissance. There are instances of such writings by Thomas Lodge, and Richard Puttenham. It was a sort of literary genre in which one could talk about the greatness of poetry in general. There were some justifiable reasons as well, for attacks on the art of poetry were in regular practice.

Stephen Gosson's vitriolic attack in his long-titled pamphlet *School of Abuse*: *Containing a pleasant invective against Poets, Pipers, Players, Jesters and such like Caterpillars of the Commonwealth* (1579), denouncing works of literature as the works of the Devil, occasioned Sidney's spirited rebuttal. Gosson was given a fitting but untitled reply by Lodge in the same year. However, Lodge does not offer enough justification for art from a purely literary perspective. Ironically enough Gosson's pamphlet was dedicated 'To the right noble Gentleman, Master Philip Sidney, Esquire.' At a philosophic level, both Gosson and Sidney might be talking about the same thing, as their attitudes are similarly based. Another view is that Gosson was not a noted figure in the realm of literary thought, and he was not worthy of Sidney's attention. In fact, he does not take direct notice of him. Sidney may have had other such attacks in mind, or the treatise might be taken as a general defence, in its own right, recapping many different Renaissance views. *Apologie* happens to be the first English text, complete and comprehensive, propounding a set of principles on the art of literature. In the words of Wimsatt and Brooks, it is 'the English locus of closest contact with Italian criticism and a brilliant epitome of what was best in that criticism.' *Apologie* is carefully crafted in the form of a rhetorical argument and the pattern is clear for analysis.

The form or plan of *Apologie* conforms to the rhetorical principle of construction. Sidney follows the general oratorical method made up of narration, proposition and proof. *Apologie* falls into seven broad divisions: 1. Exordium, 2. Narration, describing the antiquity of poetry, 3. Proposition, that poetry is imitation, 4. Division – Religious, Philosophic, Imitative, 5. Proof, 6. Refutation, and 7. Peroration. Sidney is said to have applied the Ciceronian principle of oratory to his method of developing the arguments. The argument is interspersed with recapitulatory perorations. Such a method (or form) enables him to maintain the sequence of his argument, and have control of his subject. It saves him from the sin of prolixity. Scholars have classified Sidney's text into different sections, but the main line of thought is easily traceable. The treatise opens with a prologue about the need for vindicating poetry. If simple horsemanship needs to be defended, why not the art of poetry? If poetry is subject to condemnation, it would mean that a nation's culture and its heritage are the real target. Were not the philosophers and statesmen of yore primarily poets, and other things only afterwards? Instances abound in plenty, and are available among the Romans and the Greeks, peoples of a hoary past and ancient civilisation.

> There is no art delivered unto mankind that hath not the works of nature for his principal object . . . Only the poet, disdaining to be tied to any such objection, lifted up with the vigour of his own invention, doth grow, in effect, into another nature, in making

> things either better than nature, as the heroes, demigods, Cyclops, chimeras, furies, and such like, so as he goeth hand in hand with nature, not enclosed within the narrow warrant of her gifts, but freely ranging within the zodiac of his own wit. Nature never set forth the earth in so rich tapestry as divers poets have done; neither with pleasant rivers, fruitful trees, sweet-smelling flowers, nor whatsoever else may make the too-much loved earth more lovely; her world is brazen, the poets only deliver a golden (145).

Sidney offers a definition of poetry—a poet is the maker, and poetry is the art of representation. 'Poesy therefore is an art of imitation, for so Aristotle termeth it in his word *mimesis*, that is to say, a representing, counterfeiting or figuring forth—to speak metaphorically, a speaking picture; with this end to teach and delight' (146). He classifies different categories of poetry, and adds that metre is not necessary for poetry. Poetry is proved to be superior to history and philosophy.

> Now therein of all sciences is our poet the monarch. For he doth not only show the way, but giveth so sweet a prospect into the way, as will entice any man to enter into it. Nay, he doth as if your journey should lie through a fair vineyard, at the first give you a cluster of grapes, that, full of that taste, you may long to pass further. He beginneth not with obscure definitions, which must blur the margent with interpretations, and load the memory with doubtfulness; but he cometh to you with words set in delightful proportion, either accompanied with, or prepared for, the well-enchanting skill of music; and with a tale forsooth he cometh unto you, with a tale which holdeth children from play and old men from chimney corners (151).

He discusses different generic divisions of poetry: pastoral, elegiac, iambic, satiric, comic, tragic, lyric, and heroic. He defends poetry against the charges levelled against these. Poetry is not immoral as it is charged; only its abuse is immoral. Poetry cannot be effeminate, since all men of action in warfare have felt inspired by poetry. Plato decried only the improper use of poetry. English poetry had fallen into disrepute on account of the fact that poets had not been inspired sufficiently by nature, and also because the right sort of persons fitted for the task had not taken up the art. The fault does not rest with poetry, but with the practitioners of the art.

Sidney surveys the poetic scene in England beginning from Chaucer, and bemoans the degeneracy of drama as reflected in *Gorboduc* which violates the essential unities so vital in dramatic composition. He discusses the function of tragedy, the comedy and the lyric. Then, he goes on to discuss diction and style in poetry and prose with reference to those who do not employ a natural style, but are carried away by conceits. Sidney then discusses prosody, glorifying the English language which has both the rhymed and unrhymed facilities built into its nature and system. The treatise concludes with robust claims of the greatness of poetry as an object fit for veneration. He blesses those who love and enjoy the charms of poetry, and denounces those who have no sensibility to appreciate it. Sidney's main objective in the treatise is to show the true value of poetry, and he does it by presenting to us a picture of the past. Churton Collins, one of the editors of *Apologie,* has an honest appraisal of the work: 'Its arresting charm, its distinguishing characteristic, is its genuine and all-pervading enthusiasm, which fuses into unity the main thesis and makes the work both in the effect of its general impression and in its central purpose absolutely unique.' And of this famed treatise, Saintsbury observes, 'It exhibits the temper of the generation which actually produced the first fruits of the greatest Elizabethan poetry; it served as a stimulant and encouragement to all the successive generations of the age' (57).

Apologie is in the form of a classical oration. In an age of puritan suspicion of literature, this forceful justification of poetry was a spirited defence in the truest sense of the term. Sidney's emphasis on the moral values of literature—'the ending end of all earthly learning is virtuous action'—finds its echo in many of the latter-day poet-critics too. Milton in his 'Of Education,' Pope in his 'Essay on Man,' and Shelley in his essay ('A Defence of Poetry') that echoes Sidney's title have spoken about the refinement of the moral imagination, and the morally sustaining power of literature. Sidney inaugurates that great tradition in criticism which subordinates purely technical matters in literary works, and examination of writers to enquiries into wider and deeper philosophic problems. That is why Sidney is regarded as an inalienable part of the central tradition that descends from Aristotle to the present.

English literary criticism during the Renaissance cannot be considered in isolation, since it was a part of the general credo or doctrine prevalent during the times. Historians are of the view that in the sixteenth and seventeenth centuries, English criticism developed in four different directions. The first kind of criticism called rhetoric was concerned with style and form as the characteristic ingredients of literature. Rhetoric laid down the guidelines or principles of writing. The second type of criticism was addressed to the classification of forms and metrical systems. The third stage witnessed philosophic criticism, which was also of the nature of a defence or apology. Sidney was the first exponent of this mode of criticism. With Ben Jonson, the union of criticism and creation was forged. That was the fourth stage. The fifth stage, which came about the second half of the seventeenth century, saw the French influence on English literary criticism in the shape of neoclassical principles.

Sidney's *Apologie* is an epitome of the general Renaissance criticism. The main sources of influence were Aristotle, Minturno, Scaliger, Plutarch, Virgil, Plato and a host of others. Under Minturno's influence, Sidney asserts the antiquity and superiority of poetry. The history of Greece, Rome and England confirms this. Poetry was the medium used by ancient philosophers and historians. It is the original source of all knowledge. The prophetic character of the poet was recognised in ancient times. Poets flourished and were honoured in all nations, however uncivilised or primitive.

The credit for introducing Aristotelianism should go to Sidney. Poetry is an art of imitation. It is not imitation in the narrow sense of the term. The poet transforms or transmutes with the faculty of imagination what is commonplace or actual. To quote Sidney's definition again, 'Poesy therefore is an art of imitation, for so Aristotle termeth it in his word *mimesis*, that is to say, a representing, counterfeiting, or figuring forth—to speak metaphorically, a speaking picture; with this end, to teach and delight' (146). Sidney owes these ideas to Aristotle, Plutarch and Horace. Speech and reason set men apart from the lower order of creation and it is in poetry that the gift of speech, in its highest and most exalted form, is manifested. The Horatian doctrine that poetry is delightful instruction was reiterated by Scaliger. The end of all learning is ethical improvement. Poetry, being an exercise of the imagination regulated by judgment, and being concerned with the ideal and not actual, realises its moral purposes more effectively than the traditional instructors, history and philosophy.

Sidney may be regarded as the first dramatic critic. His conception of tragedy is an amalgam of medieval notions, and Aristotle's doctrine as interpreted by the Italian critics. The classicist in Sidney is offended by the indiscriminate and purposeless intermingling of tragedy and comedy, and also by the deviation from the principle of the three unities. Aristotle had enunciated the unity of action. It was Castelvetro, who in his commentary on *Poetics,* formulated the other two unities. Sidney's review of English literature since the time of Chaucer, and his bold and frank denunciation of contemporary poetry and drama qualify him to be called, perhaps in a limited sense, the first practising critic. He was not an inflexible classicist. The two strains—the Classicist and the Romantic—are juxtaposed in him. He is a classicist when he insists that all forms of poetry serve a didactic purpose and that the dramatic unities are inviolable. The Romantic strain in him is evident in his idealisation of poetry and the poet. 'Poetry is the first light-giver of knowledge.'

Sidney's *Apologie* can make no claim to originality. Its value lies in other factors. That it is a landmark in the history of criticism is undeniable. It has brought, within a single compass, a wide range of critical principles current during the Renaissance. Critical doctrines gathered from a variety of sources have been given a recognisable shape and order. Emphasis, clarity and coherence are Sidney's virtues as the vindicator of the merits of poetry. His denunciation of contemporary literature exercised a corrective influence. By focussing attention on the shortcomings of contemporary literature, his *Apologie* stimulated interest in the art of writing as a discipline to be consciously and carefully cultivated. Sidney's *Apologie* is not a model of good prose. Many of his sentences are long, loose, and often clumsy. The rules of syntax and grammar are not always respected. But these are pardonable faults, when we remember that the language was in a state of flux in the sixteenth century, and the principle of grammar had not been laid down. But Sidney's prose bears the stamp of his personality. None can miss the crusading zeal, impassioned eloquence, earnestness, irony, indignation, and dignity running through *Apologie*.

The discussion of Sidney may be concluded with Atkins's apt remarks: 'It is therefore as the first piece of literary criticism in English that is literature itself that the *Apology* figures in critical history . . . As a fitting legacy of one of England's noblest and gentlest souls the work will continue to charm modern readers with its idealism, its sanity, its humour and its grace' (138).

Works Cited

Adams, Hazard, ed. *Literary Criticism since Plato.* 1971. New York: Harcourt Brace Jovanovich College Publishers, 1992. Unless otherwise stated, all textual references are drawn from this volume.

Atkins, J.W.H. *Literary Criticism: The Renascence.* London: Methuen and Co. Ltd., 1947.

Saintsbury, George. *A History of English Criticsm.* London: William Blackwood & Sons Ltd., 1955.

Select Bibliography

Buxton, John. *Sir Philip Sidney and the English Renaissance.* London: Macmillan, 1987.

Kay, Dennis, ed. *Sir Philip Sidney: An Anthology of Modern Criticism.* Oxford: Clarendon Press, 1987.

Sidney Journal, a semi-annual international scholarly periodical published by *The Sidney Society.* The journal is designed to provide a critical forum for scholars and students of Sir Philip Sidney.

3

English Neoclassical Criticism

ohnson's famous remark, that Dryden was the first writer who taught us the principles for determining the merit of a literary composition, is pregnant with meaning. It may be taken to mean that during the period from Dryden to the end of the eighteenth century, under the influence of Dryden, the criticism of arts in general, and poetry in particular, attained the status of an important sphere of human activity worthy of practice by the best minds. We have thus a whole lot of writers who have thought it worthwhile to write about the merits and defects of literary works, or formulate rules of composition. Some characteristics are worthy of being classified. There were works which were concerned with reducing the rules of composition to some methods or precepts; there were works on the qualities of individual works and different styles of composition; there were works on general qualities of art and their foundation on human nature; and finally, a number of writings about the problem, nature and function of criticism itself, such as Pope's *Essay on Criticism*. Despite the variety and disparity of these writings, it is possible to see a unified development in English criticism from Dryden to Johnson. Dryden had confessed that he owed his lights to Aristotle and his interpreters, and to Horace and Longinus. The criticism of the Restoration and the eighteenth century shows a preference for the Roman rather than the Greek, Horace rather than Aristotle, Quintillion rather than Longinus, and the modes of analyses sought for were more in the nature of the rhetorical rather than the poetical. Hence neoclassical criticism was concerned with what poets ought to do rather than what they might do or have done. The ends rather than the means by which they were achieved were what mattered. Discussions on art, artist, work, and audience centred on the issues of rules and the

end results. It was given to the early nineteenth century to supply a new system of enquiry and belief based on a philosophical rather than the rhetorical tradition that came as a refreshing change in Coleridge and the Romantics. In neoclassical criticism, the methodology for the analyses and discussion of works was drawn from the tradition of the rhetoric where the end is persuasion rather than pleasure. Art was a set of rules by which nature was imitated, or even improved, but dependent on nature as 'the universal light,' the ultimate source. 'Nature still, but Nature methodised' is how Pope phrased it.

JOHN DRYDEN (1631–1700)

John Dryden was such an influential personality in so many spheres of learning that the period 1660 to 1700 is rightly called the Age of Dryden. He was a poet, dramatist, translator, critic, all rolled into one. Dr Samuel Johnson called John Dryden 'the father of English criticism'. What Johnson meant was that Dryden was the one who launched this new genre of literary criticism on its way into the world of art. T.S. Eliot echoed the same sentiment when he said that Dryden was 'positively the first master of English criticism,' and added, 'the great work of Dryden in criticism is that at the right moment he became conscious of the necessity of affirming the native element in literature' (*Use of Poetry* 14). This may sound a tall claim to us, brought up, as we are, in the twentieth century critical tradition, with a great deal of exposure to close textual analysis, and rigorous evaluation of pieces of literature. We had better realise that he was the pioneer, the first practitioner of comparison and analysis in the history of criticism. It is not an exaggeration to say that English criticism evolved from Dryden. He confessed that his chief endeavour was to delight the age in which he lived. Essentially Dryden was a 'prefatory' man even as Bernard Shaw would become later. Much of his criticism is found in his prefaces. This is the starting point for criticism in the case of Dryden. For justifying his own works, he had to indulge in an analysis of his own which can be called self-criticism. Dryden uses the term 'examen' for critical analysis, and this term was originally used by the French playwright, Corneille. When

Dryden wrote prefaces to his plays, he practised dramatic criticism that was descriptive in nature. This early criticism of Dryden was defensive, trying to please his audience with what he had done. Even today the dialogue form of his famous essay *Of Dramatic Poesy* remains unique. No other critic has taken up this form for discussion. Dryden's model was obviously the Ciceronian dialogues, and Plato's later works.

For our purposes, the most relevant works of Dryden which are of a theoretical nature are 'Defence of an Essay of Dramatic Poesy,' 'A Parallel of Poetry and Painting,' 'Preface to Fables Ancient and Modern,' and the most important and widely anthologised piece *An Essay of Dramatic Poesy*. It is the only work of criticism that Dryden published as a separate work. It was revised by him, and published thrice during his lifetime. It is also the most comprehensive of his critical works. It is reported that during the plague years in England 1665–66, he retired to the countryside residence of his father-in-law, the Earl of Berkshire, at Charlton Park, and wrote this dialogue after equipping himself sufficiently well for the task on hand. Despite its overt dialogue form, it is not a dialogue in the narrow sense, since there are only long discussions and explanations of critical stands taken by the four characters (interlocutors) who engage themselves in a literary debate. It was an important document for his literary career and for us as an equally important document of critical theory. It is lively as an essay for the light conversational opening and humorous ending. On the occasion of a naval victory of the English over the Dutch, there is an exchange among the four interlocutors going on a boat expedition. The analogy between the victorious English, and Dryden's conscious attempt at asserting the strength of the English in the theatre can hardly go unnoticed. The essay had a topical interest, for the characters were real people, all men of letters, and Dryden's contemporaries. These were first identified in 1800 by the Englishman Edward Malone. Lisideius represented Charles Sedley; Crites, Sir Robert Howard, Dryden's brother-in-law; Eugenius (Greek for well-born), Charles Sackville or Lord Buckhurst; and Neander (Greek for 'new man' and an anagram for 'Dryden'), John Dryden himself.

Beginning with a light-hearted banter of the fashionable poetry of the time, the argument moves on to a different plane to discuss four themes. Are the modern poets as good as the ancients? Are the contemporaries as good as the Elizabethans? Are the English as good as the French? Of the two, which is the right choice for drama—rhyme or blank verse? The argument is restricted to the genre of drama. The main questions on the dramaturgy of the day are discussed to threadbare detail. *Of Dramatic Poesy* deals with major issues in drama: the ancients versus the moderns, the French versus the English, blank verse versus heroic verse. The dialogue form assures an impartial enquiry. Dryden is only interested in defending his profession as an English playwright. In his note, he makes it clear that his purpose was 'to vindicate the honour of the English writers from the censure of those who unjustly prefer the French before him.' Hence, his defence of the English dramatic tradition, and his justification for his use of rhyme in his tragedies forms the clinching section of his argument. Every section in the dialogue is intended to serve this end. Even the definition of the play suits this purpose. He uses Jonson's play *Silent Woman*, not to pay any tribute to him, but to build up a case for the English tradition in drama, for Jonson was the most reputed dramatist of his time. So is the case of Shakespeare who represented the living English stage. Only Neander's views are Dryden's, and he speaks for the greater part, besides possessing the advantage of being the last speaker who has the last word. The three characters echo the critical sentiments of his time in the battle of the books. Crites is the spokesman for neoclassicism, and Neander for the Aristotelian tradition. Lisideius is empirical, and Eugenius, the least strict in his views among the four. Dryden presents the different viewpoints with absolute honesty and integrity without attacking or being partial to any side. He presents various points of view in a balanced manner without refuting any or holding on obstinately to any other.

Dryden's tolerance and impartiality are evident in the entire *Essay*. He favours and defends the genre tragicomedy, rejects the addiction to the unities. He says, 'We have invented, increased and perfected a more pleasant way of writing for the Stage than was ever known to the Ancients or Moderns of any Nation, which is Tragicomedy.' Dryden had the generosity to accept the superiority of the Elizabethan drama, though he argued about the development and growth in dramatic form achieved by

Restoration playwrights. There are instances where Dryden is willing to accommodate contemporary practices in the theatre, though they may go against Aristotelian norms. Dryden's flexibility and accommodationism could even be mistaken for inconsistency. By and large, there is coherence in Dryden's theoretical stance, though we must concede that in the later Dryden one notices revisions of his earlier views and pronouncements. His basic faith in the mimetic form of art, and the Horatian function of literature is unshakeable. Dryden upholds the traditional view regarding the ultimate end of literature, and the force of the traditional literatures of the past as criteria for standards of judgment. This is convincingly stated in his *Essay*: 'For generally to have pleased, and through all ages, must bear the force of universal tradition. And if you would appeal from thence to right reason, you will gain no more by it in effect, than, first, to set up your reason against those authors; and, secondly, against all those who have admired them.'

Generally, Dryden takes a historical point of view while examining and judging past writers, but this does not mean that he is a relativist. For him, rules were invented to reform our taste and refine our judgement. Dryden's ultimate belief in literature being a mimetic art is most clearly expressed in his famous definition of the play: 'A just and lively image of human nature, representing its passions and humours, and the changes of fortune to which it is subject; for the delight and instruction of mankind.' All the four participants in the dialogue accept this as the broad-based definition of drama. Some stress the word 'just' and some others 'lively.' 'Just' may be used in the sense of decorum and correctness, and 'lively' in the sense of vivid and lifelike. The French are correct in their representation, but the plays do not stir our emotions, according to Neander. The idea of mimesis is found in other places also, such as in the use of the terms, imaging, representing, imitation of nature, following nature. Dryden pinned his faith to the universality of literature. According to Eliot, he does not seem to be very much interested in creative theory. Much of Dryden's evaluative criticism concerns itself with the language and style of poets, except for his famous evaluations of Shakespeare and Chaucer. Here is his estimate of Shakespeare:

> To begin, then, with Shakespeare. He was the man who of all modern and perhaps ancient poets had the largest and most comprehensive soul. All the images of nature were still present to him, and he drew them, not laboriously, but luckily; when he describes anything, you more than see it, you feel it too. Those who accuse him to have wanted learning, give him the greater commendation: he was naturally learned; he needed not the spectacle of books to read nature; he looked inwards, and found her there. I cannot say he is everywhere alike; were he so I should do him injury to compare him with the greatest of mankind. He is many times flat, insipid; his comic wit degenerating into clichés, his serious swelling into bombast. But he is always great, when some great occasion is presented to him (231).

On Ben Jonson, Dryden's observation is most telling. 'If I would compare him with Shakespeare, I must acknowledge him the more correct poet, but Shakespeare the greater wit. Shakespeare was the Homer, or father of our dramatic poets: Jonson was the Virgil, the pattern of elaborate writing: I admire him but I love Shakespeare' (232). Chaucer is for Dryden the father of English poetry. He is a perpetual fountain of good sense. He holds him in the same degree of veneration as the Grecians held Homer or the Romans Virgil. Here is Dryden's estimate of Chaucer in the 'Preface to the Fables':

> He (Chaucer) must have been a man of a most wonderful comprehensive nature, because, as it has been truly observed of him, he has taken into the compass of his *Canterbury Tales* the various manners and humours (as we now call them) of the whole English nation in his age. Not a single character has escaped him. All his pilgrims are severally distinguished from each other; and not only in their inclinations but in their physiognomies and persons . . . 'Tis sufficient to say, according to the English proverb, that *here is God's plenty* (190).

Aristotle, Horace and Longinus were the major influences on Dryden. His immediate follower, in many ways, was Johnson. Dryden does not arrive at any conclusion as regards the problem of the three unities, which has given rise to wide-ranging controversy among critics and dramatists. It was finally given to Samuel Johnson to have the final say in the matter when he dismissed the argument about the unity of time and place as pointless. It appears that Dryden upholds the three unities on rational and psychological grounds. By reducing the strain on human reason and imagination, the unities successfully contribute to dramatic verisimilitude. The observance of the unities adds to the credibility of the plot. Hence they are to be commended. Dryden is not dogmatic in his views on the rules of dramatic art, but appeals to commonsense. Crites, a spokesman of the ancients says, 'If by these rules we should judge our modern plays, 'tis probable that few of them would endure the trial: that which should be the business of a day, takes up in some of them an age; instead of one action, they are the epitomes of a man's life; and for one spot of ground (which the stage should represent) we are sometimes in more countries than the map can show' (218). Dryden's *Essay* is one of the acknowledged classics of literary theory. He does not reject any argument in the essay in favour of others. He presents to us a variety of views, different from one another, but, not in any sense, antithetical to one another. All of them are true and legitimate on their own terms. The balance of the essay accommodates all the views. The golden mean is the classical tradition that fuses and orders all the points of view expressed by the debaters. Historically speaking, Dryden made the classical tradition available to his age, and thus, was a civilising factor to his people. His criticism came at a time of transition, ushering in a new age.

We must learn to understand Dryden's contribution to criticism on his own terms. He wrote some three hundred years ago. We tend to overlook that fact. He is different from our conception of a modern critic. He does not analyse a text as we would do, and does not indulge in extensive theorising. His criticism was to be found in prefaces, prologues and dedications, and these were meant to defend his works and vindicate them from possible attacks. He shifts his stand to suit practical exigencies and he was a poet-critic. We are likely, therefore, to conclude that he was an amateur and connoisseur of the arts who wrote forceful prose and made observations befitting an amateur. Writing was his profession, and he wrote criticism for more than three decades, between 1664 and 1700. The inherent weaknesses in Dryden's criticism can also be attributed to the inadequacy of English critical system prevailing at that time. He himself acknowledged that he was sailing in a vast ocean without other help than the pole star of the ancients, and the rules of the

French stage which were different from those of the English. His thorough commitment to living literature and living audience makes his criticism original and informed. Dryden's comprehensive knowledge of the tradition, and his cosmopolitanism make him a great critic. The usual charge against him is that though he uses the didactical form of the dialogue, he does not reward us with any lucid argument. The *Essay* is the only attempt of Dryden in formal criticism. In his last critical essay Dryden wrote, 'I have built a house where I intended but a lodge.' This is the right summation of his achievement.

Dryden wrote his earliest critical essay in 1664, a dedicatory epistle to his first play, *The Rival Ladies.* Until the date of his death in 1700, not a year passed without his writing some criticism, either in the form of a preface, an essay or a discourse. We have thus a substantial body of criticism from Dryden, though not as large as those of Johnson or Arnold who were primarily critics. Dryden was a poet first and last, and a critic, only incidentally. No criticism existed in England before him. Sidney's *Apologie* locates criticism within a larger framework of morals and ethics and philosophy. It is said that Dryden brought criticism from the church to the coffee house. For the first time, literary works are examined with literary problems in mind. It is with some such view in mind that Johnson should have called him 'the father of English criticism,' for it was he who 'first taught us to determine on principles the merit of composition.' When Dryden came upon the scene, he had several advantages. He was a first-rate poet with a clear common sense apprehension of men and matters. He had also a sound knowledge of the ancient classics and to cap it all he had argumentative faculty, best suited to the art of criticism. According to Saintsbury, he occupied a position shared in the history of criticism only by Dante and Goethe, the position of the greatest man of letters in his own country, and 'it is in criticism that Dryden best shows that original faculty which has often been denied him elsewhere' (112). Dryden is never in the habit of contradicting the views of ancient critics and men of letters. On the value of diction and language of poetry, he was uncompromising in his views. Ancient criticism did not concern itself with this aspect, but Dryden knew that these were fundamental to poetic pleasure. To quote Saintsbury again:

> He established (let us hope for all time) the English fashion of criticising, as Shakespeare did the English fashion of dramatising—the fashion aiming at delight, at truth, at justice, at nature, at poetry, and letting the rules take care of themselves (129).

and yet again,

> We have, in short, in Dryden the first very considerable example in England, if not anywhere, of the critic who, while possessing fairly wide knowledge of literature, attributes no arbitrary or conventional eminence to certain parts of it, but at least endeavours to consider it as a whole; of the critic who is never afraid to say 'Why?'; of the critic who asks, not whether he ought to like such and such a thing, but whether he does like it, and why he likes it, and whether there is any real reason why he should not like it; of the critic, finally, who tries, without prepossession or convention, to get a general grasp of the book or author, and then to set forth that grasp in luminous language, and with a fair display of supporting analysis and argument (130–31).

No critic is free from faults, and Dryden too is not faultless. His concessions to tradition, his inconsistencies in his stand, his lack of concreteness and the resultant vagueness in argument are some of the weaknesses that do not brook any excuse. Aristotle said that it is the mark of an educated person to seek a degree of precision available to him in any sphere of knowledge, and we may reasonably conclude that this is what Dryden attempts to achieve in his famous *Essay*. It was Dryden who helped the formation of the neoclassical school of literature and criticism in England. He cast his *Essay* in the form of a dialogue deliberately with a view to presenting the different points of view and ideas that had been agitating the minds of his contemporaries rather than issuing dogmatic statements. Some hostile critics charged him with shifting politics and being a time-server for the powers that be, and that he kept the arguments deliberately inconclusive so as not to offend anyone. It is easy for us to see for ourselves that this charge is far from the truth.

We should also realise that among the English critics, he was the first to attempt descriptive criticism. Before Dryden's time, criticism was mostly judicial and legislative. No tradition as such in detailed criticism was available to the Elizabethans. In his long and distinguished career as poet and dramatist, extending beyond forty years, he wrote only one work in formal criticism, his *Essay*.

It was Dryden who had anticipated our modern methods of analysis. He can be said to belong to the lineage descending to Coleridge, Arnold and Eliot in whom an artist becomes a critic. He was the forerunner of that tradition in English criticism that treats the whole of European literature as one province. Arnold and Eliot were to follow suit later. Johnson commented in his *Lives*: 'the favourite exercise of his (Dryden's) mind was ratiocination.' George Watson concludes his chapter on Dryden with the view that he (Dryden) is most perfectly sure of what he wishes to say. Watson adds:

> It is this supreme literary tact, this talent for evasion and equivocation that allows him to play several critical roles at once. But the cost of such a sense of tact is crippling: for all the superficial vigour of his prose, real critical assertions are seldom made (The contrast with Johnson is here sharp and all in Johnson's favour). His achievement, ultimately, lies not in analysing much or in doing it well, but in providing the inestimable example of showing that literary analysis is possible at all (57).

Watson, however, is incorrect in calling Dryden's style superficial. Almost every other critic has justly praised his prose style. He is even credited with being the founder of the 'other harmony,' the art of prose. He was surely a gifted prose writer. Did not Arnold call him the 'classic of our prose?' His style is fluent and flowing, rhythmic and adorned with deft images. It is informal without being too familiar.

Dryden was a versatile professional man of letters. We get so much caught up in estimating the criticism of Dryden that we are likely to overlook his powers as a translator. The last two decades of his fruitful writing career were devoted to translating Greek and Roman classics. Of his own translation of *Aeneid*, Dryden observes, 'I have endeavoured to make Virgil speak such English as he would himself have spoken, if he had been born in England, and at this present age' (8). According to him, the primary duty of a translator is to convey to a modern audience the substance and the spirit, the tone and tenor of the original composition. In other words, what a text did in the source language should be done by its translated version in the target language. Dryden did not approve of strict literalism and word-for-word matching (metaphrase) even as he did not approve of recreation in translation (imitation). Faithful, but an autonomous restatement of the original (paraphrase) was the ideal course for him. His own translations of Ovid's *Epistles*, and Virgil's *Aeneid*, testify to his views. They are, at once, inspired and inspiring. In his *Idler*, number 70, Johnson explains Dryden's role as a translator in the following words: 'Dryden saw very early that closeness best preserved an author's sense, and that freedom best exhibited his spirit; he therefore will deserve the highest praise, who can give a representation at once faithful and pleasing, who can convey the same thoughts with the same graces, and who when he translates changes nothing but the language' (217). It is worth mentioning that Virgil left his manuscript of *Aeneid* unfinished after eleven years of toil, and his translator Dryden did not finish his translation, not being completely satisfied with it, after seven years of intermittent labour.

To conclude, then, 'by his enlightened doctrine, his literary appreciations and his critical methods he enabled readers not only to perceive fresh beauties in literature, but also to understand more clearly excellences which they had hitherto but vaguely valued; and these after all are the supreme tasks of criticism in all the ages' (Atkins 129). Dryden's work of literary criticism remains a lasting testament.

Works Cited

Adams, Hazard, ed. *Literary Criticism since Plato.* 1971. New York: Harcourt Brace Jovanovich College Publishers, 1992. Unless otherwise stated, all textual references are drawn from this volume.

Atkins, J.W.H. *Literary Criticism: 17th and 18th Centuries.* New York: Barnes and Noble, 1951.

Dryden, John, tr. *Virgil's Aeneid.* New York: Airmont Publishing Company, Inc., 1968.

———. 'Preface to the Fables.' *The English Critical Tradition.* Vol.1. Ed. S. Ramaswami & V.S. Seturaman. Madras: The Macmillan Co. of India Ltd., 1977.

Eliot, T.S. *The Use of Poetry and Use of Criticism.* 1933. London: Faber and Faber, 1964.

Johnson, Samuel. *The Idler* and *The Adventurer.* Ed. Walter Jackson Bate. New Haven: Yale University Press, 1963.

Saintsbury, George. *A History of English Literary Criticism.* London: William Blackwood & Sons Ltd., 1955.

Watson, George. *The Literary Critics: A Study of English Descriptive Criticism.* Harmondsworth, Middlesex: Penguin Books, 1962.

Select Bibliography

Eliot, T.S. *John Dryden, the Poet, the Dramatist, the Critic: Three Essays.* New York: Haskell House, 1966.

Hume, Robert D. *Dryden's Criticism.* Ithaca: Cornell University Press, 1970.

Huntley, Frank. L. *The Unity of Dryden's Dramatic Criticism.* Chicago: University of Chicago Press, 1942.

ALEXANDER POPE (1688–1744)

Though short in stature, Alexander Pope was among the tallest critics of his age. His contribution to neoclassical criticism is as important as that of the others of his period. He aimed largely at improving the literary taste, and establishing exacting standards for literary compositions. His criticism is spread over *An Essay on Criticism* (1711), *Preface to Shakespeare* (1725), *Art of Sinking* (1727–8), *Epistles to Augustus* (1733), *Preface to the Translation of the Iliad* (1715), and his *Letters.* That he was a prodigy could be seen in his youthful composition *An Essay on Criticism* written when he was barely twenty-three. It is probably the most comprehensive pronouncement of the neoclassical system. Pope's *Essay* got published in 1711 by which time neoclassical criticism had already taken deep root. He limits himself in his essay to remarks, and critical principles of literary compositions in general. He does not examine, as Dryden does, any work written during or before his time.

The *Essay* is obviously modelled on the Horatian form, and it follows a neat plan: a survey and consideration of the art of criticism in general (1–201); an examination of the important causes for literary misjudgement (202–560); characteristics of an ideal critic (561–640); and a short account of the history of criticism (641–end). It appears like a critical miscellany which discusses, with an open mind, principles which were formulated at different times. A medley of views is seen to be thrown around without a systematic organising principle. Hence, one is at a loss to build up a coherent theory out of this. On the act of literary judgement and business of criticism, Pope has much sane advice to offer: neglecting the work as a whole and judging it by parts is a fault; using conceits for the sake of using them is another; paying attention to diction, style and the media of composition without adequate attention to the content is the third; popular impressionist opinions and prejudicial views are wrong; judgement based on dogmatic views, or extreme fastidiousness in estimating a work is also bad. A true critic has knowledge of the work. He judges with modesty and discrimination, and does not exaggerate minor faults. These were the qualities possessed by great critics like Aristotle. Every poet, and every critic must read the works of the ancients, because the ancients had discovered the rules of composition, and had observed nature. Nature and Homer were the same. 'To copy Nature is to copy them.' Modern writers should be wary of transgressing rules laid down by the ancients. Pope is not in favour of the conceits of the metaphysicals. Poetry of commonsense is the best for man. 'True wit is nature to advantage dressed; / What oft is thought, but ne'er so well expressed.'

The real problem with such statements is that they are much too general. Pope lacks historical sense. According to Watson, Pope's *Essay* is 'Dryden's cultural nationalism put into verse.' What he means is that rules are good if they are ancient, and not good if they come from France. Pope's demands of a critic are beyond the reach of ordinary practitioners.

> A little learning is a dangerous thing;
> Drink deep, or taste not the Pierian Spring:
> There shallow drafts intoxicate the brain,
> And drinking largely sobers us again. (215–18)

He must possess a level of scholarship almost impossible for the common critic to acquire; he should not practise criticism unless he has established himself as a first-rate poet. One observable fact is that, despite all this fuss about idealism in critical practice, one cannot find much evidence of critical survival during the

Augustan Age. Rather the Age was characterised by a growth in periodical reviewing and criticism of the hour. Pope is Drydenesque in more senses than one, but much bolder and often brusque. There are countless saws and maxims which he has contributed to the English language. Eternal truths are presented in an epigrammatic and terse style. It is often charged that the work has nothing original except a sprinkling of commonplaces, and a collection of urbane platitudes that have grown stale.

The *Essay* of Pope remains a significant document in Augustan criticism to this day. But it has elicited widely divergent views from his critics and admirers. Atkins says of this work,

> The work is, in short, a mosaic not without its precious stones, and is the result of wide and judicious selection among 'the mazes of the schools.' Much of its contents was doubtless new to Pope's own generation; and to modern readers it remains of more than historical interest, for it comes as a reminder of some important truths not included in new-classical teaching (170).

Watson's remarks on Pope are worth our attention: 'It is clear that Pope exploited his critical interests too early to exploit them well. The *Essay* is clever, but it is the indecent, puppyish cleverness of a precocious boy, and it does not represent an advance on Dryden's except in terms of virtuosity' (63). Unfortunately De Quincey has an undeservedly poor opinion about it when he says that it was 'the feeblest and least interesting of Pope's writings, being substantially a mere versification, like a metrical multiplication table, of commonplaces the most mouldy with which criticism has baited its rat-traps.' Johnson takes a different stand when he says it 'exhibits every mode of excellence that can embellish or dignify didactic composition—selection of matter, novelty of arrangement, justness of precepts, splendour of illustration, and propriety of digression.' Decorum, or propriety was the first requisite for any literary work. It involves, among many other things, proper use of the proper words in the proper place. As Ian Jack would call it, the idiom must be level with the intention. Pope's use of poetic diction, and use of scatological words can be justified in this context. Pope was no blind adherent to the rules of composition, as many of his contemporaries were, who slavishly followed the dictum of obedience to rules. He admits that rules are useful in so far as they lead us to the works of great writers of all time, but they must be set aside if they are cramping and wooden to the extent of being dogmatic.

Much has been said of the use of the term 'wit' by Pope. It was an accepted part of the poetic vocabulary of the seventeenth and eighteenth centuries. Johnson's Dictionary of 1755 gives eight different meanings for the word, and the recent *OED* has fourteen meanings under the headword, in addition to many subordinate and compound words. William Empson who specialised in a stylistic interpretation of such words—*honour* in *Henry IV*, *honesty* in *Othello*—points out in his *Structure of Complex Words* that the key Popean term occurs 47 times in the poem, and can be found once in sixteen lines on an average count, and on every occasion the use of the term conveys a different meaning. At least four classifications of Pope's use are noticeable: 1. to refer to all mental and intellectual faculties taken together: 'So vast is art, so narrow human wit.' None can excel in all departments of the mind, and so one should keep oneself to that particular branch that suits one well. 2. to refer to the gift of the poet, the poet's genius, 'Authors are partial to their wit,'tis true/ But are not critics to their judgement too?' 3. to refer to the quality of ingenuity in a poet. This is the quality of verbal ingenuity which was found in the Restoration dramatists, like Congreve and Sheridan: 'To tell them, would a hundred tongues require, / Or one vain Wit's, that might a hundred tire.' Pope does not lay great store by this sense of the word, and 4. to refer to the poetic imagination: 'He, who supreme in judgment, as in wit, / Might boldly censure, as he boldly writ.' or 'For wit and judgment often are at strife, / Tho' meant each other's aid, like man and wife.' Imagination and judgment must coexist in happy matrimony as in 'True wit is nature to advantage drest/ What oft was thought, but ne'er so well exprest.' This has now become a philosophic aphorism, often quoted in different contexts. Pope intended these varieties of meanings to be a kind of answer to the attacks on poetry, and so he took the word associated with poetry and spoke about the complex creative process in which imagination and judgment get fused into an indivisible unity. In a sense, he was redefining poetry. And in the words of I.R.F. Gordon, 'It is the essence of poetry entailing the inspiration of genius, the mental agility of ingenuity, the fire of imagination and the control of judgment. It involves, in direct contrast to Eliot's notorious phrase, an association of sensibility' (99).

To conclude, Pope's *Essay* is not a new system, or a new exposition of a view of poetry and criticism: but it constitutes a cultural continuum. It passes on the great tradition of the past to his generation. It belongs to a lineage of literary manuals starting from Aristotle, and continued by Horace and Quintillion and a host of learned philosopher-critics. The following passage should serve as a good example of Pope's counsel to would-be practitioners of the fine art of criticism:

> First follow Nature, and your judgment frame
> By her just standard, which is still the same:
> Unerring Nature! still divinely bright
> One clear, unchanged, and universal light,
> Life, force, and beauty must to all impart,
> At once the source, the end, and test of art.
> Art from that fund each just supply provides;
> Works without show, and without prompt presides:
> In some fair body thus th' informing soul
> With spirit feeds, with vigour fills the whole;
> Each motion guides, and ev'ry nerve sustains,
> Itself unseen, but in th' effects remains. (68–79)

Readers today are likely to miss the real import of these lines. We tend to assume that the passage merely represents the critical opinion of the period: just elaborations of commonplace remarks. It is true that a work of art must be treated as a living organism. The passage, which begins by teaching us how to form literary judgments, grows into wider significance with suggestions beyond the outward meaning. Divine, bright unerring Nature is the informing soul that feeds the human body and guides it in literary creation and literary judgment alike.

Works Cited

Atkins, J.W.H. *English Literary Criticism: 17th and 18th Centuries.* New York: Barnes and Noble, 1951.

Gordon, I.R.F. *A Preface to Pope.* London: Longman, 1976.

Watson, George. *The Literary Critics: A Study of English Descriptive Criticism.* Harmondsworth, Middlesex: Penguin Books, 1962.

Select Bibliography

Crane, Ronald. 'English Neo-Classical Criticism: An Outline Sketch.' *Critics and Criticism.* Chicago: The University of Chicago Press, 1952.

Warren, Austin. *Alexander Pope as Critic and Humanist.* Princeton: Princeton University Press, 1929.

SAMUEL JOHNSON (1709–1784)

Samuel Johnson is the most widely known figure among the Augustans. This, in no small measure, is due to James Boswell's biography of that 'friend, philosopher and guide.' In a rich life, crowded with intellectual pursuits of various kinds, literary criticism for Samuel Johnson was just a part—and a small part at that of his scholarly activities, but it was an important one. His range of reading was phenomenal; he had an insatiable appetite for books. It would be unwise, therefore to treat him as a pure academic critic. In any case, such a phenomenon as academic criticism did not exist prior to the twentieth century. His old friend Oliver Edwards, who met him after many years on Good Friday of 1777, called him a philosopher and added, 'I have tried too in my time to be a philosopher; but I don't know, cheerfulness was always breaking in.' As though philosophy and cheerfulness were an irreverent combination! As a true Christian, Johnson enjoyed in full measure all the innocent pleasures available to man without indulging in them. Enjoying good books and conversation, enjoying good food, and travelling were among his innocent and harmless pursuits.

The great lexicographer always thought of himself as an ordinary person with the taste and accomplishments of an average reader, and believed that he was the spokesman for the 'common reader'. This anti-intellectualism is most characteristic of Johnson. Criticism was a subordinate activity to creative, imaginative literature. In *Rambler* 208, he says, 'Criticism, in my opinion, is only to be ranked among the subordinate and instrumental arts.' In this sense, Johnson was a philosopher, an enquirer into truth, and one who searched for wisdom in literature as one would search for it in any activity in life. How was Johnson's knowledge formed and what were his ranges of interests, wide as they were? He had a good working knowledge of the classical and European languages. He was considerably well-read in biography, history, both social and intellectual. He was acquainted with the essentials of jurisprudence too. He was interested in politics, trade, commerce and the Constitution of England. He believed in a direct relationship between life and literature, and hence, he believed too that literature is what caters to a good life and what is born of experience. Literature should help readers enjoy and endure life fully and in its entirety. Religious and moral structures were strongly embedded in his psyche. For him truth is man's guardian angel, and he praises such of those works which bring out the truth of human existence in a new and original way. A poet, for him, was a man among men: he did not possess any special powers denied to the rest of humanity. That is why he relied too heavily upon biographical criticism, relating the poet as man to the poet as artist. He was all admiration for those writings which had a universal appeal.

It was with the arrival of Dr Johnson on the critical scene that English criticism might be said to have attained some status. There are those who strongly believe that modern criticism starts with Johnson. Réné Wellek's monumental *History of Modern Criticism* in eight volumes, begins with Johnson. His greatest work in criticism *Lives of Poets* alone bears ample testimony to the greatness of this giant among criticism. Johnson sets forth his definition of criticism in *The Rambler* No 92 thus:

> It is the task of criticism to establish principles; to improve opinion into knowledge; and to distinguish those means of pleasing which depend upon known causes and rational deduction, from the nameless and inexplicable elegancies which appeal wholly to the fancy, from which we feel delight, but know not how they produce it, and which may well be termed the enchantresses of the soul. Criticism reduces those regions of literature under the dominion of science, which have hitherto known only the anarchy of ignorance, the caprices of fancy, and the tyranny of prescription.

Johnson literally believed that the aim of criticism is to establish laws with which to estimate excellence in works. He was a close textual reader, a historical critic *par excellence* and a sound scholar.

According to George Watson, Johnson's critical phase can be divided into four stages: 1. the periodical essays written during his middle years, and specially, about a dozen papers contributed to the *Rambler* (1750–2), 2. the *Dictionary* (1755), 3. his edition of Shakespeare and 4. the *Lives* (1779–81). The *Rambler* articles contain his critical theory. The *Dictionary* and the preface to Shakespeare reveal the scholar in him, and finally, the *Lives* show us his strength as a judge of poets and writers of reputation. His anti-theoretical bias is evident in his *Rambler* essays. He wishes to modify the laws laid down by the ancients and not blindly adhere to them. Poetry is forever in a process of evolution and change, and it is wrong to maintain that the old forms of poetry must survive, as they were, for all time to come. Johnson, the lexicographer felt that linguistics was both descriptive and prescriptive. His is the first dictionary in the world built on historical principles. Single-handed, he worked on his major project, *The Dictionary of the English Language* that took him eight long years to complete. It contains no fewer than 40,000 words each with illustrative examples. It is said that it took forty years for forty members of the French academy to accomplish such a stupendous task. His avowed aim, as described in the preface to *The Dictionary* was to compile, 'a dictionary by which the pronunciation of our language may be fixed, and its attainment facilitated, by which its purity may be preserved, its use ascertained, and its duration lengthened.' It shows the range of English vocabularies more fully than ever before. It provides a system of spelling that could be accepted as standard. Though it supplies quotations from the best writers, his dictionary is not unbiased in the illustration of usage, as for example, the *OED* is. The meaning of a word is settled by what the great writers have meant by it. Johnson's *Dictionary* gave rise to the tendency to regard the dictionary as the authority. The eighteenth century is considered to be the period of consolidation of the English language. Lexicography, today, has become a highly sophisticated, scientific and professional area. If we take into account the constraints and the absence of facilities in the eighteenth century, we cannot but concede that the publication of Johnson's *Dictionary*—the result of single-handed effort—was an achievement of no small magnitude.

Johnson's edition of Shakespeare (1765) was the sixth edition of the great poet in terms of history of editions (after the folio). The earlier ones were by Nicholas Rowe, Alexander Pope, Lewis Theobald and William Warburton. On his own method of textual editing and emendation, Johnson was of the view that that reading is right which requires many words to prove it wrong, and that emendation is wrong which cannot without much labour appear to be right. In form and spirit, he follows the earlier prefaces. The *Preface* is Johnson's first work in extended descriptive criticism. There are seven units in this long essay: Shakespeare as a poet of nature, a defence of his tragicomedy, his style, his defects, and attack on the unities in general, the historical background to drama, and finally, his editorial practice. The introductory remarks substantiate his theory. There are some inconsistencies in his views on tragicomedy, in his praise of Shakespeare and the later attack on him, and on his style; but these were the characteristic defects—not taken seriously—of his age.

The best of Johnson, his *magnum opus,* is his *Lives* (1779–81), written in the last stage of his life, devoted to criticism and scholarship of the best kind, when he was sixty-eight. Boswell calls it 'the richest, most beautiful, and indeed most perfect production of Johnson's pen.' Johnson was commissioned by a committee of London booksellers to undertake to review the life and works of major English poets from Chaucer to his day. These were originally meant to supply biographical prefaces to an edition of English poets, which were published in ten volumes and then reissued separately. Johnson acceded to their request, but on his own condition. He dropped medieval and Renaissance poets, and chose fifty-two lives from Cowley to Gray. Of these, except Milton and Cowley, all the rest are post-Restoration poets. It took four years for the *Lives* to be completed, and Johnson must have worked like a hack to keep up the tremendous pace of one *Life* a month on an average. Notable among the poets whose lives were not written are George Herbert and Robert Herrick. The not-so-popular poets whose names were included are Richard Duke, and William Walsh, but Johnson does not dwell much on their lives.

The lives of the poets are arranged in the order of the dates of their death. These essays follow a set pattern of a three-fold division: biography, character and criticism. The biographical part is the longest one in many cases containing the poet's birth, education, growth, etc. The second section assessing the character of the poet is usually the shortest of the three, and the third, a critical appreciation and evaluation of the poet is of middle length. Twenty-four of the fifty-two lives observe this three-fold division in a strict pattern. The three divisions are clearly demarcated. In the words of Watson, 'In the *Lives,* he (Johnson) is creating the foundations of the nineteenth-century school of historical criticism by elevating the literary life to a new critical eminence' (88). Criticism is added as a useful adjunct to biography. The three sections do not relate to one another; rather they remain as independent units. With the *Lives*, we may be said to have come to the very end of Augustan or neoclassical criticism. The elaborate theories of this school have only historical interest nowadays, and, in the words of Watson again, they have only 'the melancholy interest of deserted ruins.' Augustan aesthetic debates are not taken for serious discussion or refutation. For us, however, their contribution and achievement have a historical value. Formal analysis of works of literature did not exist before the days of Dryden, and so he found it necessary to defend the English against the dominating and domineering French works. This was taken up and continued by his followers. Johnson belongs to the next stage of consolidating the gains, and making the endeavour more scholarly and professional, and less amateurish. Being a scholar-critic, he laid the foundation for serious pursuit of literary criticism. According to Eliot, *Lives* is a masterpiece of the judicial bench. It is said of his *Lives* that when Johnson is right he is perfectly right; and when he is wrong he is entirely wrong.

Here and there we might notice some inconsistency in his theoretical stance to which he might very well answer in the words of Whitman: 'Do I contradict myself? / Very well I contradict myself. / I am large, I contain multitudes.' The range of his criticism is narrowed down to about a hundred years of British literature. Johnson lived during the pre-Romantic period when the Industrial Revolution had not yet arrived in England. His experience of literature is unlike ours in some ways. Yet, he is of immense help to us, his criticism is so bracing and the powers of his ideas come to us, in the words of John Wain, '. . .

principally, from the humanity, the learning, the generosity which irradiate them, and from the force and freshness of their expression. For he lived long, and lived deeply and strenuously; and "judgment," as he so truly said, 'tis forced on us by experience' (57). English neoclassical criticism has Dryden at the beginning, Pope in the middle and Johnson at the end. In his novel *Rasselas* (1759), in chapter 10 called 'Dissertation upon Poetry,' Johnson gives expression to his views regarding the function of writing:

> The business of a poet . . . is to examine, not the individual, but the species; to remark on the general properties and large appearances: he does not number the streaks of the tulip or describe the different shades of the verdure of the forest. He is to exhibit in his portraits of nature such prominent and striking features as recall the original to every mind; and must neglect the minuter discriminations, which everyone may have remarked, and another have neglected, for those characteristics which are alike obvious to vigilance and carelessness . . . He must divest himself of the prejudices of his age or country; he must consider right and wrong in their abstracted and invariable state; he must disregard present laws and opinions, and rise to general and transcendental truths, which will always be the same: he must therefore content himself with the slow progress of his name; contemn the applause of his own time, and commit his claims to the justice of posterity. He must write as the interpreter of nature, and the legislator of mankind, and consider himself as presiding over the thoughts and manners of future generations; as a being superior to time and place (320).

As a confirmed Tory in political belief, he had no sympathy for anything that went along with the Whig belief. T.S. Eliot remarked that Johnson had practically no influence after his own time. But his literary reviewing had left an indelible mark on many nineteenth century reviewers. He could be seen as the great culmination of the Aristotelian tradition in literary criticism.

Johnson's greatness as a critic has been confirmed by many generations that came after him. His contribution to different forms of scholarship is lasting. Lexicography, editing, biography, annotation are all forms of scholarship which cannot be combined by one person even today with all the help that is available. In his *Lives* he rewrote the cultural and intellectual history of England. 'He possessed the supreme gift of looking always to essentials, and with his mastery of language he expressed them in a style which was always monumental and often lapidary. Hence his criticism remains alive and largely valid' (Donner 103). As an editor, he was perhaps the first person to establish the principles for sound textual criticism, eschewing the easier escape route of establishing the text by emendation. He has the hallmark of humility when it came to editorial problems. Johnson overemphasised morality in art, and this perforce set narrow limits to him when it came to his judgments. He possessed a complete knowledge of the world, of men and matters. His uncompromising insistence on truth would not allow him to tolerate hypocrisy, or dishonesty in life, or in art. It is his humanity that makes him the most truthful and the most reliable of critics. For Leavis, 'Johnson's criticism, most of it, belongs with the living classics: it can be read afresh every year with unaffected pleasure and new stimulus. It is alive and life-giving' (71).

It is reasonable to suppose that Johnson's critical notions were set and formed quite early in life, and that he was open at all times to revise his notions whenever he felt it was right to do so. By nature and bent of mind Johnson was a Tory, and his view of literature was dictated by his Tory leanings. He was short-sighted and had no eye for beauty in nature. He found himself most at home in urban society. He had no ear for music. He knew his classics well. The two greatest poets of his time, Dryden and Pope, had a limited range of poetic presentation. He was nourished strictly on neoclassical thought. Johnson practised criticism in the Age of Prose, and he was the most representative spokesman of that age. Saintsbury's final verdict on Johnson is noteworthy: 'He has not merely flourished and vapoured critical abstractions, but has left us a solid reasoned body of critical judgment; he has not judged literature in the exhausted receiver of mere art, and yet has never neglected the artistic criterion; he has kept in constant touch with life, and yet has never descended to mere gossip. We may freely disagree with his judgments, but we can never justly disable his judgment; and this is the real criterion of a great critic' (229). In short, he is the orthodox eighteenth century critic in quintessence. Wimsatt and Brooks pronounce emphatically, 'As for Samuel Johnson, he is the Great Cham of 18th century English literary criticism, a mammoth personality who was more capacious than any abstract dimension of critical theory. We surround him here with the atmosphere of the classic universal because his championship of that view is a late climax in its history and appears to be his distinctive contribution to 18th century English criticism. As a classical giant, however, he is even more interesting for the complexity and sometimes inconsistent detail of his views' (323). W.R. Keast, in a masterly essay, 'The Theoretical Foundations of Johnson's Criticism' argues most convincingly that Johnson had a systematic mind, and a coherent view of literature, and a coherent body of assumptions concerning both its practice and evaluation. Only he was flexible and capable of adaptation in employing his methods and principles.

Johnson should not be classified as a mere neoclassical critic, though he shared much of the neoclassical belief. He did not effect much of a distinction between art and life. For him, the aim of fiction is to reveal truth. This is seen in all his criticism. He attacked Milton's 'Lycidas' because the emotions it expresses were insincere. He says of the poem, 'It is not to be considered as the effusion of real passion; for passion runs not after remote allusions and obscure opinions. Passion plucks no berries from myrtle and ivy, nor calls upon Arethuse and Mincius, nor tells of "rough satyrs and fauns with cloven heel." Where there is leisure for fiction there is little grief.' A clear case of what we may now call the intentional fallacy! Johnson's didactic criticism runs to extremes. He was in favour of poetic justice when he preferred a happy ending to *King Lear,* little realising that a tragic end to the play is an emotional necessity. He dismissed *Tom Jones* on the ground that it lacked sexual morality. In his '*Preface* to Shakespeare,' he called into question Shakespeare's moral purpose.

> He (Shakespeare) sacrifices virtue to convenience, and is so much more careful to please than to instruct, that he seems to write without any moral purpose. From his writings indeed a system of social duty may be selected, for he that thinks reasonably must think morally; but his precepts and axioms drop casually from him; he makes no just distribution of good or evil, nor is always careful to show in the virtuous a disapprobation of the wicked; he carries his persons indifferently through right and wrong, and at the close dismisses them without further care, and leaves their examples to

> operate by chance. This fault the barbarity of his age cannot extenuate: for it is always a writer's duty to make the world better, and justice is a virtue independent on time and place (324).

These have earned for him a dismissive attitude from the continental critics who, unmercifully, dub him 'British superstition.' For him, literature is not merely an imitation of ancient writers; it is a representation of nature in a wide and general sense. Realism consists in depicting, not copying the universal and the typical. That is why he praises Shakespeare when he says, 'in the writings of other poets a character is too often an individual, in those of Shakespeare it is commonly a species.' When he says, 'Nothing can please many, and please long, but just representations of general nature,' he means moral and truthful representations. He condemned blind adherence to rules, and this can be seen in his rejection of the unities and defence of the tragicomedy. Only 'unity of action' has to be adhered to. Johnson is categorical in his views on the 'unities,' and 'tragicomedy.' He renders them explicitly:

> The result of my enquiries, in which it would be ludicrous to boast of impartiality, is, that the unities of time and place are not essential to a just drama, though they may sometimes conduce to pleasure, they are always to be sacrificed to the nobler beauties of variety and instruction; and that a play written with nice observations of critical rules, is to be contemplated as an elaborate curiosity, as the product of superfluous and ostentatious art, by which is shewn, rather what is possible, than what is necessary . . . The greatest graces of a play are to copy nature and instruct life (327).
>
> Shakespeare's plays are not in the rigorous and critical sense either tragedies or comedies, but compositions of a distinct kind; exhibiting the real state of sublunary nature, which partakes of good and evil, joy and sorrow, mingled with endless variety of proportion and innumerable modes of combination; and expressing the course of the world, in which the loss of the one is the gain of another . . . That this is a practice contrary to the rules of criticism will be readily allowed; but there is always an appeal open from criticism to nature. The end of writing is to instruct; the end of poetry is to instruct by pleasing (322–3).

He stands committed to the neoclassical faith in maintaining decorum in the use of language and poetic diction. The lexicographer he was, it is no wonder that he aimed at purity in diction and the use of language. He could not excuse the quibble in Shakespeare for whom 'it was the fatal Cleopatra for which he lost the world and was content to lose it.' He thought that a certain amount of perfection in versification had been reached during his time, and Pope was the poet in whom it had attained a point of culmination. Johnson relied on the judgment of the common reader who is the representative of common sense for him. 'Uncorrupted by literary prejudices, after all the refinements of subtlety and the dogmatism of learning,' the common reader will 'finally decide all claims to poetical honours.' The common reader should not be mistaken for any and every reader, but the universal man in the neoclassical sense of the term. Only the critic corrupted by prejudice, and the scholar bound by dogmatism are excluded, as Virginia Woolf rightly understands the term. Johnson did not subscribe to the theory of creative imagination for poets since a poet, for him, is like any other man. Poetic imagination, for him, stood for the power of representation in artistic medium. Much of his criticism is commonsensical, and literal-minded. He always entertained a rationalistic conception of poetry. For him, prayer is a higher state than can be reached by poetic contemplation. While talking of the poetry of Waller, Johnson declares, 'The essence of poetry is invention; such invention as, by producing something unexpected, surprises and delights. The topics of devotion are few, and being few are universally known; but, few as they are, they can be made no more; they can receive no grace from novelty of sentiment, and very little from novelty of expression.' He adds, 'Omnipotence cannot be exalted; Infinity cannot be amplified; Perfection cannot be improved.' Of great European writers Johnson has nothing to offer by way of criticism. . . He was quite well read in early English literature. In his *Lives of Poets,* one gets to a close approximation to the literary history of England. He was limited to the living tradition of poetry from Cowley to Gray. Rene Wellek in his *History of Modern Criticism* ends his discussion of Johnson with these telling remarks:

> His own critical work is certainly varied enough, unified without being monotonous, strongly rooted in the tradition but still far from merely dogmatic in its acceptance of it. Johnson, while holding firm to the main tenets of the tradition of neoclassical

criticism, constantly reinterprets them in a spirit for which it is difficult to avoid a term he would have hated: liberal (104).

It is important to reiterate two statements regarding Johnson's assumptions which inform his penetrating insights into works which differ widely in the nature of their composition. The first is that his judgement, delivered with all the force at his command, is firmly grounded on the foundation of morality, and moral commitment. The second is that a poet should concern himself representing general nature, and not any particular experience. Strangely enough, British romanticism emerged as a revolt against these two basic Johnsonian propositions!

Works Cited

Adams, Hazard, ed. *Literary Criticism since Plato.* 1971. New York: Harcourt Brace Jovanovich College Publishers, 1992. Unless otherwise stated, all textual references are drawn from this volume.

Donner. H. W. 'Dr Johnson as a Literary Critic.' *Samuel Johnson: A Collection of Critical Essays. Twentieth Century Views.* Ed. Donald J. Greene. Englewood Cliffs, N J: Prentice Hall, Inc., 1965.

Johnson, Samuel. *The Rambler.* Ed. W.J. Bate. New Haven: Yale University Press, 1969.

Keast. W.R. 'The Theoretical Foundations of Johnson's Criticism.' *Critics and Criticism.* Chicago: The University of Chicago Press, 1952.

Leavis, F.R. 'Johnson as Critic.' *Samuel Johnson: A Collection of Critical Essays. Twentieth Century Views.* Ed. Donald J. Greene. Englewood Cliffs, N J: Prentice Hall, 1965.

Saintsbury, George. *History of English Criticism.* London: William Blackwood & Sons Ltd., 1955.

Wain, John. 'Johnson as Critic.' *A Collection of Critical Essays: Twentieth Century Views.* Ed. Donald J. Greene. Englewood Cliffs, N.J.: Prentice Hall, 1965.

Watson, George. *The Literary Critics: A Study of English Descriptive Criticism.* Harmondsworth, Middlesex: Penguin Books, 1962.

Wellek, Réné. *A History of Modern Criticism.* Vol. 1. New Haven: Yale University Press, 1955.

Wimsatt, William K and Cleanth Brooks. *Literary Criticism: A Short History.* New Delhi: Oxford & IBH Publishing House, 1957.

Select Bibliography

Bate, Walter J. *The Achievement of Samuel Johnson.* New York: Oxford University Press, 1955.

———. *Samuel Johnson.* New York: Harcourt Brace Jovanovich, 1977.

Bosker, A. 1930. *Literary Criticism in the Age of Johnson.* Groningen: J.B. Wolters, 1953.

Brown, Joseph E. *The Critical Opinions of Samuel Johnson.* Princeton: Princeton University Press, 1926.

Hagstrum, Jean. 1952. *Samuel Johnson's Literary Criticism.* Chicago: University of Chicago Press, 1967.

Keast, W.R. 'The Theoretical Foundations of Johnson's Criticism.' *Critics and Criticism.* Chicago: University of Chicago Press, 1952.

Krutch, Joseph W. *Samuel Johnson.* New York: H. Holt, 1944.

Leavis, F.R. 'Johnson as Critic.' *Scrutiny* 11 (1944).

Tate. Allen. 'Johnson on the Metaphysicals.' *Kenyon Review.* 11 (1949).

Wimsatt, William K. *The Prose Style of Samuel Johnson.* New Haven: Yale University Press, 1941.

4

Romantic and Victorian Criticism

n more senses than one, the romantic movement was a continental phenomenon. In a strict sense, there was no such movement in England. Coleridge himself is said to have borrowed it from Schlegel whose views on the distinction between the Romantic and the Classical came to be used by Hazlitt, Scott and others. It was Thomas Carlyle who used the terms, 'romanticism,' 'romantic,' and 'romanticist' with reference to the Germans; and in books and treatises, the term came into vogue in England in the 1850s. The French Revolution, with its slogan of liberty, equality, and fraternity, fuelled and planted in the minds of people fresh impulses demanding social and political reforms. Certain inherited beliefs concerning the very fabric of society came to be replaced by fresh thinking on morality and duty. The writings of Rousseau, the French philosopher, who pleaded for individual freedom and autonomy, William Godwin on political justice and reforms, and Mary Wollstonecraft who pleaded for the vindication of the rights of women influenced public opinion enormously. Concepts such as truth, nature, god and plenitude were redefined. In the domain of literary criticism too the impact of the changed attitudes was conspicuously noticeable.

William Wordsworth (1770–1850)

The literary theory of Wordsworth came to be written between the years 1798 and 1815. During these seventeen years, Wordsworth wrote the Preface to *Lyrical Ballads* (1800 and 1802), the three-part *Essay upon Epitaphs* (1810), and the prefaces to *The Excursion* (1814) and to the *Poems* (1815). There are also some critical observations by Wordsworth scattered about here and there. The *Preface to Lyrical Ballads* is the vital essay among all these works. It has always been regarded as the most authentic expression of the ideals of the romantic movement in English poetry. The first version of 1800 had seven thousand words. The 1802 version had another three thousand words added to it. An appendix of two thousand words was again added to the 1802 version. Wordsworth's preface is not perfectly organised as a piece of literary theory. When Johnson expressed his views in a forthright manner attacking some of the time-honoured precepts of neoclassicism, he was still held as the major spokesman of the School. It was an altogether different matter with Wordsworth.The French Revolution had completely altered the perception of life held for such a long time. The common man in the street became the epicentre; he could now claim his rights. The voice of democracy, and the rights of the people became strong contenders. Wordsworth himself became a fervent and devoted convert to the ideals underlying the French Revolution. He remained sympathetic to the French cause until the rise of Napoleon. Thus, we see Wordsworth in his preface to *Lyrical Ballads* (1800), speak as a representative man speaking to his fellow men. Kings and noblemen would not be the subject matter for poetry, and the poet need not worry about maintaining conformity to laws of creation and decorum. This is Wordsworth's declaration with respect to his objectives:

> The principal object, then, proposed in these poems was to choose incidents and situations from common life, and to relate or describe them, throughout, as far as was possible in a selection of language really used by men, and, at the same time, to throw over them a certain colouring of imagination, whereby ordinary things should be presented to the mind in an unusual aspect, and, further, and above all, to make these incidents and situations interesting by tracing in them, truly though not ostentatiously, the primary laws of our nature chiefly as regards the manner in which we associate ideas in a state of excitement (438).

There was a time when poets urged other poets to avoid rustic language, and thus what later came to be called 'poetic diction' replaced the speech of the common man for poetry. Wordsworth pleads for the retention of the common speech in poetry. And he wishes that poetry should concern itself with the 'essential passions of the heart.' To do this, the characters must be people in rural areas occupied in rural work because the passions of these persons 'are incorporated with the beautiful and permanent forms of nature.' These men constantly communicate with the best objects (in the world of nature) from which the best part of the language is originally derived. This is a point of departure for Wordsworth from neoclassical notions on poetic diction, and abstract ideas set to rules of composition.

'Good poetry is the spontaneous overflow of powerful feelings' and 'the language of a large portion in every good poem . . . must necessarily, except with the reference to the matter, in no respect differ from that of good prose.' Wordsworth's characterisation of a poet runs along these lines:

> He (a poet) is a man speaking to men: a man, it is true, endowed with more lively sensibility, more enthusiasm and tenderness, who has a greater knowledge of human nature and a more comprehensive soul than are supposed to be common among mankind; a man pleased with his own passions and volitions, and who rejoices more than other men in the spirit of life that is in him; delighting to contemplate similar volitions and passions as manifested in the goings-on of the universe and habitually impelled to create them where he does not find them (441).

This view of Wordsworth contains in essence the Romantic spirit of literature. Poetry is not a matter of rules and regulations. The poet is an uncommon man, gifted in many ways, and in some sense, superior to the common folk. The emphasis falls on the individual identity of the poet; he is not just another human being. The poet is not one who presents facts (and this is the answer to Plato), but he writes with the 'necessity of giving immediate pleasure to a human being possessed of that information which may be expected from him, not as a lawyer, a physician, a mariner, an astronomer, or a natural philosopher, but as a man.' Poetry is not just an intellectual activity. For him, it is 'the spontaneous overflow of powerful feelings; it takes its origin from emotion recollected in tranquillity; the emotion is contemplated till, by a species of reaction, the tranquillity gradually disappears, and an emotion, kindred to that which was before the subject of contemplation, is gradually produced, and does itself actually exist in the mind' (444).

Poetic communication takes place in a higher realm of emotions, beyond facts and information. Wordsworth says that the greater portion of a good poem does not differ from prose as far as the use of language and the order of words go, but the use of metre adds charm and intensifies feelings and emotions.

Coleridge, Wordsworth's collaborator—and later his devastating critic—in *Lyrical Ballads,* supplies the salutary corrective to his views on poetic language and the use of metre. Seventeen years after the preface was written, Coleridge took up some issues. Wordsworth uses a 'selection' of the language of the rustics, and when this selection is removed, Wordsworth's theory does not work. Coleridge does not accept that there is anything special in the speech of those who live in close proximity to nature. What is essential is true education, and not the mere presence of nature. He proves that Wordsworth himself did not follow his theory. Coleridge had an organic view of poetry which we shall discuss in the following chapter on Coleridge.

Coleridge's theory was written almost at the same time as Wordsworth's. There are serious charges against Coleridge that he had plagiarised a great deal from the German philosophers of his time. He had borrowed extensively from German contemporaries without acknowledging his borrowings. The only critical work published during his lifetime was the *Biographia Literaria,* and it is a collection of autobiographical pieces, religious views and comments about poets, etc. Again, it is not neatly organised. Both Wordsworth and Coleridge have been great influences on the twentieth century. Wordsworth inspired the use of ordinary subjects, and everyday language in poetry. Coleridge influenced New Criticism, especially, the concepts of organic form, inclusiveness and complexity in poetry.

Wordsworth was perhaps the first to talk of his new attempt at poetic composition when he said that the language of poetry is not different from the language of prose. This occasioned a violent attack from his friend and collaborator in the poems, later to be followed by Shelley and Keats. Raleigh and Bradley may have views to the contrary, but it is true that Wordsworth's best poems are those that do not follow his poetic principles. There seems to be no other instance when a poet so aggressively defends his own creation. After many of his theoretical positions, he chooses Gray's sonnet ('That on the death of West') to show that in the best parts of the poem there is no difference between the language of prose, and the language of poetry. Poetry is not to be equated with metrical composition. He weakly admits that there is an added charm in metrical composition. In his appendix to 'Poetic Diction,' he says that the earliest poets wrote with passion, and the later poets imitated them without any. Metre was added to this as an additional charm.

The literary criticism of Wordsworth is the manifesto of the British Romantic Movement. It effects a formal break with the neoclassical tradition. He rejected the diction of 18th century poetry; and he favoured the language of prose and said that it was the same as metrical language. His naturalism and emotionalism are quite well known. Some of these views do not stand the test of scrutiny now. His revival of the spoken idiom for poetry has many parallels. Donne maintained that his was the natural speech unlike Spenser's. Dryden, Eliot and Pound too have taken a similar stand with regard to their poetry. Wordsworth had specific reasons for his rejection. He dismissed elevated vocabulary, which excluded the trivial. He disliked personification, pathetic fallacy, periphrasis, inversions, antithesis, use of classical mythology, conceits, hyperbole, and obscurity. He is open to charges of criticism that he employed some of these in his own poems. That was the reason why Coleridge refuted his theory and practice. Wordsworth's natural language and rustic speech are hard to define. He seems to believe that there is a core language, which is common to all people, and poets should employ this language. The gaudiness and the inane phraseology of the artificial language of 18th century poets were a distortion, because it lacked the spontaneity of expression of passion of the earlier poets. His primitivism is born out of his love for folk poetry and ballad forms of composition. But his own poetic models were Spenser and Milton. For him, poetry is the release of personal emotions. Hence he sets store by sincerity of feelings, and judges poetry by the manner by which one's personal emotions and feelings are conveyed. Not for Wordsworth a poet wearing a mask and entering another person! In his oft-quoted definition of poetry, he does not advocate raw emotionalism. He says, 'the emotion is contemplated till, by a species of reaction, the tranquillity gradually disappears, and an emotion, kindred to that which was before the subject of contemplation, is gradually produced, and does itself actually exist in the mind' (444). This means, there is an amount of consciousness involved in the making of a poem. He constantly revised his work. What is important is the emotional side of poetry which arouses sympathy for fellow human beings, and other creatures. People must be made to feel the mystery of nature. He thinks that metre elevates the mind to a higher plane of consciousness, and thereby creates aesthetic distance. It 'tempers and restrains passions.' Wordsworth resisted the belief that poetry was only to teach moral lessons. Poetry stands in opposition to and disagreement with science and facts. Poetry is close to religious insight into the life of things.

Wordsworth's charge against Coleridge is that his famous definition of fancy as 'aggregative or associative power' and imagination as the 'shaping or modifying power' is much too vague, unclear and imprecise. Both of them accept the distinction that fancy is the faculty that is concerned with 'fixities and definitions,' and imagination deals with 'the plastic, the pliant and the indefinite'; only Wordsworth does not make the subtle distinction that Coleridge makes, that one is transcendental (imagination), and the other associative (fancy). Fancy is an intellectual exercise, while imagination is illimitable, and indefinite. Imagination is linked with the feeling of the world as a community of living beings. Rene Wellek demonstrates that Wordsworth's theory is built on the premise of neoclassicism. For instance, he inherits the theory of imitation of nature and adds a social dimension to it; modifies the view of poetry as passion and emotion to 'recollection in tranquillity'; amplifies the effect of poetry to a binding of society; holds that imagination has the power of offering an insight into the unity of the world. Wellek concludes: 'though Wordsworth left only a small body of criticism, it is rich in survivals, suggestions, anticipations, and personal insights' (150).

Wordsworth's hope of creating 'a class of poetry . . . well adapted to interest mankind permanently' is not realised in terms of his own professed theory. His poetry is as much dated as anyone else's. We cannot, therefore, accept that he has discovered the essence of poetry. Language is always in an evolving process of steady growth, and one can never fix it to suit poetry of all times. His theory of metre also seems woefully inadequate. His predecessors such as Spenser, Milton, Donne, and Shakespeare used unusual metrical patterns and rhythms to emphasise the meaning of words, and force them to suit the contexts. They even adapted the rhythms to fall in line with colloquial speech. Wordsworth's 'prose' was always unsuitable to the poets who came later in time. His theory regarding 'the spontaneous overflow of powerful feelings' is not applicable to all poets in general: and, sometimes, even to his own poems. It lacks the validity he claims for it, but it is a valuable statement that describes the psychological poetic process involved in the composition of some of his most successful poems, Wordsworth's theory lacks a formal system, because it is mostly occasional: but it is original and not derivative as Shelley's *Defence,* and quite different from the mere *obiter dicta* of the other romantics as, for example, Keats's *Letters.*His theory has a good deal of reference to his poetry. In sum, the ultimate value of Wordsworth's *Preface* lies in the major shift it helped to effect in the emphasis from the relationship between the poem and the reader to that between poet and poem; in other words from critical evaluation and judgment to the creative process itself. As Wordsworth himself announced most compellingly, the question 'What is poetry?' is the same as the question, 'What is a poet?'

Works Cited

Adams, Hazard, ed. *Literary Criticism since Plato.* 1971. New York: Harcourt Brace Jovanovich College Publishers, 1992. Unless otherwise stated, all textual references are drawn from this volume.

Wellek, Rene. *A History of Modern Criticism.* Vol. 4. New Haven: Yale University Press, 1966.

Select Bibliography

Barstow, Marjorie L. *Wordsworth's Theory of Poetic Diction.* New Haven: Yale University Press, 1917.

Beatty, Arthur.1922. *William Wordsworth: His Doctrine and Art in Their Historical Relations.* Madison: University of Wisconsin Press, 1960.

Eliot, T.S. *The Use of Poetry and the Use of Criticism.* 1933. London: Faber and Faber, 1964.

Heffernen, J.A. *Wordsworth's Theory of Poetry.* Ithaca: Cornell University Press, 1969.

Lucas, F.L.1936. *The Decline and Fall of the Romantic Ideal.* Cambridge: University Press, 1963.

Peacock, Markham L. Jr. *Critical Opinions of William Wordsworth.* Baltimore: Johns Hopkins Press, 1950.

SAMUEL TAYLOR COLERIDGE (1772–1834)

Coleridge's achievement as a literary critic is massive, and matchless. He is said to have delivered seven major lectures of which only three have survived, and the only critical work that came out in his lifetime was *Biographia Literaria* (1817). He was, throughout his life, engaged in attempting 'to establish the principles of writing rather than to furnish rules on how to pass judgment on what has been written by others.' The process of poetic creation obsessed him all the time. The world, according to Coleridge, is a living reality. Both as a literary critic and a speculative philosopher, Coleridge is rated as the highest in England. Saintsbury admires him: 'Coleridge is the critical author to be turned over by day and by night . . . Begin with him, continue with him, come back to him after excursions, with a certainty of suggestion, stimulation, correction, edification' (341). He rates him along with Aristotle, and Longinus. For I.A. Richards, Coleridge is the founding father of all modern criticism. References to his principle of the reconciliation of opposites; his definition of imagination as the shaping principle; and his insistence on the principle of the organic wholeness in poetry come up time and again in any discussion on criticism.

There are charges of plagiarism levelled against him that he was only echoing the sentiments of German philosophers. There are very clear and identifiable echoes from Schelling, especially in those sections in *Biographia* where he develops his theory of metaphysics, and his distinction between fancy and imagination. The fundamental epistemological ideas on which Coleridge's critical theory rests are clearly borrowed from Schelling. Coleridge uses without acknowledgement Kant's *Critique of Judgment*. We cannot credit him with intellectual honesty in many cases. Many of the key terms in his metaphysics are derivatives from German thought. He felt proud to call himself 'a High German transcendentalist.' Art is the union or reconciliation of that which is Nature with that which is human. Coleridge built up a systematic epistemology based on a unified method, a method by which creative imagination works. While defining poetry, he observes:

> The poet, described in *ideal* perfection, brings the whole soul of man into activity, with the subordination of its faculties to each other according to their relative worth and dignity. He diffuses a tone and spirit of unity that blends, and, as it were, *fuses*, each into each, by that synthetic and magical power, to which I would exclusively appropriate the name of imagination. This power, first put in action by the will and understanding, and retained under their irremissive, though gentle and unnoticed, control reveals itself in the balance or reconcilement of opposite or discordant qualities: of sameness with difference; of the general, with the concrete; and the idea, with the image; the individual, with the representative; the sense of novelty and freshness, with old and familiar objects; a more than usual state of emotion, with more than usual order, judgment ever awake and steady self-possession, with enthusiasm and feeling profound or vehement; and while it blends and harmonizes the natural and the artificial, still subordinates art to nature; the manner to the matter; and our admiration of the poet to our sympathy with the poetry (480).

He employs the distinction between fancy and imagination as value-based. 'Imagination' is the 'esemplastic' power, the power that is capable of unifying or building into one. It can be classified into the primary and the secondary.

> The primary imagination I hold to be the living Power and prime Agent of all human Perception in the finite mind of the eternal act of creation in the infinite I *am*. The secondary Imagination I consider as an echo of the former, co-existing with the conscious will, yet still as identical with the primary in the *kind* of its agency, and differing only in *degree*, and in the *mode* of its operation. It dissolves, diffuses, dissipates, in order to recreate; or where this process is rendered impossible, yet still at all events it struggles to

> idealize and to unify, It is essentially *vital*, even as all objects (*as* objects) are essentially fixed and dead. Fancy, on the contrary, has no other counters to play with, but fixities and definites. The Fancy is indeed no other than a mode of Memory emancipated from the order of time and space; while it is blended with, and modified by that empirical phenomenon of the will, which we express by the word *choice*. But equally with the ordinary memory the fancy must receive all its materials ready made from the law of association (478).

Primary imagination constitutes only perception and is unconscious, while secondary imagination is continuous with the primary imagination, but coexists with conscious will. Imagination is not only a reproductive faculty but is also recreative. Fancy merely assembles and juxtaposes images without transforming them whereas imagination, a modifying power, moulds them into a new whole. John Ruskin explains the difference in simpler terms in a section in *Modern Painters.* 'The Fancy sees the outside, and is able to give a portrait of the outside, clear, brilliant, and full of detail. The Imagination sees the heart and inner nature, and makes them felt, but is often obscure, mysterious, and interrupted, in its giving of outer detail' (Vol 2, Section 2, Chapter 3). Coleridge's philosophy of organic formalism needs to be distinguished from mechanical formalism. All art achieves its form from within, and there is no imposition from without. W.B. Yeats articulates this precisely in the concluding stanza of 'Among School Children'.

> Labour is blossoming or dancing where
> The body is not bruised to pleasure soul,
> Nor beauty born out of its own despair,
> Nor blear-eyed wisdom out of midnight oil.
> O chestnut tree, great-rooted blossomer,
> Are you the leaf, the blossom or the bole?
> O body swayed to music, O brightening glance,
> How can we know the dancer from the dance? (55–64)

Coleridge may not have an important place in the world of aesthetics, but his theory of poetry needs a closer look. He took a holistic look at the poet, his faculty, and his work with its impact on the reader. Among these three poles, there is an underlying principle of unity. The whole is more than a sum of the parts. There is first of all a true poet. He is a whole man, ideal in every way, possessing sensibility, philosophic wisdom. He is in possession of imagination, the power that unifies things—the 'esemplastic' or 'coadunating' power. 'To become all things and yet remain the same, to make the changeful God be felt in the river, the lion and the flame—this is, that is true imagination.' Genius and imagination are higher than talent and fancy. The former unify and reconcile while the latter combine mechanically. Coleridge rates the fundamental unity in the poet's mind as the highest faculty, and distinguishes different types of poetic gifts. He does not recognise the distinction between the poet and poetry. What is poetry is nearly the same question as what is a poet? His answer to the first question is involved in the answer to the second. Whereas for Wordsworth, 'metre is but an adventitious aid to composition,' Coleridge defends metre in convincing terms. If metre is superadded, all other parts must be made consonant with it. Metre must be organic and not a mere ornament. Hence, Coleridge's definition of a poem is thus worded:

> A poem is that species of composition, which is opposed to works of science, by proposing for its *immediate* object pleasure, not truth; and from all other species (having *this* object in common with it) it is discriminated by proposing to itself such delight from the *whole*, as is compatible with a distinct gratification from each component *part* (479).

Metre is a stimulant to the attention of the reader. It has a distancing power; it heightens and removes us from ordinary emotion. The reader is carried forward by 'the pleasurable activity of mind excited by the attractions of the journey itself.' There is a joy in the journey of the rhythm of the poem, a regressive and progressive advancement 'like the motion of a serpent which the Egyptians made the emblem of intellectual power; or like the path of sound through the air.' He insists on unity in a poem as is evident from his favourite passage from 'Venus and Adonis,'

> Look! how a bright star shooteth from the sky,
> So glides he in the night from Venus's eye.

He is a formalist first and last, and does not even bother about questions regarding the value of a work of literature. Coleridge's key terms are unity and wholeness. He attacks that which is particular and local, and praises that which is generic and representative. In chapter xvii of *Biographia Literaria*, he reiterates that he adopts with full faith the Aristotelian dictum that 'poetry, as poetry, is essentially ideal.' The persons in poetry must be clothed with generic attributes and not with individual traits. It was Coleridge who introduced the philosophic method in English criticism. Before him it was rather mechanical, or arbitrary and impressionistic, but never methodical or systematic. The method of creation in fine arts is based on knowledge, experience and the intuitive conception of the artist. Coleridge terms this power as 'esemplastic'.

Wordsworth had earlier said, 'Poetry is the breath and finer spirit of knowledge.' The standards of poetry must be lofty if poetry should function as the custodian of public morality. Only such poetry 'will be found to have a power of forming, sustaining, and delighting us as nothing else can.' We must be objective in our assessment of poetry, and not be driven by historical or personal opinions. Arnold develops his favourite notion of the 'touchstone' as 'a shaping power, an energy; which fuses, melts and recombines the elements of perception, and bodies them forth in a unity or synthesis which is the work of art.' According to Herbert Read, 'He (Coleridge) made criticism into a science, and using his own experiences and those of his fellow poets as materials for research, revealed to the world for the first time some part of the mystery of genius and of the universal and eternal significance of art' (111).

Coleridge did not represent any school, and the Victorians did not worry much about him. His impact on the thinking about poetry in the twentieth century is phenomenal. He noticed that the lack of English criticism lay in its inability to enquire into the deep recesses of poetic art. Coleridge's critical career extended to three decades, from 1800 to 1834. If we confine ourselves to the descriptive part of Coleridge's criticism, these fall into three units: 1. his Shakespearean criticism, 2. his critique of Wordsworth, and 3. his comments on various poets. The Shakespearean criticism of Coleridge is available in parts. They lie scattered and fragmentary, but they set a new trend in the interpretation of the essential Shakespeare. Some mistake it to be character-criticism as practised by Bradley; others mistake it as the image-school of criticism like Wilson Knight's. These are far from the truth.

Coleridge had no interest in the novel. Jane Austen, and Walter Scott were his contemporaries. He differed from the neoclassical school of criticism as practised by Johnson for whom, 'Shakespeare . . . is the poet of nature; the poet holds up to his readers a faithful mirror of manners and life.' In his analysis of *The Tempest,* he showed his dislike of the insistence on the unities. Shakespeare's characters show an organic existence and not a mechanical one. They shape themselves as botanical objects would do. As a descriptive and speculative critic, Coleridge was simply brilliant. He is the most suggestive of all English critics. As Watson would say of his manuscripts, 'They are the relics of a mind passionately in love with free enquiry, concentrated and disciplined in its determination to decipher the secret of poetic discourse' (119).

All through his life, Coleridge was interested in studying the process of artistic creation. The creative act is the result of man's union—the Coleridgean term would be 'reconciliation'—with nature. This finds a beautiful expression in the following lines from his 'Dejection: An Ode.'

> O Lady! We receive but what we give,
> And in our life alone does Nature live:
> (——————————————)
> Ah! From the soul itself must issue forth
> A light, a glory, a fair luminous cloud
> Enveloping the Earth—
> And from the soul itself must there be sent
> A sweet and potent voice, of its own birth,
> Of all sweet sounds the life and element! (47–58)

Works Cited

Adams, Hazard, ed. *Literary Criticism since Plato.* 1971. New York: Harcourt Brace Jovanovich College Publication, 1992. Unless otherwise stated, all textual references are drawn from this volume.

Read, Herbert. *Coleridge: A Collection of Critical Essays.* Ed. Kathleen Coburn. Englewood Cliffs, N J: Prentice-Hall, Inc., 1967.

Ruskin, John. *Modern Painters.* London: J.M. Dent & Sons Ltd (1920–35).

Saintsbury, George. *History of English Criticism.* London: William Blackwood & Sons Ltd, 1955.

Watson, George. *The Literary Critics: A Study of English Descriptive Criticism*. Harmondsworth, Middlesex: Penguin Books, 1962.

Select Bibliography

Bate, W.J. 'Coleridge on the Function of Art.' *Perspectives in Criticism*. Ed. H. Levin. Cambridge, Massachusetts: Harvard University Press, 1950.

———. *Coleridge*. New York: Macmillan, 1968.

Coburn, Kathleen, ed. *A Collection of Critical Essays*. Englewood Cliffs, N.J.: Prentice Hall, 1967.

Fogle, Richard. H. *The Idea of Coleridge's Criticism*. Berkeley: University of California Press, 1962.

Leavis, F.R. 'Coleridge in Criticism.' *Scrutiny* 9 (1940).

Mckenzie, Gordon. *Organic Unity in Coleridge*. Berkeley: University of California Press, 1939.

Read, Herbert. 'Coleridge as Critic.' *Sewanee Review* 56 (1948).

———. *The True Voice of Feeling: Studies in Romantic Poetry*. London: Faber and Faber, 1953.

Richards, I.A. *Coleridge on Imagination*. 1934. Bloomington: Indiana University Press, 1960.

Shawcross, J., ed. *Biographia Literaria*. 2 vols. Oxford: Oxford University Press, 1907.

Sherwood, Margaret. *Coleridge's Imaginative Conception of the Imagination*. Wellesley, Massachusetts: House Bookshop, 1937.

Snyder, Alice. D. *S.T. Coleridge's Treatise on Method*. Norwood, Pa.: Norwood Editions, 1976.

Willey, Basil. *Coleridge on Imagination and Fancy*. Oxford: Oxford University Press, 1946.

THE VICTORIAN AGE

The pages of history are replete with critical controversies, one of the most conflicting and contradictory of them being the one between the neoclassical school of the eighteenth century and the Romantic school of the early nineteenth century. The rules of composition framed and followed by the former were summarily dismissed by the latter. Old order, as always, changes yielding place to new. The age that followed the Romantic Age, the Age of Queen Victoria, that spanned almost the whole of the nineteenth century, was an age of consolidation in many respects. Increase of wealth, the general prosperity of England as a whole on account of its colonial hold over other countries, immense growth in scientific, and industrial development, are some of the clearly noticeable characteristics of this age. The publication of Charles Darwin's *On the Origin of the Species* (1859), with its theory of human evolution, was a major blow to traditional religious orthodoxy, challenging the Biblical version of creation, the very foundation of Christianity. On the other side, 'The Oxford Movement' that initiated a higher conception of the institution of the Church as possessing the privileges, and sacraments ordained by Christ attracted some of the best intellectuals of the time such as Cardinal Newman, Keble and Froude. Greater faith in the principles underlying democracy, opening up of new universities, and introduction of free education widened the scope of the reading public, and thereby changed the modes and practices of the people. The Victorian novel—with all its abundance and variety—can be seen as a product of this age, reflecting its values and its life.

MATTHEW ARNOLD (1822–88)

Critics and prophets of the Victorian Age such as Matthew Arnold, Carlyle, and Ruskin and others, became the major spokesmen setting public standards in morality, religion, and the arts. The enslavement to machinery and the vulgarised middle classes with their newly acquired prosperity posed a great threat to the stability of the society as a whole. Inspired by indignation and pity, John Ruskin attacked the nation for despising art, literature, and the right values of life. The nation, he proclaimed, had become incapable of thought in its insanity of avarice. The greatest of all the critics was Matthew Arnold, the son of Thomas

Arnold, the great headmaster of Rugby School. Matthew Arnold did not like the mid-nineteenth century scene. Though England had advanced by leaps and bounds industrially, on the moral front there was much left to be desired. Morally, the nation was found wanting; in terms of culture, the aristocrats were mere barbarians, the middle-class mere 'philistines,' and as for the common populace the less said about them, the better. The English nation was provincial and uncivilised, lacking in the basic foundations of culture. These views find vigorous expression in the concluding lines of his famous poem, 'Dover Beach'.

> And we are here as on a darkling plain
> Swept with confused alarms of struggle and flight,
> Where ignorant armies clash by night.

Such a view should not be misunderstood as cynical; Arnold felt it was his duty to awaken the nation from the stupor into which it had fallen; that he must create a climate for the creative artist to function properly, and the people must be brought to an awareness of the best that is written and thought.

As a true democrat, powered by the spirit of nationalism, Arnold preached his social philosophy of culture (sweetness and light) as the only cure for the spreading ills that afflicted national life. The Arnoldian concept of culture lays stress on the harmonious development of human nature. Culture is not just personal equipment, but a social force leading to social progress. Culture is described by Arnold in the first essay 'Sweetness and Light' in *Culture and Anarchy* 'as having its origin in the love of perfection; it is a *study of perfection*. It moves by the force, not merely or primarily of the scientific passion for pure knowledge, but also of the moral and social passion for doing good' (45). Arnold further observes:

> Culture which believes in making reason and the will of God prevail, believes in perfection . . . It is in making endless additions to itself, in the endless expansion of its powers, in endless growth in wisdom and beauty, that the spirit of the human race finds its ideal. To reach this ideal, culture is an indispensable aid, and that is the true value of culture. Not a *having* and a *resting* but a *growing* and a *becoming* (italics mine) is the character of perfection as culture conceives it (48).

And the pursuit of perfection, for Arnold, is the pursuit of what Swift calls in his *The Battle of the Books* 'the two noblest things, *sweetness and light.*'

In the words of Eliot, Arnold's justly notable essay 'Study of Poetry' is a classic in English criticism: so much is said in so little space, with such economy and with such authority. Arnold opens with the following clarion call:

> The future of poetry is immense, because in poetry where it is worthy of its high destinies, our race, as time goes on, will find an ever surer and surer stay. There is not a creed which is not shaken, not an accredited dogma which is not shown to be questionable, not a received tradition which does not threaten to dissolve. Our religion has materialized itself in the fact, and now the fact is failing it. But for poetry the idea is everything; the rest is a world of illusion, of divine illusion. Poetry attaches its emotion to the idea; the idea *is* the fact. The strongest part of our religion today is its unconscious poetry (603).

As the dogmatic foundations of religion have come to be shaken, poetry alone can provide self-assurance, and nourishment to mankind. It is, therefore, necessary that we keep the best of poetry as our models. Charlatanism should not be allowed to prevail. We must steer clear of the two fallacies of estimating poetry, the historical and the personal.

Arnold's touchstones have aroused a lot of controversy. He claims, 'short passages, even single lines, will serve our turn quite sufficiently.' Lines of intense poetic quality must be treasured by us, and lodged well in our minds, as guiding touchstones to great poetry. This view, naive in every way, has come in for a lot of controversy among the latter-day critics of Arnold. His touchstones have sometimes been likened to the fellow who carried a brick to show what a house was made of. One is reminded of a humorous incident in Aristophanes' *Frogs* in which poetry is sold by the pound. It is even suggested that these touchstones show his personal taste only; they do not have a universal quality about them. But the answer to this charge would be that he did not wish his touchstones to be compared unimaginatively with some other passages of other poets. Here is what he says: 'If we are thoroughly penetrated by their power, we shall find that we have acquired a sense enabling us, whatever poetry may be laid before us, to feel the degree in which a high poetical quality is present or wanting there.' Arnold's absolutism and dogmatism are subject to attack. He contrasts his 'real estimate' with the personal (relativism) and the historical (again relativism). It is true that Arnold, in the words of Eliot, is a propagandist for criticism. It is equally true that his essays constitute, according to Leavis, high pamphleteering. Some of the elements in his famous essay 'The Study of Poetry' seem outmoded concepts now. But we should agree with his view that when other forms of social life do not unify mankind, literary culture and tradition should be strengthened. For Arnold, greatness in poetry and genuineness in poetry are one and the same. Again defending his 'touchstone,' Leavis says in the essay, 'Arnold as Critic' that, 'it is a tip for mobilizing our sensibility; for focusing our relevant experience in a sensitive point; for reminding us vividly of what the best is like.'And in Leavis's view, 'we read Arnold's critical writing because for anyone interested in literature it is compellingly alive' (268). Arnold gave importance to the unity, wholeness and totality of a work of art. He preferred the use of the term architectonic with reference to *Paradise Lost,* and *King Lear.* His proposal for the touchstones as an infallible test for great poetry runs counter to this principle of totality in a work. Arnold does not want anyone to apply this test mechanically. He quotes eleven passages, three from Homer, three from Dante, three from Milton, and two from Shakespeare; all of them have a tone of melancholy about them.

Again, for him, poetry that does not possess 'truth and high seriousness,'—that which gives to our spirits what they can rest upon—cannot be ranked as great poetry. He has his notions of moral seriousness in his concept of high poetry. 'The best poetry is what we want; the best poetry will be found to have a power of forming, sustaining, and delighting us, as nothing else can.' This noble sphere of poetry must be kept inviolate and inviolable. He denies such a status to Chaucer and Burns for lack of this poetic quality, the high seriousness of the classics. We must realise that Arnold had a rather narrow conception of poetry. In attempting to exalt it, he narrowed down its range. If poetry must stand as a substitute to religion, it must perforce be morally spirited and high. The American 'New Humanists' propounded the same philosophy as Arnold.

Though historical criticism was the fashionable thing in the nineteenth century, Arnold consistently opposed it. The first prose work of Arnold was the Preface to the *Poems* of 1853, and for the remaining thirty-five years of his life, he indulged with great relish in prose writing. Like Dryden before him, and Eliot after him, he was trying to justify himself as a poet in his prose works. In his Preface, he was modest enough to confess his own failure as a poet. He rejected the poetry of the Romantics and the Elizabethans, and favoured poems which are 'particular, precise and firm,' dealing with human actions which 'most powerfully appeal to the great primary human affections; to those elementary feelings which subsist permanently in the race.' Arnold became Professor of Poetry at Oxford at the comparatively young age of thirty-five; and he held the position for ten years. From 1862, he published a series of essays on various authors and to this he added the opening essay, 'The Function of Criticism at the Present Time,' originally published in the *National Review*, in 1864. This has provoked a number of essays on the same pivotal theme by Eliot, Helen Gardner, Terry Eagleton and many others.

Essays in Criticism, first series, marks the end of the first phase of Arnold's critical career. The second phase was spent in theological and religious controversies, and the second series of *Essays in Criticism* marks the third phase. The two series are divided by a long gap of twenty years. The two complement each other. Watson holds that Arnold was an 'adapter rather than a coiner of terms.' The critic has a social function to perform. His 'disinterestedness' does not mean an 'art-for-art's sake' attitude. Arnold makes his position unambiguously clear in his essay, 'The Function of Criticism at the Present Time' in which he asks the critic to steer clear of the practical and political considerations. 'And how is criticism to show its disinterestedness? By keeping aloof from practice; by resolutely following the law of its own nature, which is to be a free play of the mind on all subjects which it touches; by steadily refusing to lend itself to any of those ulterior, political, practical considerations . . . Its business, is, as I have said simply to know the best that is known and thought in the world, and by in its turn making this known, to create a current of true and fresh ideas' (597).

The two well-known custodians of the consciousness of the people, *The Edinburgh Review*, and the *Quarterly Review* were in the service of the political interests of the Whigs and the Tories respectively. Hence, Arnold's insistence on the need for good criticism to create 'a current of true and fresh ideas'. Critical activity is essentially disinterested. The critic's job is to pave the way for high culture. Criticism needs to regard 'Europe as being, for intellectual and spiritual purposes, one great confederation.' His function of criticism, 'a disinterested endeavour to learn and propagate the best that is known and thought in the world' is derived in word and spirit from Sainte-Beuve. 'Philistine' is borrowed from German, and 'sweetness and light,' from Swift.

Arnold rated the English romantics very low in comparison with their continental counterparts. Though Goethe and Byron possessed equally productive resources, Goethe's poetry was nourished by an intense critical effort providing true material, whereas Byron's was not.'The English poetry of the first quarter of this century, with plenty of energy, plenty of creative force, did not know enough. This makes Byron so empty of matter, Shelley so incoherent, Wordsworth even, profound as he is, yet so wanting in completeness and variety' (594). Arnold's views were a reaction to the ideals that romanticism preached. He called Shelley a 'beautiful and ineffectual angel beating in the void his luminous wings in vain.' Coleridge, for him, was a 'poet and philosopher wrecked in the mist of opium.' The letters of Keats were the 'love-letters of a surgeon's apprentice.' In 'Function of Criticism,' Arnold says that for good literature to flourish, two powers are necessary—the creative and the critical. While the critical power is of a lower order than the creative, it is this power that affords the intellectual stimulation of which the creative power can avail itself profitably. It is the business of the critical power, 'in all branches of knowledge, theology, philosophy, history, art, science, to see the object as in itself it really is' (593).The critical power establishes an order of new ideas, or at least makes the best ideas prevail. Out of these fresh ideas, creative epochs are born. The Romantic Movement in England did not possess the glow of life that Elizabethan society had; nor did it possess the force of learning and culture that German society had. Hence the movement was poor and premature. Alas! Arnold's judgment appears far too unfair and even prejudiced.

Between these two critical works, come his body of writings dealing with education and humanistic matters: *Culture and*

Anarchy (1869), and *Literature and Dogma* (1873). Arnold considered both literature and religion as two indivisible parts of culture. As a critic, Arnold has not been successful in demonstrating a first-rate effort as either Johnson or Coleridge has done. His 'disinterested endeavour' often proves to be questionable. He fails to provide us with any theory of poetry. The following passage illustrates some of the obvious things: in any case, nothing by way of critical theorising.

> In poetry, as a criticism of life under the conditions fixed for such a criticism by the laws of poetic truth and poetic beauty, the spirit of our race will find...its consolation and stay. But the consolation and stay will be of power in proportion to the power of the criticism of life. And the criticism of life will be of power in proportion as the poetry, conveying it is excellent rather than inferior, sound rather than unsound or half-sound, true rather than untrue or half-true (604).

He talks much about the right subject for poetry, but is not quite precise in his suggestions. The only point he affirms is that the true subject of poetry 'is an excellent action' appealing to 'the great primary human affections.' Human actions which have an inherent interest are the 'eternal objects of poetry'. Arnold maintained that it was a fallacy to believe that a dull subject can be made interesting by the poet's treatment of the subject. 'Vainly will the latter imagine that he has everything in his power; that he can make an intrinsically inferior action equally delightful with a more excellent one by his treatment of it: he may indeed compel us to admire his skill, but his work will possess, within itself, an incurable defect' (587). Such a view is not sustainable in our time. He excluded from his collection *Poems* 'Empedocles on Etna,' a dramatic poem in which the Greek philosopher, disillusioned with life, throws himself into the crater of Etna. Arnold was of the view that tragic circumstances should be so represented as to be enjoyable. He felt that circumstances 'in which suffering finds no vent in action' are not to be treated as subjects for good poetry. Prolonged mental distress, which is unrelieved and irresolvable, cannot be the right choice of subject for poetry. In the twentieth century, the poetry of World War I and II has elicited quite a sympathetic response from sensitive readers of poetry. It is only in war poetry that felt experiences get transmuted. And that is what accounts for its strength.

Arnold is the most important critic of the second half of the nineteenth century. It is suggested that he reverts to the classical age in his views. He does not exhibit much of an advance from the previous age. H.W. Garrod calls his tone 'High-Church ceremonial.' His literary criticism is always seen alongside his religious and social criticism. In a sense, he was a literary critic by accident. The evangelical side in him attracted his attention to extra-literary considerations. His preface to his *Poems* of 1853 is, in effect, the whole of Arnold's view on literature. And these views were sympathetically shared by quite a few of his contemporaries. 'On the Modern Element in Literature' (1857), his inaugural lecture as Professor of Poetry at Oxford, shows his view that Greek literature should serve as the right model for English poets of his era. *On Translating Homer* (1861) was the first volume of criticism and his *Essays in Criticism: First Series* (1865) contains most of his criticism of this first period. Most of the essays are about individual continental authors. These essays show that he is needlessly biased towards continental literature. *Essays in Criticism, Second Series*, published posthumously in 1888 contains essays on British, and more particularly, romantic poets. The other essays that deal with literary subjects were published in 1910 under the title, *Essays in Criticism, Third Series.*

Creative theory was not Arnold's forte. He does not seem to hold the view that poetic creation is organic; otherwise, how could we accept his touchstones. Evaluation of literature was his speciality. It stands to reason why Eliot called him a propagandist for literature rather than a critic! Literary criticism for Arnold was just one part of social and religious criticism. In his 'Study of Poetry' he says:

> In poetry, which is thought and art in one, it is the glory, the eternal honour, that charlatanism shall find no entrance; that this noble sphere be kept inviolate and inviolable. Charlatanism is for confusing or obliterating the distinctions between excellent and inferior, sound and unsound or only half-sound, true and untrue or only half-true. It is charlatanism, conscious or unconscious, whenever we confuse or obliterate these. And in poetry, more than anywhere else, it is unpermissible to confuse or obliterate them. For in poetry the distinction between excellent and inferior, sound and unsound or only half-sound, true and untrue or only half-true, is of paramount importance. It is of paramount importance because of the high destinies of poetry (604).

Arnold always took a serious view of literature. He did not have much respect for the literature of his own time. He liked evaluating the literature of the past generations. He did not like Elizabethan lyrics and seventeenth century poetry very much. His judgments on the romantic poetics are perhaps his best.

Among the English critics up to the nineteenth century, Arnold happens to be the most influential and the most convincing too. According to Eliot, academic literary opinions were formed by Arnold. R.A. Scott-James asserts, 'For half-a-century Arnold's position in England was comparable with that of Aristotle in respect of the wide influence he exercised, the mark he impressed upon criticism, and the blind faith with which he was trusted by his votaries.'

'In poetry, as a criticism of life under the conditions fixed for such a criticism by the laws of poetic truth and poetic beauty, the spirit of our race will find, we have said, and as time goes on and as other helps fail, its consolation and its stay.' His famous phrase, 'Literature is a criticism of life' has meant many things to many people. Leavis defends Arnold's definition (literature is the criticism of life) most convincingly: 'We make (Arnold insists) our judgments about poetry by bringing to bear the completest and profoundest sense of relative value that, aided by the work judged, we can focus from our total experience of life (which includes literature), and our judgement has intimate bearings on the most serious choices we have to make thereafter in our living' (*Selections from Scrutiny,* vol 1, 263). A work that possesses organic unity is a criticism of the chaos of life even as a good man is a criticism of a bad one. Sidney's 'golden world' is a salutary corrective to the 'brazen world.' Arnold talks about the function of poetry. Lionel Trilling interprets it thus: 'Criticism is not what poetry is; it is what poetry does . . . In so far as poetry helps us to live, not merely by occupying us or by delighting us but by clarifying us with delight, it is a criticism of life' (196).

Arnold's criticism does not have much to do with criticism in the usual sense. Its primary function is 'to see the object as in itself it really is.' The quality of criticism is to be disinterested. It ought not to espouse any cause, or drive any belief into anyone. Arnold adds, 'Its business is, as I have said, simply to know the best that is known and thought in the world, and by in its turn making this known, to create a current of true and fresh ideas. Its business is to do this with inflexible honesty, with due ability; but its business is to do no more, and to leave alone all questions of practical consequences and applications, questions which will never fail to have due prominence given to them' (597). Arnold's definition of poetry and his view of the poetic moment have had many detractors. Saintsbury gives an overall picture of his abilities:

> Systematic without being hidebound; well-read (if not exactly learned) without pedantry; delicate and subtle, without weakness or dilettantism; catholic without eclecticism; enthusiastic without indiscriminateness, Mr Arnold is one of the best and most precious of teachers on his own side . . . Then he is one of the best and most precious of critics (490).

In his essay 'Arnold and Pater,' Eliot's appraisal runs thus: 'Arnold had little gift for consistency or for definition. Nor had he the power of connected reasoning at any length: his flights are either short flights or circular flights. Nothing in his prose works, therefore, will stand very close analysis, and we may very well feel that the positive content of many words is very small' (431).

Arnold's place as the most important critic of the latter half of the nineteenth century is unquestionable. Eliot and Leavis among others have shown allegiance to his system of beliefs. Arnold offers us: an apology for culture; a respect for the Greek ideals; a plea for a return to the study of the humanities against the urge for science, and utility subjects; an attack against the growing philistinism of the middle class; and a call for improvement of criticism, and its standards. More than all, he preaches a religion devoid of dogmatism. When Arnold calls for a replacement of religion by literature, he recommends his own world view—a poetic view of life in which 'morality touched by emotion' governs our being. He is a strong apologist for criticism by which he means a critical spirit; he advocates 'disinterestedness,' a circulation of fresh and free ideas, freedom from British provincialism, and an acceptance of European ideas, especially drawn from Germany and France. Disinterestedness also may mean absence of prejudice and intellectual curiosity. Literary criticism, for him, is descriptive and interpretative. The function of criticism is to create an intellectual climate for the flowering of creative literature. He also firmly emphasises the role of judicial criticism for setting the right standards in art. That is why he pleads for the 'real estimate' as against the other two, which are fallacious, the one subjective and the other governed by antiquarian considerations. In his 'real' estimate, the literature of the eighteenth century is provincial and the literature of the Romantic age lacks intellectual vigour. In fact, he possessed a very good sense of the historical facts. As pointed out earlier, he had a very low opinion of his contemporaries. Carlyle was a 'moral desperado,' Ruskin, 'eccentric,' Tennyson's 'Maud' a 'lamentable production,' and Swinburne a 'pseudo-Shelley.' Like Coleridge before him, Arnold had no interest at all in the genre novel. One of the main strengths of the nineteenth century lies in fiction.

Judged by contemporary standards, many of Arnold's beliefs and assumptions on poetry, and its function are vulnerable for attack. His definition of poetry is that it is a criticism of life. It means that literature is capable of interpreting life, and in this simplified sense it is a gross and didactic misrepresentation of the function of art. His didacticism in expecting high seriousness from poetry is too narrow. His high seriousness is sometimes ridiculed as churchyard solemnity. Arnold gets into difficulties when he argues that 'all depends on the subject,' the choice of a fitting action. To say that style and content are two different things independent of each other is a fallacy. Again, his conviction that the Alexandrine and the couplet are inadequate for poetic expression is another fallacy. His insistence on particular metrical patterns begs the question of the very nature of poetry. According to Arnold, grand style arises when a gifted poet treats, with simplicity or with severity, a serious subject. His range of great poetry is severely restricted. The touchstones have only a short range. Single passages do not prove his theory. Great authors and centuries of national traditions cannot be represented in a line or two. Such a game, for Rene Wellek, is not worth the candle.

As a practical critic, Arnold arranged the English poets, showed discrimination between the major and the minor poets. Réné Wellek remarks, 'Arnold's defence of the critical spirit, his theory of criticism with its emphasis on the real estimate, and even his discussion of the concept of poetry (limited as it is by his didacticism) were a great contribution to English criticism. Arnold, almost single-handedly, pulled English criticism out of the doldrums into which it had fallen after the great Romantic Age' (4: 180).

Arnold's approach to literary criticism is moralistic. He treats literary criticism as an important branch of criticism in general. The purpose of the critical power is 'to see the object as in itself it really is.' For this purpose criticism should be 'disinterested.' It should 'endeavour to learn and propagate the best that is known and thought in the world.' For him the value of a work of art cannot be discussed by analysing it. Its value has to be felt and recognised. Poetic quality is indefinable. Critical power, and sensitivity to respond to works of art grow through liberal education. The power of true judgment is cultivated, and literary sensibility is enlarged through liberal education.

Works Cited

Adams, Hazard, ed. *Literary Criticism since Plato.* New York: Harcourt Brace Jovanovich College Publishers, 1992. Unless otherwise stated, all textual references are drawn from this volume.

Arnold, Matthew. *Culture and Anarchy.* Ed. J. Dover Wilson. Cambridge: Cambridge University Press, 1963.

Eliot, T.S. 'Arnold and Pater.' *Selected Essays.* 1932. London: Faber and Faber Limited, 1972.

Leavis, F.R. 'Matthew Arnold as Critic.' *A Selection from Scrutiny.* Vol. 1. Cambridge: Cambridge University Press.

Saintsbury, George. *History of English Criticism.* London: William Blackwood & Sons Ltd., 1955.

Trilling, Lionel. *Matthew Arnold.* New York: Columbia University Press, 1949.

Select Bibliography

Anderson, W.D. *Matthew Arnold and the Classical Tradition.* Ann Arbor: University of Michigan Press, 1965.

Brown, E.K. *Arnold: A Study in Conflict.* Chicago: University of Chicago Press, 1948.

Donovan, Robert H. 'The Method of Arnold's *Essays in Criticism.*' *PMLA* 71 (1956): 922–31.

Eels, John S. 1955. *The Touchstones of Matthew Arnold.* New York: AMS Press, 1971.

Eliot, T.S. 'Arnold and Pater.' *Selected Essays.* 1932. London: Faber and Faber Limited, 1972.

———. 'Matthew Arnold.' *The Use of Poetry and the Use of Criticism.* 1933. London: Faber and Faber, 1964.

Elton, Oliver. *A Survey of English Literature, 1830–1880.* 2 vols. New York: The Macmillan Company, 1920.

Garrod, H.W. *Poetry and the Criticism of Life.* Cambridge, Massachusetts: Harvard University Press, 1931.

Grierson, H.J.C. *The Background of English Literature.* London: Chatto and Windus, 1925.

Leavis, F.R. 'Arnold as a Critic.' *Scrutiny* 7 (1938).

James, D. J. *Matthew Arnold and the Decline of English Romanticism.* Oxford: Clarendon Press, 1961.

Jamison, William A. *Arnold and the Romantics.* Copenhagen: Rosenkilde and Bagger, 1958.

Robbins, William. *The Ethical Idealism of Matthew Arnold.* Toronto: University of Toronto Press, 1959.

Tillotson, Geoffrey. *Criticism and the Nineteenth Century.* London: University of London, Athlone Press, 1951.

Trilling, Lionel. *Matthew Arnold.* New York: University of Columbia Press, 1949.

5

Twentieth Century Criticism

T.S. Eliot (1888–1965)

t is said, with some justification, that between the years 1910 and 1939, there was a renaissance in English literature and criticism comparable, in some measure, to the periods 1590–1612, 1710–35, and 1798–1822. A complete change came about imaginative literature and criticism. And, in no small measure, it is due to the contribution of Thomas Stearns Eliot.

In his well-known preface to *For Lancelot Andrews* (1928), Eliot openly described himself as a classicist in literature, a royalist in politics, and an Anglo-Catholic in religion. Such a public revelation of his political, and religious position naturally elicited protests. But his declaration sets the tone for his lifelong commitment to criticism. He held some very strong and dogmatic beliefs, as for example, his conviction that only those who believed in the doctrine of the original sin could understand his writings. In *After Strange Gods* (1934) he declared, 'at this point I shall venture to generalize, and suggest that with this disappearance of the idea of *Original Sin,* with the disappearance of the idea of intense moral struggle, the human beings presented to us both in poetry and in prose fiction today, and more patently among the serious writers than in the underworld of letters, tend to become less and less real.' For Eliot, his faith in religion, belief in politics, and concept of literature form one seamless whole. His general attitude to literature, and the critical stand he took remained uniform throughout his life, though sometimes he revised his notions regarding individual writers like Milton, for example. He recanted in 1947 his earlier estimate of Milton made in 1935. In 1919, he wrote a very important essay, 'Tradition and the Individual Talent'. It appeared in two instalments in the journal *The Egoist,* which is an invaluable document so far as literary criticism in our time is concerned. It heralded a new dawn in our thinking about literature. It is considered as the unofficial manifesto of T.S. Eliot's criticism. The term 'tradition,' the key to the essay, does not mean 'a blind or timid adherence,' but

> it involves, in the first place, the historical sense, which we may call nearly indispensable to anyone who would continue to be a poet beyond his twenty-fifth year; and the historical sense involves a perception, not only of the pastness of the past, but of its presence; the historical sense compels a man to write not merely with his own generation in his bones, but with a feeling that the whole of the literature of Europe from Homer, and within it the whole of the literature of his own country, has a simultaneous existence and composes a simultaneous order. . . (761).

Talking of 'historical sense', Eliot says, 'This historical sense, which is the sense of the timeless as well as of the temporal and of the timeless and the temporal together, is what makes a writer traditional.' He uses 'historical sense' not in the usual sense. He wants the critic to see literature, 'not as consecrated by time, but to see it beyond time; to see the best work of our time and the best work of twenty-five hundred years ago with the same eyes.' His view of tradition is negative in so far as it distrusts novelty or originality, or any kind of revolution or individualistic attempt, and it is positive in that it recommends that the poet should have a sense of the history of poetry. It is this 'historical sense' which makes a writer traditional. This sense denies chronology and conceives the past as timeless and existing here and now. 'Honest criticism and sensitive appreciation is directed not upon the poet but upon the poetry.'

The individuality of the poet is no concern at all in the created object. Eliot first disposes of the idea that a poet is great in proportion as he is original. No poet can be understood in his terms only. The most valuable parts of a work are those in which 'the dead poets, his ancestors, assert their immortality most vigorously.' All existing monumental works of literature form an ideal order, and whenever a new work comes on the scene, it alters the whole order, ever so slightly. Therefore, every new writer is to be judged by the standards which exist already in the past. Every poet worth the name must be a shareholder of the past, and be knowledgeable about the current of literature. He must possess 'the historical sense, which we may call nearly indispensable to any one who would continue to be a poet beyond his twenty-fifth year.' The writer should be (in fact *is*) conscious of the dead writers: the conscious present is but an awareness of the past. The mind of Europe (the word 'tradition' is synonymous here because Eliot is part of the European ethos) is more important than the individual poet. The poet must subordinate himself to this tradition, because it is more important than himself, and his personality as a poet. 'The progress of the artist is a continual self-sacrifice, a continual extinction of personality.'

In order to make the relationship between the process of depersonalisation and tradition clearer, Eliot gives us the example of a chemical reaction, a catalysis. When a piece of platinum is introduced into a gas chamber containing sulphur and carbon dioxide, the two combine to form sulphurous acid, but the platinum itself remains unchanged. The mind of the poet is this platinum. The emotions and feelings are sulphur and carbon dioxide. The more perfect he is as a poet, the less involved is his own personality. The artist's mind keeps forming new compounds, but he remains separate in the whole process of creation. The mind that suffers is different from the man that creates. Eliot dismisses the romantic expressive theory of self-expression. The experiences, which are important to the poet as man, do not have much of a place in his poetry, and those that are quite important in his poetry have practically nothing to do with the poet's personality. That is why he is dismissive of Wordsworth's theory of 'emotions recollected in tranquillity.' 'Poetry is not a turning loose of emotion, but an escape from emotion; it is not expression of personality but an escape from personality.' Some of these ideas are found in the neoclassicists too and in those who have opposed individualism in poetry. The poet must constantly surrender himself to tradition. 'The emotion of art is impersonal.' Some commentators have accused Eliot of what might be called 'antipoetic coldness'. The Eliot's point about 'depersonalisation' may be likened to Keats's *negative capability* which he defines as that state of mind, 'when a man is capable of being in uncertainties, mysteries, doubts, without any irritable reaching after fact and reason,' or the psychical distance which is a necessary condition for successful composition. A willing submission to things as they are is a prerequisite to poetry. It is only then a poet can get into a state of impartial freedom, and range freely without being committed to any dead weight of a doctrine.

In the essay, 'The Function of Criticism', Eliot says that the problem of criticism is one of establishing order. A critic must listen to his inner voice alone. He must have a highly developed sense of fact, for fact cannot corrupt taste whereas opinion can. The major characteristics of Eliot's critical method are easy to identify. He practises the method of evaluatory or judicial criticism, and does not indulge in close analysis of texts as recommended by the New Critics. This may be because his taste and judgments predate the thirties when New Criticism came into vogue. He is a follower of Arnold, creating an audience for him. When he discusses the writers of the past, he quickly arrives at value judgments and even rates them. Eliot has the readers of his own poetry in his mind when he evaluates other poets, particularly the dead ones.

Eliot's poetic career falls into three stages: the first one between 1919 and 1928 with interest in the sixteenth and seventeenth century dramatists and poets published in *Sacred Wood: Essays on Poetry and Criticism* (1920), *Homage to John Dryden: Three Essays* (1924), and *For Lancelot Andrews: Essays on Style and Order* (1928); the second one between 1929 and 1939, of social and religious criticism in *Dante* (1929), *Thoughts after Lambeth* (1931), *The Use of Poetry and the Use of Criticism* (1933), *After Strange Gods* (1934), and *Elizabethan Essays* (1934); and finally, the post-war period which shows a return to the earlier interests, though not in the form of the first phase. His later critical works, such as *Notes towards the Definition of Culture* (1948) and *To Criticise the Critic* (1965) show the shift of his focus from purely literary criticism to a deep-seated concern with culture and civilisation, in general. In the midst of all these preoccupations as a social and literary critic, he found time to edit the quarterly *Criterion,* which set a considerably high standard of literary publication. The essays collected in the volume *Selected Essays* contain in a nutshell his best criticism, quite enough for a reappraisal of his contribution to literary criticism.

Eliot gave the title 'The Sacred Wood' to his first book of criticism. He borrowed it from Frazer's *The Golden Bough* in which a ritual is described, where the priest occupies a sacred wood driving away any contender to the priesthood. Eliot implied that as critic or poet, he was entering this sacred wood, challenging any contender for the position. *The Sacred Wood* is central to Eliot's achievement in one sense. Criticism becomes a by-product of his private poetry-workshop in judging others by his own standards as a practising poet. His essays written during the 1920s and the 1930s helped in changing the course of English literary history considerably. It is now almost impossible to talk at length about the poetry after 1600 without reckoning Eliot's writings in some measure. Eliot replaced the critical orthodoxy of Arnold. For him, there has been a decline in English poetry from Shakespeare and Milton to the eighteenth century, with the possible exception of Wordsworth. This is compensated for by a rise in quality in prose writings. Genuine poetry is composed in the soul, whereas Dryden and Pope composed their poetry in their wits. Eliot looked upon the scene a little differently from Arnold. In his famous essay, 'The Metaphysical Poets' (one of the pieces in *Homage to John Dryden*), a review of Herbert Grierson's *Metaphysical Lyrics and Poems of the Seventeenth Century* (1921), he asserts, 'In the seventeenth century a dissociation of sensibility set in, from which we have never recovered.' The result was a decline in poetic quality. In the Jacobean dramatists and the Metaphysical poets there is 'a direct sensuous apprehension of thought or a recreation of thought into feeling.' In the later poets thought and feeling got dissociated more and more.

> A thought to Donne was an experience; it modified his sensibility. When a poet's mind is perfectly equipped for its work, it is constantly amalgamating disparate experience; the ordinary man's experience is chaotic, irregular, fragmentary. The latter falls in love, or reads Spinoza, and these two experiences have nothing to do with each other, or with the noise of the typewriter or the smell of cooking; in the mind of the poet these experiences are forming new wholes (183).

There are attempts at a unification of sensibility in Keats and Shelley, but Tennyson and Browning only ruminated. It is said that ratiocination gave way to reflection and rumination. For Eliot, the high watermark of English poetry was the seventeenth century after which there was a steady decline which, he felt, had to be arrested by Eliot himself. The metaphysical poets possessed the power to 'amalgamate disparate experiences,' and the lapse of this power to 'amalgamate' results in the separation of thought and feeling. Eliot calls this the 'dissociation of sensibility.' The fusion of the emotion with the intellect is best poetry for him. Poets until the seventeenth century thought and felt, and knew that these two exist together; but in the seventeenth century, a split occurred with the onset of scientific rationalism. Poets only thought, and after the Romantic revolution, they only felt. Again in the nineteenth century, there was a return only to thinking which he calls 'rumination'. Eliot pleads for a reintegration of these two—thought and feeling.

In many ways, Eliot has proved himself to be the most important critic of our century. He helped in correcting the taste of the poetry reading public; he re-evaluated the English poets. He initiated a critical theory of his own. His concept of the impersonal theory of poetry, unified sensibility, his emphasis on the perfection of the spoken idiom for poetry, and his formulae, such as, the 'objective correlative' are all invaluable aids to the understanding and appreciation of poetry. Though he had competence in abstract thinking, Eliot did not build a coherent system of aesthetics on poetry. He felt it was none of his concern. Despite a remark of this kind, it is possible to see observable cohesion in all his writings, leaving out his contribution made for specific purposes and on special occasions. He says that his criticism is 'workshop criticism,' 'a by-product of my private workshop.' He associated scholarship with permanent interest in a work, and criticism with the immediate. This does not always sound true. He maintained three types of criticism: creative criticism, historical criticism, and criticism proper. Arthur Symons, and Walter Pater belong to the first type, Herbert Grierson, and W.P. Ker to the second type; the poet-critic belongs to the third type. He himself belongs to the enlightened company of Dryden, Johnson, Coleridge, and Arnold, who were poet-critics. Somehow, he did not like interpretation and judicial criticism, but in his own practice he was a successful judge of other people's writings.

Frequently, Eliot was in the habit of ranking poets and dramatists. He does not approve of interpretation and judicial criticism. For him, interpretation is valid only 'when it is not interpretation at all, but merely putting the reader in possession of facts which he would otherwise have missed.' For him, the critic 'must simply elucidate; the reader will form the correct judgment for himself.' He ridicules interpretation as belonging to the 'lemon-squeezer school of criticism.' And 'taking the machine to pieces' kills the enjoyment of the poems that are analysed. The aim of criticism is 'the return to the work of art with improved perception.' Eliot's 'impersonal theory' employs a notorious metaphor of referring to the poet's mind as a platinum shred, in which case, the poet is merely a passive medium, and so, the reference to the poet's mind as a catalyst is not quite right. How is it then that we speak of 'Shakespearean' imagination, or the 'Wordsworthian' elements, or 'Joycean' qualities in a work? However, in practice, Eliot is fond of discovering a pattern in the works of artists. This pattern is a sort of evolution of the poet. He ranks writers in terms of this personality as an evolution in their works. The Elizabethan dramatists are ranked on such a scale of personal contribution. There are instances when Eliot speaks of transmuting private and personal experiences into something universal and impersonal. For, all great poetry has a universalising of emotion, which may or may not be personal in its origin.

Eliot makes a distinction between art emotion, and life emotion which is transformed into art. Art emotion or significant emotion is a complex one; and personal emotion may be 'simple, crude and flat.' The early Eliot believed in the total autonomy of art; the later Eliot defended two types, the artistic, and the moral and philosophical. In his essay, 'Religion and Literature,' Eliot observes: 'Literary criticism should be completed by criticism from a definite ethical and theological standpoint. . . The 'greatness' of literature cannot be determined by solely literary standards; though we must remember that whether it is literature or not can be determined only by literary standards' (43). This dichotomy between 'artness' and 'greatness' is another way of creating a divorce between form and content. Eliot held widely disparate views on poetry and belief at different times, but finally this passage clarifies his position. 'When the doctrine, theory, belief, or "view of life" presented in the poem is one which the mind of the reader can accept as coherent, mature, and founded on the facts of experience, it interposes no obstacle to the reader's enjoyment, whether it be one that he can accept or deny, approve or deprecate.' Coherence is as much artistic as it is logical. A work of art is mature because of its inclusiveness, coherence, complexity, and its correspondence to reality. In fact, the strength of belief and sincerity in feeling have nothing much to do in the criticism of a work.

Here is another formulation of Eliot's theory about the impersonal art. It appears in his essay, 'Hamlet and his Problems.' Eliot describes his 'objective correlative' in the following terms:

> The only way of expressing emotion in the form of art is by finding an 'objective correlative'; in other words, a set of objects, a situation, a chain of events which shall be the formula of that particular emotion; such that when the external acts, which must terminate in sensory experience, are given the emotion is immediately evoked (766).

This view of the 'objective correlative' places the emphasis squarely on the work as an artefact. The poet cannot transmit his emotions directly to the reader, and so takes recourse to some medium. This may be a situation, a set of objects or a chain of ideas. What the poet has to convey gets objectified through this medium, and hence, interaction between the poet and the reader takes place. The reader responds to the medium, and through that, to the work of art. As a successful instance of objective correlative, Eliot gives the example of the sleepwalking of Lady Macbeth, where there is a 'complete adequacy of the external to the emotion.' But in the case of Hamlet, he 'is dominated by an emotion which is inexpressible, because it is in *excess* of the facts as they appear.' And, precisely for this reason, 'far from being Shakespeare's masterpiece, the play is most certainly an artistic failure.' The term generally means the right kind of situation, the right plot, or a set of symbolic objects in a play, or a novel which generates the emotion of the characters in the play or novel. Eliot might have lighted on the term as the 'equivalent' of the author's emotion, which is the successful objectification of the emotion in a work of art.

Eliot always held the view that poetry should approximate to the spoken language as it is spoken during the poet's lifetime. That is why he admires Dante's language which is a 'perfection of the common language,' and Dryden's language 'which restored

English verse to the condition of speech.' This does not, however, mean that poets should use colloquialisms. He maintained that Milton corrupted the language by subjecting it to 'a peculiar kind of deterioration,' and wrote 'English like a dead language.' Later in 1947, when he recanted much of his argument, he said that he felt Milton was a bad influence on him, and the poets of his generation who wanted to restore the spoken idiom to poetry. His standards were the same even for prose. He did not favour the poetic prose of the nineteenth century. Even for his plays, he wanted to use a form of language close to the music of the spoken form. While he seems to favour prosaic style in poetry, he attacks poetic style in prose. He calls Kipling's poetry 'verse'. He says, 'Good poetry is obviously something else besides good verse; and good verse may be very indifferent poetry.' He likes poetry of statement, poetry without imagery, like the poetry of, say, Dryden or Goldsmith. He introduces another criterion in poetry: the criterion of intensity, especially, in long poems or in drama. The entire criticism of Eliot deals with poetry or drama (poetic drama), which he tried his best to revive and defend. *The Three Voices of Poetry* deals with this. The lyric is the first voice overheard by the reader; the dramatic monologue, the second voice; and the drama with imaginary characters the third voice. All the three voices are present in drama.

Eliot's contribution to the criticism of the novel is not noteworthy. He admired Joyce and he said that *Ulysses* is 'a book quite as Irish in material as a book can be, but a book so significant in the history of the English language that it must take its place as a part of the tradition, of that language. Such a book not only realises untried possibilities in a language, but revivifies the whole of the past.' There are some who think that after his religious conversion, he declined as a critic. But Réné Wellek counters such a charge in the following words:

> He used his gifts as well as ever. But his interests shifted away from literary criticism and thus he was apt to use literature as documents for his Jeremiads on the modern world. He embraced a double standard which dissolves the unity of a work of art as well as the sensibility which goes into its making and the critical act itself. He thus weakened (on behalf of what he felt to be higher interests) the impact of his achievement as a literary critic. Taken in its early purity his literary criticism seems to be very great indeed (5: 220).

George Watson's estimate of Eliot's achievement runs thus: 'Eliot made English criticism look different, but in no simple sense. He offered it a new range of rhetorical possibilities, confirmed it in its increasing contempt for historical processes, and yet reshaped its notion of period by a handful of brilliant institutions' (177).

Finally and quite importantly, more than all the critical pronouncements Eliot had made, and more than all reappraisals of major literary reputations he had established (Dante, Dryden, Pope, the Elizabethan dramatists and the metaphysical poets), he had a significant role to play in unearthing and recognising new talents wherever they lay. That he was deeply interested in contemporary writing can be seen in his criticism of Joyce and Yeats, among others. The major charge against him is that his interest was restricted to poetry, and he turned a blind eye to American literature, and American literary tradition.

Works Cited

Adams, Hazard, ed. *Literary Criticism since Plato.* 1971. New York: Harcourt Brace Jovanovich College Publishers, 1992. Unless otherwise stated, all textual references are drawn from this volume.

Eliot, T.S. 'Religion and Literature.' 1936. *Five Approaches of Literary Criticism.* Ed. Wilbur Scott. London: Collier Macmillan Publishers, 1979.

———. 'The Metaphysical Poets.' *The English Critical Tradition.* Vol.2. Ed. S. Ramaswami and V.S. Seturaman. Madras: Macmillan, 1970.

Watson, George. *The Literary Critic: A Study of English Descriptive Criticism.* Harmondsworth, Middlesex: Penguin Books, 1962.

Wellek, Réné. *History of Modern Criticism.* Vol. 5. New Haven: Yale University Press, 1986.

Select Bibliography

Austin, Allen. *T.S. Eliot: The Literary and Social Criticism.* Bloomington: Indiana University Press, 1971.

Brombert, Victor. *The Criticism of T.S. Eliot: Problems of an 'Impersonal Theory' of Poetry.* 1949.

Buckley, Vincent. *Poetry and Morality: Studies in the Criticism of Matthew Arnold, T.S. Eliot and F.R. Leavis.* 1950. London: Chatto and Windus, 1959.

Eliot, T.S. *The Sacred Wood: Essays on Poetry and Criticism.* London: Methuen & Co. Ltd., 1920.

———. *For Lancelot Andrewes.* London: Faber and Gwyer, 1928.

———. *Selected Essays 1917–1932.* London: Faber and Faber, 1932.

———. *The Use of Poetry and the Use of Criticism.* 1933. London: Faber and Faber, 1964.

———. *After Strange Gods.* London: Faber and Faber, 1934.

———. *On Poetry and Poets.* London: Faber and Faber, 1957.

———. *To Criticise the Critic and other Writings.* London: Faber and Faber, 1965.

Frye, Northrop. *T.S. Eliot.* New York: Grove Press, 1963.

Granta, Michael. Ed. *T.S. Eliot: The Critical Heritage.* 2 vols. London: Routledge & Kegan Paul, 1982.

Jay, Gregory S. *T.S. Eliot and the Poetics of Literary History.* Baton Rouge: Louisiana State University Press, 1983.

Leavis, F.R. 'T.S. Eliot as Critic.' *Anna Karenina and other Essays.* London: Chatto and Windus. 1967.

Lucy, Sean. *T.S. Eliot and the Idea of Tradition.* 1960. London: Cohen and West, 1967.

Matthiessen, F.O. *The Achievement of T.S. Eliot.* New York: Oxford University Press, 1959.

Rajan, B, ed., *T.S. Eliot: A Study of His Writings by Diverse Hands.* New York: Funk and Wagnall's, 1948.

Ransom, J.C. 'T.S. Eliot: The Historical Critic.' *The New Criticism.* Norfolk, Conn.: New Directions, 1941.

Stead, C.K. *The New Poetic: Yeats to Eliot.* London: Hutchinson. 1964.

Tate, Allen, ed. *T.S. Eliot: The Man and His Work.* New York: Delacorte Press, 1966.

Unger, Leonard, ed. *T.S. Eliot: A Selected Critique.* New York: Rinehart, 1948.

Vivas, Eliseo. *Creation and Discovery: Essays in Criticism and Aesthetics.* New York: Noonday Press, 1955.

I.A. RICHARDS (1893–1979)

Ivor Armstrong Richards is often referred to as the critical consciousness of our age. There is a lot of truth in such an observation. John Crowe Ransom begins his book *The New Criticism* with the remark that any discussion of the New Critics must start with Dr Richards. The New Criticism very nearly began with him. Many others have the same opinion that he is the creator of modern criticism. He was many things: poet, dramatist, speculative philosopher; but primarily he was a psychologist, and semanticist. A lot has been written on Richards's contribution to modern criticism. We shall, however, limit our discussion to some of the concepts as the theory of value, theory of communication, and poetic language.

Let us start with the theory of value in the arts. Richard says that the aesthetic state is not any different from the ordinary state in our life. 'When we look at a picture, or read a poem, or listen to music, we are not doing something quite unlike what we were doing on our way to the Gallery, or when we dressed in the morning.' Aesthetic experience is not different from any other experience. It has nothing special to commend it: only in an aesthetic experience there are 'a greater number of impulses which have to be brought into coordination with one another.' In art experience, there is a resolution, an inter-animation and balancing of impulses. 'Impulses' are those stimuli that motivate 'attitudes' in us and the 'attitudes' are the 'imaginable and incipient activities or tendencies of action.' This psychological theory is not his creation, but he was the one who used it in relation to criticism and defence of poetic creation. Poetry organises our impulses and attitudes. Poetry organises our mind, gives it certain order, renders us happy, and makes our minds healthy. 'The best life is that in which, as far as possible, our whole personality is "engaged" without confusion.' That state of mind in which waste and frustration are reduced is the valuable state of mind. Art in general (and literature in particular) is valuable for us in this sense that it integrates our activities, resolves our mental conflicts and tension, and leads us to a liberated state. Richards calls this harmonised state, this balancing of conflicting impulses, 'synaesthesis'. In the experience of synaesthesis, there is a sense of detachment that is conducive to the formation of a completely coordinated personality.

Some of these claims may have to be taken with a pinch of salt; otherwise how could we account for madmen, criminals, suicides and wholly disorganised men among poets. Richards's psychologism shows that he is not concerned with the poetic object *per se* enclosing a certain structure in itself, but only with our responses to the object. The poem is located in the reader. The poem is the reader's response to it. Such confessedly open subjectivism leads him to the conclusion that poetic language is ambiguous, plurisignant, open to different and diverse meanings. Similarly metre in poetry is that which patterns us in some way. The balance or organisation is not to be found out there in the object, but in our response to it. Richards along with C.K. Ogden expounded a theory of language. They distinguished between two uses of language—the referential and the emotive. In 'Two Uses of Language', Richards makes the distinction:

> A statement may be used for the sake of the *reference*, true or false, which it causes. This is the *scientific* use of language. But it may also be used for the sake of the effects in emotion and attitude produced by the reference it occasions. This is the *emotive* use of language. . . We may either use words for the sake of the references they promote, or we may use them for the sake of the attitudes and emotions which ensue (112).

Richards distinguishes four different kinds of meaning, or rather, the four aspects of it. They are sense, feeling, tone and intention. When we make an utterance, we direct the attention of our hearer to what we utter. We use language to convey the feelings that we wish to convey in our utterance. We arrange the tone depending on whom we are addressing. Finally, we have some intention, conscious or unconscious, and this modifies our utterance. There is interplay of these functions in any communication, written or spoken.

Poetry is made of 'pseudo-statements' which cannot be empirically tested and proved true or false. 'A pseudo-statement is "true," if it suits and serves some attitude or links together attitudes which on other grounds are desirable. . . A pseudo-statement is a form of words which is justified entirely by its effect in releasing or organizing our impulses and attitudes; a statement, on the other hand, is justified by its truth, that is, its correspondence, in a highly technical sense, with the fact to which it points (Stallman, 330).' Poetry is emotive and cannot be expected to provide us with knowledge. Poetry communicates feelings and emotions, and has nothing to do with meaning or knowledge. To counter the cognitive value of poetry, Richards opens up a discussion on poetry and belief, which is whether a poet should convey any ideas, whether the readers should have belief in the doctrine of the poet. Richards holds the view that there is no intellectual doctrine in poetry at all. 'We must free poetry from entanglement with belief.' Doctrinal adhesion is a vice in poetry. That is why he admires *The Waste Land* which 'effects a complete severance between poetry and all beliefs.' Richards's psychological theory about effective communication and worthlessness of the experience that is communicated, with reference to chosen poems in his *Practical Criticism,* is unverifiable. How do we accept the fact that H.S.'s poem 'The Pool,' has value but lacks the communication of experience, and how do we accept his findings about the sonnet by Ella Wheeler Wilcox? Richards defines a poem as a class of experiences, 'composed by all experiences, occasioned by the words,' which do not differ within certain limits from 'the original experience of the poet.' This standard experience for him 'is the relevant experience of the poet when contemplating the completed composition.' Many of his suppositions on the psychological factors governing poetic experience cannot hold sway now in the context of contemporary theories. He employs purely biological systems when he equates the mind with the nervous system in the well-known diagram in chapter 14 of his *Principles.*

However, we must concede that his influence depends largely on his *Practical Criticism* (1929). He analyses factors responsible for misreading of poems and exposes our dependence on props such as the name of the author or our sense of the history of the poem. He demonstrates how the readers of poetry are crippled in their responses, and documents the main difficulties of sensitive criticism. They are 1. the difficulty of making plain sense of poetry—failure to grasp the sense of the poem, insensitivity to the form and meaning of words in a sequence, 2. the difficulty of sensuous apprehension of poetry, 3. the difficulty presented by imagery, principally by the visual imagery, 4. mnemonic irrelevances—the intrusion of private and personal associations, 5. stock responses, based on privately established judgments, 6. sentimentality, 7. inhibition, 8. doctrinal adhesions, 9. technical presuppositions, and 10. general critical preconceptions—prior demands made upon poetry. Richards believes in the validity of specific interpretations and their correctness, and he points out how and where the poem fails in its confused imagery, or sentimental theme. The conclusion that Richards comes to is, 'the critical reading of poetry is an arduous discipline. . . The lesson of all criticism is that we have nothing to rely upon in making our choices but ourselves. The lesson of good poetry seems to be that, when we have understood it, in the degree in which we can order ourselves, we need nothing more' (*Practical Criticism* 329). As a formalist, he is not enamoured of relating poems to particular ideologies. He places works in the long Western tradition from Plato, and interprets them on the basis of an accepted view of the unity of mankind. If he is freed from the entanglements of psychological theories, he is at one with the tradition of poetic theory, descending from Aristotle. Richards's rejection of aesthetics, reducing a work of literature to a mental state, his defence of poetry as emotive language organising our impulses and contributing to mental health—all these appear rather naive today. So poetry, whether it is good or bad, is meant to organise our impulses, and that is about all there is to it. One entertains a feeling that poetry is just reduced to mental therapy, whereas the quality of the poetic object is wholly neglected. Réné Wellek comments that

> Richards's lack of interest in the kind of stylistics practised on the Continent has rather widened the gulf between English and American criticism and developments on the Continent. . . But all of this hardly matters: the stimulus that Richards gave to English and American criticism (particularly Empson and Cleanth Brooks) by turning it resolutely to the question of language, its meaning and function in poetry, will always insure his position in any history of modern criticism (238).

Eliot and Richards are jointly associated as pioneers of the movement of New Criticism. Both of them were among the most influential critics of the twentieth century; only Eliot was descriptive and Richards theoretical. The latter provided the foundations for verbal analysis of poetry. His major influence is based on his two early books, *Principles* and *Practical Criticism.* He is dismissive of all early theories, and thinks that literary criticism must be strong with experimentalism. Richards seems to encourage 'unhistorical' readings of poems. Helen Gardner took serious objection to Richards's experiment in his *Practical Criticism.* This is how she contradicts: 'the experiment proved, I think, not the incapacity of the readers, but the futility of the method. Quite apart from the inhibiting anxiety of many of the readers to say the right thing or not to be taken in, it was clear that, divorced from their human and historical context, works were deprived of their power to speak to the heart and conscience' (19). With him, this method of interpretation (demonstrated in *Practical Criticism*) originated in England, later spread to the US, and finally, has come to dominate academic criticism the world over. This anti-historical criticism became New Criticism. Now we tend to forget that its origins are to be located in England with Richards as one of its primary founding fathers.

Works Cited

Gardner, Helen. *The Business of Criticism.* London: Oxford University Press, 1959.

Richards, I.A. 'The Two Uses of Language.' *Twentieth Century Literary Criticism.* Ed. David Lodge. London: Longman, 1972.

———. *Practical Criticism.* New York: Harcourt, Brace & World, Inc., 1929.

Stallman, R.W., ed. *Critiques and Essays in Criticism.* New York: The Ronald Press Co., 1949.

Wellek, Rene. *History of Modern Criticism.* Vol 5. New Haven: Yale University Press, 1986.

Select Bibliography

Constable, John, ed. *I.A. Richards and his Critics: Selected Reviews and Critical Articles.* London: Routledge, 2001.

Crane, Ronald, ed. *Critics and Criticism.* Chicago: University of Chicago Press, 1952.

Hyman, Stanley E. 1948. *The Armed Vision.* New York: Vintage Books, 1955.

Krieger, Murray. *New Apologists for Poetry.* Minneapolis: University of Minnesota Press, 1956.

Ransom, J.C. *World's Body.* 1938. Baton Rouge: Louisiana University Press, 1968.

Richards, I.A. *The Meaning of Meaning.* New York: Harcourt Brace & Company, 1923.

———. *Principles of Literary Criticism.* 1924. New York: Harcourt Brace Jovanovich, 1961.

———. *Science and Poetry.* London: K. Paul, Trench and Trubner, 1926.

———. *Practical Criticism: A Study of Literary Judgment.* London: K. Paul, Trench and Trubner, 1929.

———. *Coleridge on Imagination.* 1934. Bloomington: Indiana University Press, 1960.

———. *The Philosophy of Rhetoric.* 1936. New York: Oxford University Press, 1965.

———. *Speculative Instruments.* Chicago: University of Chicago Press, 1955.

Schiller, Jerome. P. *I.A. Richards's Theory of Literature.* New Haven: Yale University Press, 1969.

Vivas, Eliseo. *Creation and Discovery.* New York: Noonday Press, 1955.

Vendler, Helen, Rouben Brower and John Hollander, eds. *I.A. Richards: Essays in His Honor.* New York: Oxford University Press, 1973.

THE NEW CRITICISM

The most noteworthy movement in twentieth century criticism which effected a total transformation, as it were, of the discipline of English studies, goes by the name of New Criticism. The new emphasis that was given to criticism earned the title 'New' for it. It is, of course, no longer new. How did this movement come about? What is its philosophic foundation? In what manner has it affected English studies the world over? What are its strengths and weaknesses, its merits and demerits? We shall try to seek answers to these basic questions in this chapter. More or less, around the same period of time, roughly in the first half of the twentieth century, this movement grew in stature on both sides of the Atlantic, in England and in the United States. There seems to have been some discontent with the literary situation, in both these countries, at the turn of the century. Trade and industry had shown phenomenal growth; but literary art, and criticism had not kept pace with this. In the academic circles, there were discussions on where to lay the emphasis, on history or on criticism, on the background and the life of the author, or on the work itself. Hence, the full nomenclature for it is Anglo-American New Criticism.

T.S. Eliot wielded a great deal of influence among his contemporaries. When his *The Sacred Wood* (1920) came out, it started a trend in criticism, mainly descriptive then, which came to be called New Criticism. The term was put into circulation by Joel. E. Spingarn, and all its major practitioners have been either English, or American. Spingarn is an authoritative historian of Renaissance criticism. He explained the theories of Croce in a booklet called *The New Criticism* in 1911, and later, in 1941, the poet John Crowe Ransom, the founder of *Kenyon Review,* wrote a book, reviewing the criticism of I.A. Richards, T.S. Eliot, and Yvor Winters, rather disparagingly, to which he gave the title *The New Criticism* (1941). This title has now come to stay. In Ransom's book, there is an essay 'Wanted: an Ontological Critic,' where he pleads for an establishment of an intellectual movement that deserves to be named New Criticism. Ransom made a formal announcement:

> I suggest that the differentia of poetry as a discourse is an ontological one. It treats an order of existence, a grade of objectivity, which cannot be treated in scientific discourse. . . Poetry intends to recover the denser and more refractory original world which we know loosely through our perceptions and memories. By this supposition it is a kind of knowledge which is radically or ontologically distinct (148).

But by the time Ransom published his book in 1941, New Criticism had become an established school in academia. In the US, it came and settled itself as a reaction against certain prevailing modes of criticism which are discernible in the following trends: mere subjective aesthetic impressionism, otherwise called 'appreciation,' which was noticeable in the first decade of the twentieth century; the philosophical humanist movement of Irving Babbitt and Paul Elmer More; and the Marxism of Granville Hicks, and Edmund Wilson. Imagism in poetry, and Hulme's influential essay 'Classicism and Romanticism' gave a stimulus to the prevailing situation. The pioneer of New Criticism, John Crowe Ransom, taught his students, Allen Tate, and Robert Penn Warren, some early lessons such as those that Eliot held in his *After Strange Gods*. Eliot's essays in his *The Sacred Wood* (1920) show clearly that he was in favour of technical criticism as against glib moralism and impressionism. The two essays, complementing each other, 'The Perfect Critic,' and 'The Imperfect Critic,' supply ample evidences to prove his stand. That criticism is bad which is just an expression of one's personal predilections, and emotions. Good criticism, on the other hand, is the result of refined sensibility. To be a good critic, one has to be a being of a higher order. For such a person, technical and aesthetic analyses are necessary, but not sufficient conditions for sound criticism. As an orthodox Anglo-Catholic, he felt that non-literary considerations should be taken into account for a comprehensive, and fuller treatment of a work. His essay 'Religion and Literature' confirms this position. And in Eliot's case, this meant conformity to the faith and doctrine established by the Church of England. Early on in his *World's Body* (1938), Ransom had declared his much-favoured programme of criticism that would be aristocratic in manners, ritualistic in religion and traditional in art. This was probably meant to be an echo of Eliot's oft-quoted declaration in his preface to *For Lancelot Andrews* (1928). Ransom strongly believed that teaching literature meant concentrating on 'criticism.' This meant defining and enjoying the aesthetic characteristics of literature. The proper concern is to treat literature as an art with its own laws of governance. The earliest criticism, carrying this method, could be found in the poetry magazine, *The Fugitive* (1922–25).

The American New Criticism was a reactionary movement in its contempt for historical criticism. Its anti-historicism became manifest, when it spread to the academia with its useful anthologies *Understanding Poetry* (1938), and *Understanding Fiction* (1943). If poetry (literature) is worth teaching at all, it is worth teaching as poetry (literature). The altogether changed tone and tenor in criticism can be noticed, for instance, in the works of John Crowe Ransom, Allen Tate, R.P. Blackmur, Kenneth Burke, Yvor Winters; and later, in Cleanth Brooks, Robert Penn Warren, and William Wimsatt. If one looks for the probable date, it could be settled around 1923. Eliot's influence with his *Sacred Wood* (1920), and the influence of Richards's *Principles of Literary Criticism* (1924) were also contributory factors. On the English side, besides Richards, Empson, and the Scrutiny critics, Leavis, L.C. Knights, and Derek Traversi can be cited as those who preferred and practised this criticism. We ought not to have the wrong idea that all these critics formed a guild, and subscribed to the same philosophic notions on criticism. Though they shared many attitudes, they were by no means unanimous in their beliefs. Eliot was a pioneer in New Criticism. But his insistence on the theological judgment of Anglo-Catholic Christianity was not shared by his followers. They followed a different path. Ransom, Tate, Brooks and Warren were the Southern critics. Burke and Blackmur stand apart, and so do their British counterparts Richards, Empson and Leavis. Winters stood all by himself in his critical writings. The pronouncements made by the critics were widely different from one another's. New Criticism does not represent a coterie. Ideally, these critics should be treated individually in any discussion of criticism. What brought them together was their opposition to the system of academic literary scholarship that existed during their time. Scholarship was pure and simple, limited to historical scholarship, and philological methods of study. In his paper, 'Criticism, Inc.' (1937), Ransom argued for criticism to be made a subject of study. 'What we need,' he said, 'is Criticism, Inc., or Criticism, Ltd.' New Criticism had to fight hard against a hostile atmosphere that prevailed in academic institutions. The New Critics questioned their basic assumptions, and exposed the weaknesses in applying biology, psychology, economics, or sociology to literary studies. Tate wanted criticism to judge literature, and not leave it to history to do it. Blackmur, and Winters too attacked what may be termed 'extrinsic' criticism. Scholarship can only supply facts at the service of interpretation.

New Criticism first started as a movement replacing the bio-critical and historical methods that dominated literary studies in the nineteenth and early twentieth centuries. Books in the *EML* series are good examples of this kind. In these approaches, instead of the text itself, the biographical–historical contexts of the text were examined whereas the text is the sole evidence for interpreting it. The life and times of the author, may be of interest to the historian, but not necessarily to the critic. The text ought not to be confused with its origins (the intentional fallacy), nor with the emotions it arouses (the affective fallacy). These two lead to impressionism and relativism, respectively: they do not possess, or provide objective standards for interpreting literature. The text itself provides all evidences which can be examined and corroborated through its formal elements such as the image, metaphor, plot, character, rhyme, and metre. The literary work is a timeless, autonomous, verbal object. It is the same for all time, and for all people. Its meaning is as objective as its physical presence. Its complex meaning cannot be explained just by paraphrasing it, or by translating it into some other language.

New Criticism takes a stand that the nature of literary language is different from the scientific, or everyday language. The latter is denotative depending on a one-to-one correspondence between words, and the objects they stand for. Scientific language does not call attention to itself, but points to the world outside. Literary language, on the other hand, organises linguistic resources into some special kind of arrangement, into a complex and unique unity in order to create an aesthetic experience. And the form of literary language is inseparable from its content, and its meaning. What a text means, and how it means it are one and the same. And the work has an ideal, organic unity in which all elements contribute to create an indivisible whole. This unity is that by which the New Critics value a literary work. The organic unity makes for the complexity of a work. The interpretation of a work, and its evaluation become one and the same for the New Critics. By explaining its unity, they are also establishing its value. The complexity of a work is often the result of multiple and conflicting meanings.

These meanings are produced by such devices as irony, paradox, ambiguity, tension, etc. If a work should achieve some order, all these devices should help resolve the conflicts, and tensions produced in the work. Thus, they should contribute to the harmony of the work which is an interpretation of human experience, and if a text is great, the theme comments upon human values. What is to be seen is whether the theme is established by the formal elements of the text which produce an organic unity. A scrupulous examination of these formal elements which contribute to the unity of the work, is close reading. There are also figurative elements which unify a work such as images, metaphors, symbols, myths, similes.

The New Critics maintain that their interpretations are based entirely on the context and the language of the text. Hence, their critical practice goes by the name 'intrinsic' criticism. This means that their criticism exists within the confines of the text. All other methods are called 'extrinsic,' because they go outside the text (its external causes) for the tools they require to interpret the text. The New Critics thought that a single and the best interpretation was possible, and could be discovered by finding out which is the one which best accounts for its organic unity. New Criticism insisted on focussing on the text. A close reading of the literary text drew a lot of critics together, differing widely in the methods of close reading. One critic may emphasise symbols, the other myths, and the third, metaphors. The concentration of the New Critics on the linguistic aspects of a poem has immensely benefited the study of poetry. They have contributed enormously to the widening of the audience for reading poetry. Basically New Criticism is founded on the premise that the text is an autotelic artefact. It is complete and wholesome in itself, and it exists for its own sake. Its relationship with the world beyond itself is not of much interest to the New Critic.

Cleanth Brooks in his essay, 'The Formalist Critic,' published in *The Kenyon Review*, 1951, subscribes to some of the articles of New Criticism:

- That literary criticism is a description and evaluation of its object.
- That the primary concern of criticism is with the problem of unity. . . the kind of whole, which the literary work forms or

fails to form, and the relation of the various parts to each other in building up this whole.

- That the formal relations in a work of literature may include, but certainly exceed, those of logic.
- That in a successful work, form and content cannot be separated. That form is meaning.
- That literature is ultimately metaphorical and symbolic.
- That the general and the universal are not seized upon by abstraction, but got at through the concrete and the particular.
- That literature is not surrogate religion and the purpose of literature is not to point a moral.

Two full accounts of New Critical manifesto appeared as 'The Intentional Fallacy,' and 'The Affective Fallacy,' authored jointly by Wimsatt and Beardsley. The twin essays constitute the most uncompromising theoretical statement of the manifesto that objective criticism is that in which attention is focused upon the meaning of the work itself without being distracted by enquiries into the origins of works in personal experiences. New Criticism is more pragmatic in its concerns, and it ought not to be construed merely as a doctrine.

Réné Wellek's essay 'The New Criticism: Pro and Contra' weighs the merits of New Criticism after the movement has grown out-of-date. Today when the movement stands rather outmoded, four charges are made against it. Wellek cites these charges. Its 'esoteric aestheticism' shows no concern with the social function of literature, and it is like the revival of the 'art for art's sake movement.' They (the New Critics) are often called 'formalists' to expose their lack of social concerns. It is unhistorical, because it isolates a work from its origins, and context. It aims to make criticism 'scientific.' It is just a pedagogical tool like the French *explication de texte*, useful only at the level of trying to learn to read literary texts, and poetry in particular (87).

The hostility to New Criticism is most powerfully, and memorably expressed by Geoffrey Hartman in his essay, 'Beyond Formalism' in these words:

> There is good reason why many in this country, as well as Europe, have voiced a suspicion of Anglo-Saxon formalism. The dominion of Exegesis is great: she is our Whore of Babylon, sitting robed in

> Academic black on the great dragon of Criticism and dispensing a repetitive and soporific balm from her pedantic cup. . . Yet our present explication-centred criticism is indeed puerile, or at most pedagogic: we forget its merely preparatory function, that it stands to a mature criticism as pastoral to epic (56–57).

The objections to New Criticism also came from other sources, before the final rejection came from the continental movements. The Chicago critics referred to the New Critics as 'the radical reformers of literary study,' inspired by the *res et verba* 'Hellenistic–Roman–Romantic–Rhetorical' tradition. They termed the movement as 'reactionary and obscurantist,' and repudiated it mainly for the following reasons:

- Its method of reasoning is deductive, dialectical and *aprioristic*. Its procrustean methodology forces everything into a predetermined scheme. It is, therefore, inappropriate to literary study.
- Its practical criticism is reductive, bringing the enquiry to an end before it is begun.
- It is unsound in its principles, and incompatible with enquiry, for it concerns itself with only the two elements which constitute a work—the subject, and the words in which it is expressed. The material cause of a literary work is just one of the several factors governing its being.

The myth critics also attacked the New Critics. Myth as a system of symbols, or metaphors is a central device in New Criticism. But the myth critics identified myth with literature: myth is the handmaiden of literature. They began to discuss myth as part of the content apart from the poem itself. They had no concern with judgment, or evaluation. Later, the Geneva School, the structuralists, and the Russian formalists attacked New Criticism. Many do not share the religious or political views of the New Critics. Its methodology is accused of being sterile, and often boring, routine and stereotyped. A quick inventive mind can interpret a work in any manner it likes. Réné Wellek, in his essay, 'The New Criticism: Pro and Contra' observes, 'The New Criticism has become a victim of the general attack on literature and art, of the "deconstruction" of literary texts, of the new anarchy that allows a complete liberty of interpretation, and even of a self-confessed "nihilism" ' (102).

It is true that New Criticism has somehow proved to be rather restricted in its area of operation to the English and provincial literature, not showing a broader preoccupation with the wealth of the literature of the world at large. By way of defending the New Critics, it should be said to their credit that they were not averse to historical knowledge (as so often they are charged), but they felt it should stand in subordination to the interpretation of the poem. It should serve as a means to another end. Many New Critics, such as Brooks and Winters, are sound historical scholars. In all their attempts at a revisionary literary history, they have based their faith on a historical scheme, and have used history as a basic standard for judgement and interpretation. The role that the New Critics assign to criticism is good for poetry, and good even for society. For them, poetry is not cut off from the world, but is always directed to it and bound by it. Witness, for instance, Warren's essay 'Pure and Impure Poetry.' Words in a poem do point to the world outside. They are called 'formalists'. This does not mean that they pay attention to the outward form only in the traditional sense. For them, form and content coexist inseparably. They stand for the organicity of the poem. They are concerned with the meaning of a literary work of art in all senses, including the world view that is conveyed. They are formalists because they see the poem not only as an act of communication but as an artefact endowed with a certain shaping principle of organisation.

New Critics are opposed to science, and this comes as a revelation to many who maintain that they make criticism a science. They do not have any sympathy for the 'mechanistic technological' views held by the Russian formalists. They have stressed the cognitive value of poetry; the knowledge it gives is greater than the knowledge one gets from science. It is an object of knowledge, *sui generis*. It has a special ontological status. This normal knowledge, required for understanding the world, can be acquired only by a union of feeling and intellect. Such a union is nowhere better achieved than in poetry. Therefore, criticism is not just a lifeless and neutral science. The close reading that they encouraged, and developed later got institutionalised as a pedagogical weapon. Close reading, and *explication de texte* are not one and the same. Close reading is not a sterile activity, but leads to judgment and discrimination between good and bad poems. The New Critics feel that unless a work of art is set off from all its antecedents, it cannot be fully approached as a coherent body of knowledge. The critic's job is to see the work 'as a totality, a configuration, a gestalt, a whole.'

There are many home truths New Criticism has taught us, and these cannot be ignored by the succeeding generation of critics. A work of art is a structure with its norms; it has coherence and unity, and it is not dependent upon its origins or effects. It does not yield abstract knowledge. It has taught us how to discriminate between good and vulgar art. To quote yet again from the same essay of Wellek:

> The humanities would abdicate their function in society if they surrendered to a neutral scientism and indifferent relativism or if they succumbed to the imposition of alien norms required by political indoctrination. Particularly on these two fronts the New Critics have waged a valiant fight, which, I am afraid, must be fought over and over again, in the future (103).

New Criticism became prominent within American universities when liberal humanism and radical criticism, which were fashionable in the 1930s, declined. By the early 1940s this movement established itself in the universities, and younger scholars were in favour of this school in the post-war years. Close textual analysis came to replace arid historical scholarship, and theories about the language of poetry helped in strengthening the claims of the New Critics. Learned literary journals, *The Southern Review, The Kenyon Review,* and *The Sewanee Review,* and later even the conservative journals accepted, and espoused their mode of critical writings. What about the name New Criticism given to it during its origin? Is it appropriate now in the present context? The equivalent terms such as aesthetic formalism, and analytical criticism have also been suggested because these describe the actual practice of the school. For Mark Schorer, in his 'Technique of Discovery,' form is the 'achieved content' of the work. But there are other common grounds. As noted earlier, it is mostly associated with John Crowe Ransom, and his followers who have subscribed to similar notions on literary, social and political ideas.

All said and done, the New Critics have done much to advance literary criticism, and the understanding of literary form. Walter Sutton succinctly sums up the contribution of New Criticism in the following words:

> Their sophistication, intelligence, and informed sensibilities are apparent in many excellent and stimulating essays. When achievements are set against limitations, one is impressed by the thought of what the New Criticism might have accomplished with a less hermetic theory. The task of the present is to develop a criticism of form resting upon a theory that fully acknowledges and explores, as the New Critics have not, the social and historical dimensions of literature (151).

The position that New Criticism occupies now in the area of literary studies is rather strange. For one thing it is not strictly speaking contemporary but the habit of reading it promoted during the '40s through '60s is prevalent even now. Some important concepts it taught us are now absorbed in all theories today. Concrete evidences from the text are shown to validate the interpretations. The 'close reading' of texts that New Criticism taught us is now practised as a regular pedagogical method in teaching and learning. In this sense, New Criticism is never to be invalidated. On all other grounds, New Criticism seems dated, and outdated. Structuralism opposes its focus on individual works in isolation. Deconstruction's view of language rejects New Criticism's assumptions. New historicism's view of objectivity is different from that of New Criticism.

That which was its strength when it first came on the scene, later proved its downfall? It dominated critical discourse for well over four decades. In the late 1960s, its hegemony and influence waned, when there was a growing interest in the ideological content of literary texts. New theories are emerging today, extending the narrow limits of New Criticism through revision, and expansion of its formal concepts, such as connecting the author formally with his works, rather than historically or biographically. The works of E.D. Hirsch, and the more recent works of structuralists, and phenomenologists are a positive contribution in this direction. There can be no pure 'innocent' reader, for there is a whole array of presuppositions, beliefs, etc., which come in the way intruding upon the reader in his response to a work. In this sense, there can be no sanctified and objective texts storing a wealth of content in them. What matters is the process by which the content is formulated and realised in limitless ways. New Criticism is a realisation of the assumptions drawn from Aristotle, Kant, and Coleridge, recreated and fused together, culminating in the modernist literary tradition. With the influence exerted by the continental thinkers, the dinosaur of New Criticism got killed. One might add that it died of exhaustion, or, better still, died of its own success, whichever way one prefers to look at it. In conclusion, we might very well recall a few notions which are central to the philosophy of the movement.

- The notion of deviationism which holds the view that the language of a poem is the aesthetic medium (like painting) that is manipulated into a form. The language of poetry is different from the usual language used in everyday communication.
- The notion of totalisation that holds the view that the poem is an organism like the body. It is an organised whole in which every part is related to every other part, and these stand in harmony with one another.
- The principle of closure which is a notion related to the previous one that a poem is a system of language which is a self-justified and autonomous entity.
- The poem is a special object which is ontologically present (principle of presence).
- The work is a sacred object (verbal icon). The critic is the adorer and the work is the idol.

The New Critics underemphasised the reader and the poet by overemphasising the object (the poem). The underemphasis or the banishment of the poet has led to the countermovement hermeneutics, and the banishment of the reader has led to the reader-response theories and reception aesthetics. Structuralists and poststructuralists emphasise the flow of textuality. There is no way of separating the text from the intertextual swing. There is no special form of language for poetry. Language is one monolith, and we just have to face it. Rejecting positivistic literary scholarship, the New Criticism with its empiricism, exercised its influence on the institution of English studies for four decades—and still plays a significant role—and later with the entry of European literary theory its prestige has been on the wane. New Criticism stands eclipsed—almost. However, one cannot hide the truth that only after the arrival of the New Critics, such other related disciplines as women's studies, Black studies, and comparative literature began to establish themselves.

In this sense, at least, New Criticism paved the way for widening the scope of the discipline of English studies in various directions. This, then, is the legacy of the movement.

Works Cited

Hartman, Geoffrey. 'Beyond Formalism.' *Beyond Formalism: Literary Essays 1958–1970.* New Haven: Yale University Press, 1970.

Ransom, John Crowe. 'Wanted an Ontological Critic.' *The New Criticism.* Norfolk, Conn.: New Directions, 1941. *Selected Essays of John Crowe Ransom.* Ed. Thomas Daniel Young. Baton Rouge: Louisiana State University Press, 1984.

Sutton, Walter. *Modern American Criticism.* Englewood Cliffs, New Jersey: Prentice Hall, Inc., 1963.

Wellek, Rene. 'The New Criticism: Pro and Contra.' *The Attack on Literature and other Essays.* Chapel Hill: The North Carolina University Press, 1982.

Select Bibliography

Brooks, Cleanth. *Understanding Poetry.* New York: H. Holt, 1938.

———. *Modern Poetry and the Tradition.* Chapel Hill: University of North Carolina Press, 1939.

———. *The Well Wrought Urn.* New York. Harcourt, Brace & World, 1947.

———. 'The Formalist Critic.' *The Kenyon Review.* 1951.

Empson, William. *Seven Types of Ambiguity.* 1930. Harmondsworth, Middlesex: Chatto and Windus, 1961.

———. *Some Versions of Pastoral.* 1935. New York: New Directions, 1968.

———. *Structure of Complex Words.* London: Chatto and Windus, 1951.

———. *Milton's God.* 1961. London: Chatto and Windus, 1965.

———. *Using Biography.* Cambridge, Mass: Harvard University Press, 1984.

Foster, Richard. *The New Romantics: A Reappraisal of the New Criticism.* Bloomington: Indiana University Press, 1962.

Krieger, Murray. *The New Apologists for Poetry.* Minneapolis: University of Minnesota Press, 1956.

Lentricchia, Frank. *After New Criticism.* Chicago: University of Chicago Press, 1980.

Ransom, John Crowe. *The New Criticism.* Norfolk, Conn.: New Directions, 1941.

———. *The World's Body.* 1938. Baton Rouge: Louisiana State University Press, 1968.

Richards, I.A. *Principles of Literary Criticism.* 1924. New York: Harcourt Brace and Jovanovich, 1961.

———. *Practical Criticism.* London: K. Paul, Trench and Trubner, 1929.

Schorer, Mark. 'Technique as Discovery.' *Hudson Review* (1948). *Twentieth Century Literary Criticism: A Reader.* Ed. David Lodge. London: Longman, 1972.

Sutton, Walter. *Modern American Criticism.* Englewood Cliffs, N.J.: Prentice Hall, Inc., 1963.

Tate, Allen. *Collected Essays.* Denver, Colorado: A. Swallow, 1959.

Wellek, Réné. *A History of Modern Criticism.* Vol. 6. New Haven: Harvard University Press, 1986.

Wimsatt, W.K. *The Verbal Icon: Studies in the Meaning of Poetry.* Lexington, Ky.: University of Kentucky Press, 1954.

———. *Hateful Contraries: Studies in Literature and Criticism.* Lexington, Ky.: University of Kentucky Press, 1965.

RUSSIAN FORMALISM

Writings from Russia had long been concealed behind the Iron Curtain. We are not as much acquainted with these writings as we are with the literature from Western Europe. The best achievements of the Russians lie in the novel, and the short story. Some of these are world's classics. As for criticism, the second and the third decades of the twentieth century noticed a lively debate in Russia on matters relating to poetic art and its understanding. Criticism of the previous century was largely didactic, or moralistic in tone and tenor, as in Tolstoy, for example. Many other schools proclaiming symbolism or aestheticism were also prevalent in lesser degrees of importance, but the major breakthrough came about in the form of Russian formalism (also referred to as East European formalism, to distinguish it from Anglo-American formalism which is just another name for New Criticism), the repercussions of which are felt on many theories that have followed it. The movement itself became institutionalised by the year 1919, the *annus mirabilis* of modernism, with the establishment of *Opojaz* (Petersburg Society for the Study of Poetic Language).

The theory of formalism was the result of the discussions that emerged from two groups—the *Opojaz group,* and the Moscow Linguistic Circle. The movement falls into three periods: 1916–21, when the focus was on poetic language, and prose composition; 1921–8, when there was a serious attempt to re-examine many literary problems; and 1928–35, when the movement disbanded, and disintegrated owing to several factors, political/historical being one of them. On account of the suppression of this movement by the Soviet Republic, and the rise of Stalinism, its centre of operation moved to Czechoslovakia, with the result that the pioneers of this movement Roman Jakobson, Victor Shklovsky, and Baris Elchenbaum, devoted their attention to other fields of literary study, such as text exegesis. The movement had no immediate impact outside the Soviet Union. Despite the historical events that put an end to intellectual developments in Russia, the movement had its impact on other movements such as structuralism, for instance. Russian formalism got absorbed in these systems of thought, and lost its identity as a separate literary movement. Now, it remains just a matter of historical importance.

In the context of literary studies, Russian formalism was a major reaction against the biographical determinism, and the positivism of the nineteenth century. The Russian formalists started attacking the historical, sociological, and other extrinsic approaches to literary study. They vehemently opposed the symbolists for whom language was only a medium. The mysticism of the symbolists, and the separation of poetic form from the language was anathema to them. They also stood firm in their opposition to the impressionistic, and subjectivistic practices in literary studies. In a sense, the symbolist, and the futurist movements paved the way for Russian formalism.

The term 'formalism' generally denotes the kind of criticism that lays stress on the form of a work, rather than on the content. Anglo-American New Criticism also goes by the name 'formalism' in academic circles. Coleridge employed the term 'organic formalism' to refer to the poetic object, because all elements in it are organically related to one another, as in a plant, or the human body. A work is an artefact governed by its own laws of existence, without reference to the author or the external world. Both Russian formalism and New Criticism had their roots deeply planted on the idealism of Immanuel Kant, as illustrated in his *Critique of Judgment* (1790). Whereas New Criticism directs its effort to exploring the relationship between art and life, Russian formalists would keep them apart, treating them as mutually exclusive. Russian formalism is the earliest attempt to justify the existence of literary study, and place it on a firm scientific footing. It was an attempt to create an independent science of literature which studies literary material specifically. In the words of Roman Jakobson, 'the object of study in literary science is not literature but "literariness", that is, what makes a given work a literary work.' What constitutes literature is its difference from other orders of facts. In Jakobson's words, 'Poeticity is present when the word is felt as a word and not a mere representation of the object being named or an outburst of emotion, when words and their composition, their meaning, their external and inner form, acquire a weight and value of their own instead of referring indifferently to reality.' The term 'form' is used in a very broad sense.

Russian formalists use the term 'deformation' in a positive sense. It suggests the changes imposed on the material of the poem, and the resultant effects. These include all the poetic devices and artistic instruments, which help in the creation of the aesthetic effects. They do not negate the social function of art. For them, the function of art is to 'make us see things, not to know them. Art is there to awaken us from the usual torpor.' The term used is *defamiliarisation,* or making strange. Art refreshes our life and our experience of life. As Ransom would have it, art offers us the 'world's body.' Art defamiliarises things which have become habitual. Defamiliarisation is the opposite of automatisation. The usual example given for this is that walking is a habitual activity, and it goes generally unnoticed by us. Dancing too uses the movements of the limbs, but dance is seen and enjoyed. It forces its attention upon us. 'A dance is a walk which is felt . . . It is a walk constructed to be felt.' Similarly, the everyday language we use in our daily commerce is rendered strange in poetry on account of the formal devices, such as rhyme and rhythm acting upon it. Gogol's 'Overcoat,' or Sterne's *Tristram Shandy* lay bare the form and emphasise the technique of discovery.

In literature, the author is no more than a craftsman. A work of literature is related to all literature in general, and not at all to its author, or his personality. If Columbus had not discovered America, someone else would have discovered it. It would have been discovered without Columbus. There is only poetry, and there are no poets. 'The object of literary science is an authorless literariness.' For the Russian formalists, Shakespeare would be an anonymous literary figure. Literariness, as we have seen, consists in defamiliarisation, the opposite of automatism. It is literariness that distinguishes literature from non-literature. And literariness could be studied by focussing on the artistic devices used in the work. Victor Shklovsky defined a work as the 'sum-total of all stylistic devices employed in it.' It was held to be a structured system, an ordered hierarchical set of artistic devices. The important essay for them, 'Art as Technique' was written in 1917 by Victor Shklovsky, in which he states:

> And art exists that one may recover the sensation of life; it exists to make one feel things, to make the stone *stony*. The purpose of art is to impart the sensation of things as they are perceived and not as they are known. The technique of art is to make objects 'unfamiliar', to make form difficult, to increase the difficulty and length of perception because the process of perception is an aesthetic end in itself and must be prolonged. *Art is a way of experiencing the artfulness of an object; the object is not important* (754).

Russian formalists developed the concepts of *fabula* and *syuzhet.* The former (*fabula*) refers to the chronological sequence of events, the story, while the latter (*syuzhet*) refers to the order of presentation in the narration, the plot. E.M. Forster in his *Aspects of the Novel* made the distinction in simple terms. A plot is a narrative of events, the emphasis falling on causality. 'The king died and then the queen died' is a story. 'The king died and then the queen died of grief' is a plot. *Fabula* is 'the action itself' while *syuzhet* is 'how the reader learns of the action.' *Syuzhet* creates a defamiliarising effect upon *fabula*. These concepts are put to effective use in narratology and fictional poetics. The writer of prose fiction uses his raw material, rearranges it and gives it a shape in such a manner as to create a literary object out of it. The process involves, not a direct, chronological, and literal representation of the material, but selection, concealment, focalisation, distancing, and taking up different points of view, all of which go to create the object. Wayne C. Booth, Tzvetan Todorov, among others, have made extensive contribution to the analysis, and understanding of prose fiction based on these concepts. Since the main interest of the Russian formalists was on poetic language, and its difference from everyday language, it is no wonder that their area of specialisation was rhythm, rhyme, metre, and those elements which contribute to deviations in language—the hallmark of poetic language.

Russian formalists had no use for the usual literary history. Roman Jakobson once said, 'The old literary historians remind us of policemen who, in order to arrest a certain individual, arrest everybody and carry off everything from his lodgings, and arrest also anyone who passed by on the street. The historians of literature use everything—the social setting, psychology, politics, and philosophy. Instead of literary scholarship, they give us a conglomeration of home-grown disciplines.' They always maintained that great art evolves from the lowly, and hence, hierarchies in art get shifted back and forth. The process of 'rebarbarisation' goes on, relentlessly. This must be conceded to them that they placed literature at the centre, relegating all related matters to the margin. They condemned the insistence on the image as the basis for interpretation. They placed importance on the role of the metaphor, and other linguistic devices. It is in this sense that Russian formalism can be seen as a forerunner to structuralism; only the latter has widened the scope of study to include the social structure rather than the work of literature alone.

The two concepts which are quite fundamental for them are *defamiliarisation* and *retardation.* The object of art is not the presentation of life and nature by means of realistic images but through distortion-using devices. Innovation seems to be the end of all art. Defamiliarisation makes the mode of expression different from other modes: there is a renewed perception of life, and literary history proves it by throwing up several discontinuities. In retardation, the process of perception is prolonged. Literary criticism took on the shape of a scientific method in its insistence on the internal organisation of a literary work, and the functional relationships between individual parts of a work.

There are many weaknesses in the formalists' theory of art, however. As Réné Wellek points out (and rightly so), they have chosen a technical, scientific approach to art that would dehumanise art, and destroy criticism. To insist on novelty as a criterion of value would be wrong in the long run. Art is not accepted as creation, but a discovery of pre-existing forms. The individual artist is ignored in preference to a collective nameless history. They too are deterministic and historical relativists. Poetry is often reduced to a game, or puzzle.

Julia Kristeva condemns the 'mechanical idealism' of the formalists. In her essay, 'The Ruins of a Poetics,' she says that the literary text is reduced to mere linguistic categories and theories 'with no grasp of the individual character of the literary object in the history of modes of meaning, nor of the fact that this treatment disorganizes the 'poetic' discourse, since it is an inventory and a self-trial rather than objective knowledge.' Russian formalists went to the other extreme, when they took exception to what they called the genetic fallacy of other schools of criticism. The formalists neglected the individual artist with the result that in their evaluation they were exposed by their extreme aesthetic relativism. Their criterion of evaluation was often personal judgment. The Russian formalists have turned a blind eye to non-literary elements in a work. This is conveniently neglected in their theory which leans much too heavily on the language segment of literature. And their view of language is pre-Saussurean. Marxists called their ideology, reactionary, and attacked them for ignoring the social dimension, and utilitarian function of art. Leon Trotsky led the attack dubbing the theory of

Russian formalism superficial, childish, narrow, and defective. It had separated the 'superstructure' from the 'base.' Russian formalism is an easy target for the Bakhtin school which holds the view that all use of language is sociological and ideological. The major drawback of Russian formalism is that it did not extend its theory to spheres other than language. And for this good reason, politically oriented theories of recent years have discarded it. Their view about language is also invalidated by reader-response critics, and new historicists.

Works Cited

Shklovsky, Victor. 'Art as Technique.' *Literary Criticism since Plato.* Ed. Hazard Adams. 1971. New York: Harcourt Brace Jovanovich College Publishers, 1992.

Select Bibliography

Erlich, Victor. *Russian Formalism: History, Doctrine.* 1955. New Haven: Yale University Press, 1981.

Lee, Lemon T. and Marion J. Reese, eds. *Russian Formalist Criticism: Four Essays.* Lincoln: University of Nebraska Press, 1965.

Ladislav, Matejka and Krystyna Pomorska, eds. *Readings in Russian Poetics: Formalist and Structuralist Views.* 1971. Normal, IL: Dalkey Archive Press, 2002.

Medvedev, P.N. and M.M. Bakhtin. *The Formal Method in Literary Scholarship.* Baltimore: Johns Hopkins University Press, 1978.

Thompson, E.M. *Russian Formalism and Anglo-American New Criticism.* The Hague: Mouton, 1971.

ARCHETYPAL CRITICISM

Archetypal criticism marks the transition from New Criticism to structuralism. In an earlier chapter, we saw how New Criticism encouraged focusing one's whole attention on the words on a page. This concentration on the language, and multiple meanings resulting from irony, ambiguity, paradox, etc., surely yielded rich benefits in the matter of meaningful interpretations. But it also suggested to readers that the meaning of a work could go beyond what only the words could convey. Archetypal criticism can be rightly understood in the context of the study of the myth made by cultural anthropologists. The most influential book in this respect is *The Golden Bough,* in twelve volumes, by the Cambridge anthropologist James Frazer. This book of reference made a complete and comprehensive survey of the myths, rituals, and religious practices of the different societies of the world, especially the primitive ones. It is a remarkable encyclopaedia of the mythologies of the world. The Swiss psychologist Carl Jung (1875–1961), often referred to as Freud's renegade disciple, used the term 'archetype' to refer to the experiences of our ancestors which get lodged in what he called 'the collective unconscious' of the whole race. By 'collective unconscious' is meant, 'the psychic disposition shaped by the forces of heredity.' The contents of the 'collective unconscious' are the archetypes. These buried experiences seek expression in myths as well as in literature. Vico, the seventeenth century Italian philosopher, and recently, the German philosopher Ernst Cassirer (1874–1945) have done remarkably perceptive work on the nature and function of myths and rituals. Myth can be understood 1. as a story or a complex of story elements, expressing the deeper aspects of the human experience, and 2. as a perspective, i.e., an activity of the mind that synthesises received knowledge. In this sense, it is a mode of envisaging experience. Myths are the reflections of a profound reality. They are said to be the greatest falsehoods which tell us the greatest truths. Among the most noteworthy practitioners of archetypal criticism are Leslie Fiedler, Francis Fergusson, Richard Chase, Philip Wheelwright, Wilson Knight and Maud Bodkin whose *Archetypal Patterns in Poetry* (1934), was a trailblazer in every sense. Wheelwright used the term 'plurisignation' to describe how literature acquires multiple meanings, and resonance from the unconscious association with myths and religious essences. These critics dig up the mythical pattern in literary works, and subject them to close analysis.

However, the one critic who is synonymous with archetypal criticism, and who might verily be considered its founding father, and foremost practitioner is the Canadian mythologist, and scholar-critic, Northrop Frye (1912–91). Three of his works, *Fearful Symmetry* (1947), *Anatomy of Criticism* (1957), and *Fables of Identity* (1963), stimulated a deeper interest in the study of myths. His *Anatomy of Criticism*, the critical *tour de force,* is a touchstone in archetypal criticism, and perhaps the first attempt at erecting a grandiose theory of literary cartography. At the time of the publication of the work, his was the sole voice inveighing against the uncompromising attitude of New Criticism. He was a strident believer in treating a work of literature as part of a larger system, and not as a purely isolated phenomenon. 'Literature imitates the total dream of man.' For him, the whole body of literary works of any society constitutes what might be called a self-contained, autonomous universe. The natural world and the human world are brought together by the human imagination. Poetic thought is categorical, mystical, and so powerful in its impact on the human mind that in our innermost being the natural world is assimilated to the human world. The term 'archetype' stands for a recurring pattern of experience which can be identified in works of literature, and human sciences. These can be identified in the form of recurring actions, characters, images, metaphors, analogues, figurative language, etc. These archetypes are the reflections of primitive, universal thoughts which are essentially poetic. They are the primordial images which reside deep in our psyche, and which seek an outlet in works of art. Have we not known that in the earliest stages of any culture, language was ritualistic and prelogical? When the archetypes are embodied in literary works, they awaken in us our profound feelings which are socially sharable. Frye gives an example from an Egyptian tale of 'The Two Brothers' in his book *The Anatomy of Criticism.*

> An elder brother's wife attempts to seduce an unmarried younger brother who lives with them, and, when he resists her, accuses him of attempting to rape her. The younger brother is then forced to run away, with the enraged elder brother in pursuit. So far, the incidents reproduce more or less credible facts of life. Then the younger brother prays to Ra for assistance, pleading the justice of his cause; Ra places a large lake between him and his brother and, in a burst of divine exuberance, fills it full of crocodiles. This incident is no more a fictional episode than anything that has preceded it, nor is it less logically related than any other to the plot

> as a whole. But it has given up the external analogy to 'life': this, we say, is the kind of thing that happens only in stories. The Egyptian tale has acquired, then, in its mythical episode, an abstractly literary quality (135).

The incorporation of this simple myth of goddess Ra transforms an otherwise sensational realistic short story (good enough for a tabloid newspaper) to a work of literature. The acted part of the myth is the ritual, and the spoken part of the ritual is the myth. The myth is the central informing power that gives significance to the ritual. The central myth of literature is the quest myth.

In his much-anthologised essay, 'The Archetypes of Literature', Frye expresses his dissatisfaction with New Criticism. What is missing from it is a coordinating principle that will place works of art as parts of a larger whole, a larger system. And so, he would rather approach them from two opposite ends, the inductive (centripetal) and the deductive (centrifugal). In great works, especially, one can discover growing, emerging patterns of significance, spreading out from the centre, like the ripples in a pond when a stone is cast upon it. He illustrates this from Yorick's soliloquy in the gravedigger scene in *Hamlet*. The text opens out from the literal meaning of words, to images of decay and corruption, to psychological relationships among characters, to archetypal patterns, and so on. Critics interpret the play based on what their assumptions happen to be. From the other end, the deductive one, one can discover in works of literature analogies of the recurrent rhythms of the natural cycle (of births, deaths, seasons, etc.). Literature enacts these. Frye classifies the literary universe into four categories—he calls them *mythoi*—corresponding to the four natural seasons: comedy corresponds to spring, romance to summer, tragedy to autumn and satire to winter. For him, educated imagination is that which is nurtured by classical mythology. Using this as his base, he develops his brand of cultural criticism. He can thus reach out to wider worlds of ethical, and social criticism enshrining deep human values. His view of life, and his view of literature are one and the same; only life, structured as concrete universals, is refracted and made available to us in a heightened form through the medium of literature. And so, only through literature can we be interested in larger questions pertaining to life. Hence Frye says, ' Art deals not with the real but with the conceivable, and literary criticism, though it will eventually have to have some theory of conceivability, can never be justified in trying to develop, much less assume, any theory of actuality' ('The Archetypes of Literature', 431).

Frye chooses two Platonic levels of knowledge from *The Republic*—'nous' and 'dianoia' for his discussion of the basic kinds (and degrees) of criticism. At the primary, literal level, criticism is concerned with the knowledge about things. This is seen in the gathering of what constitutes the sense of fact in Eliot's sense (the sense of the past, for Lionel Trilling): in the acquiring of all related facts, ideas and thoughts, which constitute the foundation for building up the context for literary study. But, this knowledge about literature has to seek a transformation as knowledge of literature, which we generally associate with wisdom. In this ideal situation, the reader and the work become one and the same. In the words of Frye, 'Criticism in order to point beyond itself needs to be actively iconoclastic about itself.' The higher level of teaching–learning nexus Frye suggests is quite close to the concept of the *sahrudaya* in our Indian aesthetic theory. As different from Western empiricist metaphysics, Indian theory of art has a strong faith in mystical, intuitive, inspirational response to and understanding of a literary work. Art is born out of a detached contemplation of life, and its delight is realised on the part of the student, the *rasika* in his disinterested pursuit. Our aestheticians use the metaphor of the body and the soul in any discussion of a composition, the *kavya.* In the case of the *sahrudaya,* there is a total identity achieved with the soul of the work, referred to as *rasanubhava,* a sensitive but non-involved state of aesthetic contemplation. Only for Frye, literature is not only an object to be contemplated, but also a power to be absorbed.

There is a whole tradition of value judgments in the arts right from Aristotle. Quite a large number of thinkers hold the view that any valid criticism should prepare us for, and lead us to, an evaluation of the work. Johnson, for example, was judicial in his proclamation, which he delivered with a New Testament conviction. Of Milton's 'Lycidas' he says, 'Passion plucks no berries from the myrtle and the ivy. . . Where there is leisure for fiction, there is little grief.' Arnold, Eliot, Leavis, all belong to the tradition of arriving at value judgments, sometimes on the basis of their avowed assumptions about literature in general, or the work discussed in particular, or a commonsense apprehension, even intuitive, as in the instance above. There is the other point of view of which Frye is the spokesman that literary exegesis need not (and does not) lead to judgment. For him, 'the sense of value is an individual, unpredictable variable, incommunicable, indemonstrable, and mainly intuitive reaction to knowledge.' Evaluation has its right place in book and theatre reviewing; in fact it may be even necessary for various reasons. Frye's view of literature is that it is a 'reservoir of potential values.' Our value sense is not part of our critical discussion, and for this very reason value judgments have no place in literary scholarship.

Frye uses the term 'structure' in several related senses. Indeed, it was he who had anticipated structuralism in literary criticism. He was a structuralist without being aware of it. Theme is referred to as the structural principle in a poem. Sometimes, he calls the images the structural units; at other times, he holds myths as the conventional structures in literature. These are, for him, the units which form the organising principle of literary work. Structuralist poetics treats literature as a system of conventions in which signs are embedded. These signs take on a meaning, not on account of an inherent property in the form of any ontological meaning in them, but by virtue of a signification within a larger system. By 'structuring' is meant relating one signifying element with another with a view to discovering relationships among them. Frye's view is that any literary work—secular scripture for him—exists as a 'displacement' from the larger mythos. The critic's job is to realign it with the larger framework and situate it there, for, literature, as we have argued before, is reconstructed mythology. The concept of *vraisemblablisation* of the structuralists has close affinities with Frye's theory. A text has to be recuperated, naturalised and placed in a larger framework so as to make it both legible and intelligible. Frye's view of literature 'as a total order of words,' and that works of literature are created out of literature anticipates again the structuralist view of intertextuality. Only in the case of Frye, coherence is to be achieved by conformity, whereas for the structuralists it is through a play of difference. Frye restricts the associations with other texts to mythological images and to the metaphysical agents by which analogies and identities are established.

Frye's focus in his literary discussions has been solely on western literature, and its classification. He was a deeply devoted Biblical scholar. His evangelical background, and theological training give him a good grounding in Christian eschatology: hence, his cartography based on Judeo-Christian myths. His exemplary insights are, without any doubt, often invigorating. His critics charge him with arbitrariness in his taxonomy and categorisation of literary works. He subordinates works to an overarching mythological framework drawn from religion. In this process, the uniqueness and the artistic integrity of individual works get ironed out to desert uniformity. All works, great and small, are subjected to the same treatment. There is no generic distinction. His interpretations raise questions and doubts regarding poetry and belief. In the hands of a less sensitive critic, Frye's approach has the danger of degenerating into crude, and unverifiable myth hunting. The heydays of archetypal criticism were the years between 1950 and 1970. Its impact can be still seen in the interpretation of children's literature, science fiction, and feminist criticism. Historically, archetypal criticism prepared the ground for the arrival of structuralism in the US and later in England. Leavis's resistance to theory could not be sustained for long.

Frye lived in a comparatively quieter intellectual climate. His Protestant spirituality would not allow him to share the philosophic nihilism of his European counterparts. As a born teacher, he clarified difficult texts, and interpreted Western culture to his students. And that prompted his distinguished student, Margaret Atwood, to pay him the following tribute: 'He did not lock literature into an ivory tower; instead he emphasized its centrality to the development of a civilized humane society.'

Works Cited

Frye, Northrop. *The Anatomy of Criticism: Four Essays*. Princeton: Princeton University Press, 1957.

——. 'The Archetypes of Literature.' *Twentieth Century Literary Criticism*. Ed. David Lodge. London: Longman, 1972.

Select Bibliography

Barber, C.L. *Shakespeare's Festive Comedy.* Princeton: Princeton University Press, 1959.

Casirer, Ernst. *Language and Myth.* Trans. Susanne Langer. New York: Harper & Bros., 1946.

Chase, Richard. *The Quest for Myth.* Baton Rouge: Louisiana University Press, 1946.

Fergusson, Francis. *The Idea of a Theatre.* Princeton: Princeton University Press, 1949.

Frazer, Sir James. G. *The Golden Bough.* 12 vols. London: Macmillan Press, 1907–15.

Frye, Northrop. *The Anatomy of Criticism: Four Essays.* Princeton: Princeton University Press, 1957.

Graves, Robert. *The White Goddess.* New York: Farrar, Strauss & Cadahy, 1948.

Jones, Ernst. *Essays in Applied Psycho-Analysis.* London: Hogarth Press, 1951.

Jung, C.G. *The Archetypes and the Collective Unconscious.* Trans. R.F.C. Hall. New York: Harcourt, 1930.

Wheelwright, Philip. *The Burning Fountain: A Study in the Language of Symbolism.* Bloomington: Indiana University Press, 1954.

6

Contemporary Theories

n the last two decades, in the realm of literary and cultural studies in all parts of the world, critical theory (or theories?) has assumed considerable importance. Theory has grown into an independent discipline. But if we look back one hundred years, literary scholarship was equated with philology (in the old sense of the term), still preserved in the name of the journal, *Modern Philology*. This philological tradition in literary scholarship should have been inherited from the Germanic tradition in the nineteenth century. It was given to Eliot and Richards at the turn of the twentieth century, to veer its course away towards criticism. The era of criticism, in turn, gave room to the era of theory in the latter part of second half of the twentieth century. Theory is of continental origin. Its philosophy (very different from the pragmatism, and logical positivism of England) is rooted in existentialism. Hence, it makes a clean break from liberal humanism. The term 'theory' should remind us that its primary concern is not with the interpretation of specific works, but with human discourse in general. There is a view that theory has changed the very nature of English studies in the world. Whether one likes it or not, it has become an indispensable discipline in higher education. Many teachers and students feel helpless, because it is so jargon-ridden these days. The anthologies available in the market contain the difficult and tangled writings of these theorists: students who are not initiated into these systems, find themselves floundering. Why is it necessary for us to learn these theories? Do they, in any way, help us in understanding literature better? Do they not stand in the way of our personal response to literature? Why should anyone bother about them? These are some relevant questions which merit consideration.

There is so much of discussion of non-literary matters, so much of discussion about problems whose relation to literature is almost non-existent, that we tend to raise the question whether it is necessary at all to get to know these theories. There is too much of reading of philosophical, political, and psychoanalytic meanings into literature. In literary studies, theory does not mean an account of the nature and function of literature, or methods of study alone. Réné Wellek's useful book, often prescribed for research scholars, *Theory of Literature,* might lead us to think along these lines, though such matters are part of what constitutes theory. It is a body of thinking and writing which is pretty hard to define. Writing from outside the field of literary studies, by thinkers like Derrida, Foucault, Lacan, and Althusser have been taken up by people from literary studies because their analyses of language, mind, history, etc., offer new and persuasive insights into textual criticism, and cultural matters. The genre theory comprises works of anthropology, art history, film studies, science, and social studies and what not! These works are helpful, besides being serviceable, for a study of literature.

In recent times, sadly though, knowledge of these critical theories has become a status symbol. On the positive side, such knowledge can help us in many ways to comprehend the world better, and think more logically. Each theoretical system tries to compete, and gain dominance over the other. These theories offer different interpretations of history and the current events of this world, and every theory is grounded on certain key concepts. There is no unmediated, personal, and natural response to literature. When we respond to some work, we have internalised some assumptions about what a piece of literature is, and what it should mean based on our assumptions. All interpretations are based on beliefs about the world, language, etc. Theories make explicit what these assumptions are and how our understanding of literary works is based on these assumptions. Theory involves a questioning of some of the basic hypothetical assumptions we make in our study of literature. What is an author? What is meant by 'meaning' of a text? What happens when we read? How should we read a text and why? What is the difference between a 'work' and a 'text'? The 1980s were the high watermark of theory. It started off as a rejection of and reaction to the traditional modes of understanding literature, or what we call 'liberal humanism' which prevailed during 1930–50. The basic premises of theory can be summed up as follows:

- There can be no disinterested enquiry in the artistic phenomenon. Our mind is not an empty slate. An ideological commitment preconditions our mind, and our thinking is controlled by it.
- There are no fixed unalterable 'essences.' What we consider as basic 'essences' (such as selfhood) is constructed socially. There is no such thing as a 'fixed' and absolute truth.
- It is language that shapes reality and not the other way round. Language does not record reality but creates it.
- There is no definitive reading of a text. Language generates a web of meanings with infinite possibilities. All texts are self-contradictory. Literary texts are independent structures made of language.

Peter Barry in *Beginning Theory* (1995) sums up the recurrent ideas in theory succinctly as follows: 1. politics is pervasive, 2. language is constitutive, 3. truth is provisional, 4. meaning is contingent, 5. human nature is a myth. With these newer notions available to us, it is but proper that we move towards a newer critical practice in our study of literature. Hillis Miller makes a robust plea for literary theory:

> The future of literary theory is immense (to paraphrase Matthew Arnold) because it is the fundamental tool of both the tasks of humanistic study in the coming years as I have defined them: the work of archival remembering and the work of the teaching of critical reading as the primary means of combating the disastrous confusion of linguistic with material reality, one name for which is 'ideology' (111).

Work Cited

Miller, Hillis. 'The Function of Theory at the Present Time.' *The Future Literary Theory.* Ed. Ralph Cohen. London: Routledge, 1989.

STRUCTURALIST CRITICISM

Developed in the twentieth century, structuralism is basically a movement of thought in the human sciences. It has affected many disciplines such as philosophy, anthropology, and literary criticism. The word 'structure' (of Latin origin, meaning mode of construction) does not necessarily mean structuralist activity. When we read and interpret a poem, we are not engaged in structuralist activity. However, we are engaged in structuralist activity, if we examine a large number of poems, or lyrics to discover the basic principles that govern their composition, say, in terms of the use of images, metaphors, etc. We are also engaged in structuralist activity if we take a single poem, and discover in its composition an example of the basic principles in a stuctural system of poems. Structuralism is a human science that tries to understand the basic structures that underlie all human experience and behaviour. It is generally defined as the internal relationship through which constituent elements of a whole are organised. Structural analysis, therefore, consists in discovering the significant elements, and their order. It is not a field of study, or a system of philosophy *per se*. Any phenomenon is conceived of as a whole, and the task of structuralist criticism is to analyse its workings so as to reveal its inner laws. In the structuralist view, the conceptual system of any discipline is a web of internal correlations. It is a method of systematising human experience, which is used in various fields of study as anthropology, linguistics, psychology, literature, etc.

Structuralism divides the world into two units: the visible, or palpable, or observable (surface structure), and the invisible, or underlying (deep structure). The visible world has all that is seen and felt, the *surface phenomena,* and the invisible world, the structures that organise and order these phenomena so that we can make sense of them. These structures are created and generated by the human mind. Whatever order we see in the world is the order that our mind has imposed on it. These structures are innate in us, and we project them onto the world outside. Reality is out there, but concepts are generated by the human consciousness to organise reality. Structures are conceptual frameworks we use to organise, and understand physical entities. As a conceptual system, a structure has three characteristics: 1. wholeness—a system functions as a unit, 2. transformation—a system is dynamic and capable of change, 3. self-regulation—transformations do not lead beyond the system.

Structural Linguistics: This discipline was developed by the Swiss linguist Ferdinand Saussure (1857–1913), in his trailblazing work, *Course in General Linguistics*, published posthumously in 1915. It was an outcome of a series of lectures, delivered at the University of Geneva, in 1906–11. Before his discovery of the new system of linguistics, language and its changes were studied *diachronically,* and the assumption was that words stood for the objects they imitated. Saussure said that language is not a collection of individual words, but a structured system of relationships among them, at a given point of time, existing *synchronically*. Structuralism is not interested in finding the origins of language, but in finding out the rules that govern the functioning of language. It is interested in its structure. Saussure called the structure of language, *langue* (French for speech, language), and individual utterances *parole* (French for speaking). The structures are units that interact with one another. We perceive them as existing differentially. The usual example is that red is red, because it is different from blue or green or orange. In the traffic signal, there is no natural bond between 'red', and 'stop'. Culture (the rule of the road, in our example) erects the bond, as it were. Each colour in the traffic system signifies, not by asserting a positive, univocal meaning, but by making a difference, a distinction within a system of opposites and contrasts. The human mind perceives, most readily, differences that are opposites; these are called *binary oppositions*.

Saussure made another discovery when he said that words do not refer to the objects they stand for. Language is a structure, a system of signs. Individual components of this system can be understood only in relation to one another, and in relation to the system as a whole, and not in relation to any external 'reality' that exists outside the system. A word is just a linguistic sign consisting of two inseparable parts, like the two sides of a coin, and they are the *signifier* and the *signified*. A sign comes into being only when it acquires a meaning. The relationship can also be understood using an analogy of a piece of paper. The front side of the paper cannot be cut without cutting the back of the paper at the same time. A *signifier* is the sound image and the *signified* is the concept to which the signifier refers. A sound image becomes a word when it is linked with a concept. *The relationship between the signifier and the signified is arbitrary.* The yoking of words with concepts is the result of a social contract, and cultural conventions. There is no law governing the intrinsic relationship between the two. It is only a matter of social customs bound by cultural requirements. Signifiers do not refer to things in the world but to concepts in the mind. Saussure's pronouncement runs:

> Everything that has been said up to this point boils down to this: in language there are only differences. Even more important: a difference generally implies positive terms between which the difference is set up; but in language there are only differences *without positive terms.* Whether we take the signified or the signifier, language has neither ideas nor sounds that existed before the linguistic system, but only the conceptual and phonic differences that have issued from the system (120).

Structuralists always maintain that our perception of the world is a result of the conceptual framework that is innate to man as part of his consciousness. It is not as though the world lies out there, and man discovers it. We create the world according to the inherent structures within our consciousness. Language is the most fundamental way by which we convey our belief from one generation to another. It is only through language, we learn to perceive the world. Language creates the world. It is language that structures human experiences. This fundamental idea is of paramount importance: vital, and indispensable to our understanding of the basic concept governing structuralism.

Structural Anthropology: In the late 1950s, the French cultural anthropologist, Claude Levi-Strauss, used the structuralist principle to organise some aspects of human life, in spite of the differences in the cultures of human beings. Kinship ties, myths such as initiation to adulthood, are some aspects of the relationship. The existence of structural similarities among widely differing cultures was his area of interest. For him, 'culture, in all its aspects, is a language.' He said that all the myths of the different cultures could be reduced to a set of relations called *mythemes*, the fundamental units of myths. Using these, we can reduce and understand the large number of myths of this world. If myths are taken to be forms of narrative, *mythemes* are narrative structures. His theories have had a good deal of influence on the growth and development of what goes by the name of narratology, an aspect of structuralism. A.J. Greimas, Tzvetan Todorov, and Gerard Genette identify the formula that structures a narrative, or group of narratives, and use that formula to address larger questions about literary meaning, and its relationship to human life.

Semiotics: The term 'semiotic' (or 'semiology') is derived from the Greek word for sign. This science of signs has been in existence throughout the world, but only in recent times it has been subjected to a systematic, principled enquiry. Semiology established a clean break from New Criticism. It applies structuralist insights to the study of sign systems. A sign system is a non-linguistic object which can be analysed like language. Advertisements, and popular cultures rely on semiotic systems. Semiotics recognises language as the fundamental sign system: only for semiotics, sign=signifier+signified. Semiotics likens signs to symbols. Unlike the index and the icon, a symbol is a sign in which the relationship between the signifier, and the signified is neither natural nor necessary, but arbitrary. This relationship is decided by the conventions of community or society. The symbol is a subject matter for interpretation. Semiotics isolates and analyses the symbolic function of sign systems, synchronically. For semioticians, the whole world is a sign system, and structuralism provides them with the framework to interpret it. A work of literature is not purely a formal construction, or an image of its author's view, or a reflection of a certain milieu. Semiotic aesthetics is a negation of all forms of determinism. It stands in opposition to all other views on art: the mimetic, the expressive, the formalist, and the sociological. The different kinds and forms of art, such as music, painting and literature, follow different sign systems, and these signs are different from one another in their modes of signification. Each art has its own signifying system, specific to its form and mode of existence.

Structuralism and literature: For students of literature, structuralism has great significance. The medium of literature is language, and literature is a way by which the mind structures the world and explains it. Hence, the close relationship between literature as a field of study, and structuralism as a method of analysis. Structuralism deals mostly with the narrative domain, because narratives share many structuralist features as plot, setting, and character. Structuralism does not try to interpret what an individual text means, or whether a given work is good or not. It finds out the *langue* of literary texts, often called grammar, because of the basic rules that govern literary elements. It focuses on three areas of literary study: the classification of literary genres, the description of narrative options, and the analysis of literary interpretation.

It is good to get an overview of the historical growth of structuralism as applied to literary study, because it effected a break from New Criticism which held its sway over the academy since the twenties of the last century to the sixties and seventies. It is often said that New Criticism died of its own excess, of expiration. A wholesome view of life and literature, as opposed to a partial one, was the felt need. A change in envisioning the world was long overdue. Structuralism is sometimes described as a revolution. It reached its peak in 1967–8. It evolved outside the universities, and educational institutions. It can be adopted only as an alternative—not an addition—to traditional methods. It is somewhat revolutionary, because it challenges some of our long-addicted, and cherished beliefs. We have always held the view that a literary work is the outcome of the author's imagination. It is the noble expression of the human spirit. This commonsense view is also called liberal humanism. A literary work is the child of the author's creative life, expressing the author's self. We enter into a communion with the author—his thoughts, his feelings—through his work. A good book tells us, or at least ought to tell us, the truth about human life. Did not Milton declare that 'a good book is the precious life-blood of a master spirit, treasured up and embalmed on purpose for a life beyond life'? The structuralists, on the other hand, persuade us that the author is 'dead,' and literary discourse has no function of truth. Roland Barthes, in his essay, 'The Death of the Author', makes a celebrated statement that 'the birth of the reader must be at the cost of the death of the author.' He further remarks, 'Writing is the destruction of every voice, of every point of origin. Writing is that neutral, oblique, composite space where our subject slips away, the negative where all identity is lost, starting from the very identity of the body writing' (168)

The hegemony of the linguistic model acquires a special significance in the sphere of literature. Literature is like any other form of social or cultural activity. Literature is not only organised like language; it is made of language. Literature is always about language. As Todorov would say in a different context, 'the writer does nothing more than read language.' Saussure's view of language excludes the referential dimension. His concept of the sign is that it is a combination of the signifier and the signified. Words, for him, do not depend on reality for their meaning. Language is a self-sufficient system. It is not the speaker who imparts meaning to an utterance, but the linguistic system as a whole that produces it. Therefore, structuralism excludes both the author and reality as points of reference for interpretation. It will concentrate on signifiers at the expense of the signified. Its aim is to release the signifier from the tyranny of the signified. It will be concerned with the way meaning is produced rather than with the meaning itself. It is the type of criticism that emphasises the aspect of constructing the meaning rather than deciphering it. Lacan uttered what has now become a home truth: 'It is the world of words that creates the world of things.' Again Saussure's interest was on the synchronic study of language. This emphasis on the synchronic aspect was also influential in turning the attention of the structuralist critic to the given work with regard to its internal relationship, and its relation to the system of literature rather than to its genesis, or the subjective intentions of its author. The structuralist method consists in an analysis of the 'immanent' (indwelling) structures of work.

Genette's aphorism runs: 'Literature had been regarded as a message without a code for such a long time that it became necessary to regard it momentarily as a code without a message.' The language of literature is not subordinated to the message supposedly carried by the text. The emptiness of the content illustrates the primacy of the language. Literature, in its freedom from any referential obligation, demonstrates the supremacy of language over all other activities. Language is foregrounded by literature. Literature's very being, its finer breath, is language. The shift of focus from individual work to literature, in general, has brought a new awareness of the types of discourse about literature—reading, criticism and poetics. Criticism is no longer to be held as an extension of the reading process. It is not a straightforward, transparent, and unproblematic response to a given work of art. For Roland Barthes, reading is a process of identification with a work. Criticism consists in actively constructing a meaning for the text, and not in passively deciphering a meaning. There is no single meaning in literary works. The plurality of meanings in a text is a consequence of the absence of authorial intention in literary works. Hence, there is always an irreconcilable multiplicity of meanings. Meaning is the result of rules and conventions of different signifying systems. It is polysemic. Private meanings and intentions have no role to play. This is what is meant by 'decentring of the subject,' the fuller consequences of which are worked out by Jacques Derrida in his monumental work, *Of Grammatology*. Without the authorial guarantee, the critic's job is no longer to retrieve the meaning, but produce one which realises just one of the possibilities contained in the text. A work is 'eternal,' not because it imposes one meaning on different persons, but because it suggests different meanings to the same person. The absence of the real, argues Tzvetan Todorov, is what gives the characters in Henry James's 'The Real Thing' their essential value, so necessary to a work of art. In the realm of art, there is nothing that is preliminary to the work, nothing which constitutes its origin. It is the work itself that is original; the secondary becomes the primary. As Oscar Wilde put it with his characteristic, ready wit, 'life imitates art!' And so, structuralist criticism differs from traditional criticism by not pretending to retrieve a single, definitive meaning from the literary text.

Social and cultural phenomena have no 'essences,' but are defined by a network of internal and external relations. A phonetic sequence (human utterance), for example, is understood because of an astonishingly wide repertoire of conscious and unconscious knowledge—grammatical, phonological, semantic, etc.—otherwise called 'internalised grammar.' A poem has meaning with respect to a set of conventions which the reader has assimilated all his life. Conventions play the greatest role in literature. For a structuralist, a system of conventions is the matrix in which individual signs are embedded. The individual signs mean nothing in themselves; they acquire meaning and significance within a total structure. The process of discovering relationships is called structuring. Literary competence lies in developing these conventions. The sole objective of the discipline of English studies should be to nurture literary competence in students. Literature is an institution. We always read against the background of these conventions of the discourse. For a competent reading—a reading that involves a wholesome experience of the pleasures of the text—we are advised against what Culler calls 'premature foreclosure' of the text, and the 'unseemly rush from the word to the world.' We have to stay in the system for as long a time as possible. We naturalise or recuperate the conventions and bring them to our ken, our sphere of understanding. The French word that most accurately describes this process is *vraisemblablisation.*

Structuralism is not a recondite, or abstract theory. Structuralism does not put forth fancifully new, or astounding interpretations; nor does it move towards a definite meaning. It is not a new way of interpreting works, but only an attempt to understand how works have meaning for us. In other words, it is an attempt to catch the force of the text, its power, and reduce the possibilities of boredom. It is an aesthetic based on the pleasure of the text. The reader makes explicit the conventions of reading. Structuralism refutes the Aristotelian 'mimetic' criticism that believes that literature is the imitation of reality. Structuralism rejects the Romantic 'expressive' criticism which views literature as the expression of the feelings of a creative artist. Structuralism replaces the atomism and individualism of New Criticism by its trust in and reliance on universalism. Above all, structuralism undermines, and radically departs from the assumptions of traditional criticism, and the traditional ways of perceiving the word, the world, and the text.

Works Cited

Barthes, Roland. 'The Death of the Author.' *Modern Criticism and Theory: A Reader.* Ed. David Lodge. London and New York: Longman, 1988.

Saussure, Ferdinand de. *Course in General Linguistics.* 1915. Trans. W. Baskin. London: Fontana/Collins, 1974.

Select Bibliography

Barthes, Roland. *Writing Degree Zero*. Trans. Annette Lavers and Colin Smith. London: Jonathan Cape, 1967.

———. *The Pleasures of the Text*. 1973. Trans. Richard Miller. New York: Hill and Wang, 1975.

———. *S/Z: An Essay*. London: Jonathan Cape, 1975.

———. 'The Death of the Author.' *Modern Criticism and Theory: A Reader*. Ed. David Lodge. London and New York: Longman, 1988.

Culler, Jonathan. *Structuralist Poetics: Structuralism, Linguistics and the Study of Literature*. London: Routledge and Kegan Paul, 1975.

Ehrmann, Jacques, ed. *Structuralism*. Garden City, New York: Doubleday, 1970.

Hawkes, Terence. *Structuralism and Semiotics*. London: Methuen, 1977.

Jameson, Frederic. *The Prison-House of Language: A Critical Account of Structuralism and Russian Formalism*. Princeton, New Jersey: Princeton University Press, 1972.

Lane, Michael, ed. *Structuralism: A Reader*. London: Jonathan Cape, 1970.

Lentricchia, Frank. *After the New Criticism*. Chicago: University of Chicago Press, 1980.

Levi-Strauss, Claude. *Structural Anthropology*. Trans. C. Jacobson and B.G. Schoepf. London: Allen Lane, 1968.

Lodge, David. *The Modes of Modern Writing: Metaphor, Metonymy and the Typology of Modern Literature*. London: Edward Arnold, 1977.

———. *Working with Structuralism*. London: Routledge, 1986.

Macksey Richard and Eugenio Donato, eds. *The Structuralist Controversy: The Languages of Criticism and the Sciences of Man*. Baltimore: Johns Hopkins University Press, 1970.

Propp, Vladimir. *The Morphology of the Folktale*. Austin: University of Texas Press, 1968.

Riffaterre, Michael. *Semiotics of Poetry*. Bloomington: Indiana University Press, 1978.

Robey, David, ed. *Structuralism: An Introduction.* Oxford: Clarendon Press, 1973.

Saussure, Ferdinand de. *Course in General Linguistics.* 1915. Trans. W. Baskin. London: Fontana/Collins, 1974.

Scholes, Robert. *Structuralism in Literature: An Introduction.* New Haven: Yale University Press, 1974.

Strurrock, John. *Structuralism and Since.* New York: Oxford University Press, 1979.

Todorov, Tzvetan. *Literature and its Theories.* London: Routledge, 1988.

DECONSTRUCTION

Structuralism includes many disciplines, but all these subscribe to the Saussurean notions of 1. synchronic analysis of language, 2. the distinction between *langue* (the system) and *parole* (the particular use), and 3. the arbitrary nature of the linguistic sign, and the associative bond that unites the *signifier* and the *signified.* Language as a total system is independent of reality. Poststructuralism may be looked upon as an attempt to question some of the assumptions of structuralism. Contemporary theorists—Marxists, psychoanalysts, feminists, and others—have all expressed their uneasiness with structuralism.

Poststructuralism deflates the scientific certainties and pretensions of structuralism, making a mockery of structuralism. For example, according to Saussure, there is stability in signification. Signifier and signified form a unified whole, and preserve a certain identity of meaning. Saussure recognised the signifier and signified as two separate systems, but he could not envisage how unstable units of meaning can be when the two systems come together. He tried to retain a sense of the sign's coherence. Poststructuralists—and this is the point of departure—have, in various ways, prised apart the two halves (the signifier and the signified) of the sign. They have discovered the unstable nature of signification. Sign is not, therefore, a unit with two sides; but a momentary 'fix' between two moving layers. Answering a child's innocent query, for instance, takes us on from one sign to another. We may feel, when we look up the meaning (signified) of a word (signifier) in a dictionary, that the unity of the sign is confirmed. But the contrary is true, and our dictionary confirms it. There is an endless deferment of meaning. We not only find several signifieds for one signifier, but each of the signifieds, in turn, becomes yet another signifier which can be traced in the dictionary with its array of signifieds. There is no uncontaminated signifier. 'The signified is always already in place elsewhere as signifier.' To quote Derrida, 'the absence of the transcendental signified extends the domain and interplay of signification *ad infinitum.*' The signifier 'crib' has several signifieds: manger, child's bed, hut, a job, a plagiarism, a literal translation, discarded cards, and so on and so forth. As a signifier 'bed' has several signifieds: a place for sleeping, a garden plot, layer of oysters, a channel of a river, a stratum, and so on. The relay of signifiers thus continues endlessly, with chains and crosscurrents of meaning.

Jacques Derrida inaugurated the theory of deconstruction in the late 1960s; it became a great influence on literary studies in the late 1970s. His writings are both a continuation and a critique of structuralism. His quarrel is with the way in which structuralism has betrayed the principles on which it was sought to be founded. Derrida's rigorous exploration of Saussure's claim that 'in language there are only differences without positive terms' leads him on to question the two key concepts of structuralism, namely 1. sign and 2. structure. He does this in his much-anthologised paper, 'Structure, Sign and Play in the Discourse of Human Sciences', 1969, which inaugurated a new movement in the US, influencing literary study the world over.

Deconstruction is a radical destabilisation of all earlier movements in literature. It is the most philosophically oriented, and the most theorised movement we have known so far. The Derridean movement is no longer a new phenomenon now, having been absorbed in contemporary critical thought. There are many things that deconstruction teaches us. It adds to our understanding of literature with a greater sense of critical perception. Our life and experiences are governed by certain ideologies which are built into our language, and it is good for us to try to see ourselves rid of these ideologies. For Derrida, language is not a reliable mode of communication that we believe it is. It is fluid and slippery. The word 'tree,' for example, never reaches to a point when it refers to a concept, a signified. One signifier that is uttered refers to a chain of signifiers in the mind, and this in turn evokes a chain of signifiers in the mind of the person who hears. And every signifier in those chains is constituted by another chain or chains of signifiers. Language, therefore, does not consist of merely a simple union of signifiers and signifieds. Instead, it consists of a chain of signifiers. Structuralism believes that language is non-referential because it does not refer to things in the world, but only to concepts of things in the world. Deconstruction takes it one step further, when it maintains that language is non-referential, because it refers neither to things in the world nor to our concepts of things, but only to the play of signifiers of which language itself is made. Our mind does not contain stable and unchanging concepts, but a continually changing play of signifiers. These signifiers, though they seem to be stable, are not stable in reality. Each and every signifier produces other signifiers in a never-ending *deferral* or postponement of meaning. We may try to find a stable meaning, but it is not possible because we can never get beyond the play of signifiers, that is language.

According to Derrida it is only the mental *trace* left behind by the signifiers that we take to be the meaning. And that trace is made of differences by which we make a word. Only because we distinguish between words, we associate a particular meaning with a particular word. If all the objects in the world were made of the same colour, we will not read the word red as red at all. We call a colour red, because it is different from blue and green. Hence, the word red carries with it the trace of all the signifiers it is not. If it does not sound equivocal, Derrida's 'trace' is the mark of the absence of a presence, 'an always already absent present.' The characteristics of language are that its play of signifiers continually defers meaning, and any meaning that a word seems to have is the result of the differences by which we distinguish one signifier from another. The meaning of a sign, in some sense, is always absent from it. Meaning cannot be fixed. There is a constant flickering of absence and presence, at one and the same time. Derrida coins a word *differance* (his master concept) for the meaning that language seems to convey.

We have to use language as the only available tool for communication. It does not possess the stability or the solidity we assume it possesses. That is the very reason why we can improvise and stretch it to suit newer ways of thinking about the world and ourselves. Derrida uses the term *bricolage* to refer to this activity. Bricolage is the process of assembling something from materials at hand. In the Derridean usage, it refers to the act of borrowing concepts from different sources, and redesigning them to suit one's needs. He demonstrates this activity by putting words *under erasure*, that is, first by writing them, and then crossing them out. We use, and erase language at the same time. There is no escaping from language; it is language that forms us, and we exist in the language we are born into. Hence, the need for stretching or distending the language for our benefit. The way we understand the world, and the way we see ourselves are governed by the language we are taught, and the language we have learnt. Our experience of the world and of ourselves, is mediated by language. Language carries along with it conflicting, ever-changing, and dynamic systems of ideologies.

Structuralism has told us that we have a way of conceptualising our experience in terms of polar opposites, which is called *binary oppositions*. We get to know what is good by contrasting it with what is evil. These oppositions build hierarchies in which one term in a pair is privileged. By finding out the binary oppositions in a work we can know something about the ideology advanced by it. Derrida observes that this neat pairing of opposites advanced by structuralism does not work that way. The two oppositions overlap and share some common elements. The example of the 'objective,' and the 'subjective' would prove the point. Language does not operate in any tidy way. It always overflows with contradictions and associations that we carry: it is replete with opposed ideologies. It is through language that we conceive, and perceive the world. This language, from the deconstructive point of view, is a different ground of being from the ones associated with our system of traditional philosophies.

Every philosophical system in the world has a base, a fundamental grounding, an organising principle based on which we try to understand the meaning of the world we live in. Plato's system believes in an ideal, abstract dimension of thought. Descartes said, 'I think; therefore I am.' For structuralism, it is the innate structures of the human consciousness that generates human experiences. Derrida's argument is that these grounding principles produce an understanding of the world around us. And yet, these concepts, which produce those that are always changing, are held to remain stable! How can we accept this paradox? Is not the centre that controls the structure also a part of the structure? Derrida calls this philosophic system, 'logocentric' (more of it, later). It places at the centre (*centric*) of its understanding of the world a concept (*logos*) that orders and organises the world, while itself remaining outside the world it organises. This, according to him, is an illusion in Western philosophy. Here is Derrida, in the essay, 'Structure, Sign and Play in the Discourse of the Human Sciences':

> Thus it has always been thought that the centre, which is by definition unique, constituted that very thing within a structure which while governing the structure escapes structurality. This is why classical thought concerning structure could say that the centre is, paradoxically, *within* the structure and *outside it.* The centre is at the centre of the totality, and yet, since the centre does not belong to the totality (is not part of the totality), the totality, *has its centre elsewhere.* The centre is not the centre (84).

Hence Derrida questions the basic assumptions of Western philosophy since Plato. And, according to Nietzsche, Derrida's godfather, it is from Plato that man has learnt to think of the world of appearance in preference to the world of reality. Human understanding is structured by the world of appearance, and we always escape to this illusory world from the world of reality. The notion of 'structure' has presupposed a centre. The centre governs a structure, but is itself not subject to structural analysis (to find the structure of the centre would be to find another centre). We desire a centre; it guarantees being as presence. Our physical and mental life centres on an 'I.' This is the principle of unity that underlies the structure of all that keeps happening in the world. Western thought has given birth to many concepts and terms that act as centring principles, such as God, truth, man, form, and so on.

Derrida calls this desire for a centre 'logocentrism'. 'Logos' (Greek for word) carries in it the concentration of presence. Logocentrism is the belief that the first and the last things are the 'logos,' the word, the divine mind, the infinite understanding of God. In philosophic parlance, 'logos' means the rational principle that develops and governs the world. In theology, it is the divine word, incarnate in Christ. In the *New Testament* in the *Gospel* according to St John, ch. 1, verse 1, 'In the beginning was the *word*, the *word* was with God, and the *word* was God.' Word was the origin of all things; everything was the result of this one cause. God's *word* is spoken. A spoken word is closer to the original thought than a written word. Privileging of *speech* over writing is 'phonocentrism.' Logocentrism and phonocentrism are both governed by the human desire to point to a central presence at the beginning, and at the end. It is this longing for a centre that spawns hierarchical oppositions: the superior term belongs to 'presence' or the 'logos.' Speech has its full presence, felt and heard at once, while writing is secondary, and therefore, contaminated speech. Western philosophy, according to Derrida, has always supported this hierarchy in order to preserve this concept of presence. This traditional hierarchy of binary oppositions has infected all systems of thought including literature, criticism of art, in fact, the whole culture. Rev Fr Walter Ong, a spokesman for the traditional philosophic system, refutes this view. In his *Orality and Literacy*, he observes:

> The interaction between the orality that all human beings are born into and the technology of writing, which no one is born into, touches the depths of the psyche . . . It is the oral word that first illuminates consciousness with articulate language, that first divides subject and predicate and then relates them to one another, and that ties human beings to one another in society. Writing introduces division and alienation, but a higher unity as well. It intensifies the sense of self and fosters more conscious interaction between persons. Writing is consciousness-raising (178–9).

This ranking can be reversed, and Derrida proposes it. Both speech and writing share the same features, the writerly features; both are signifying processes and both lack presence. Writing ought not to be conceived in the usual material sense of graphic notation. Writing is the name of the structure always already inhabited by the trace. In fact, writing is speech and speech is one form of writing. Writing is constructed on the same principle as speech. Such a reversal of the traditional hierarchy is the first step in Derridean deconstruction. Jonathan Culler, the best commentator on Derrida, explains it in his book *On Deconstruction* with some striking examples, one of which, at least, is worth citing.

Paradise Lost rests on a basic distinction between good and evil. Good originates with God. Evil came later to contaminate the good. If we examine this a little more closely, we can see it operating the other way round. When was good without evil? Did it exist before the fall of Satan who warred in heaven against heaven's angel? If that were so, who was it who caused Satan's fall? Pride goeth before a fall, it is said. Then who created Pride? It should be the same God who created angels, and later humans, free to sin. On this analogy, one can never reach a moment of immaculate and uncorrupted pure goodness. Let us try for a moment reversing the hierarchy, and say, that there are no good acts by humans until after the Fall. Adam's first act of sacrifice is an expression of affection coupled with devotion to his wife, the fallen Eve. Hence 'goodness' comes after Evil. It is the result of evil. It is evil that causes goodness. In *Areopagitica* Milton opposes licensing of books, because we can be virtuous only if we are given the freedom to oppose evil. God's prohibition is in itself an act of evil; or, at least, it presupposes evil. The poet, William Blake, was of the view that Milton was on the side of Satan. Shelley too held the view that, as a moral being, Satan was much superior to Milton's God. They reverse the hierarchy (and thereby deconstruct *Paradise Lost*) substituting evil for good. To use from Culler again: the basic principle of the universe is causality. Cause produces effects. Causal sequence is 'pin' to 'pain' but the cause (pin) gets imagined after the effect (pain) has occurred. It is the result of a tropological operation. To deconstruct causality, one must operate within the notion of the cause. Derrida reverses the hierarchical operation of the causal scheme. 'If the effect is what causes the cause to become a cause, then the effect, not the cause, should be treated as the origin' (88). Therefore, origin is no longer originary; it loses its metaphysical privilege—a non-originary origin.

The centring principle is itself a human product of human language. How can it lie outside the control of the instabilities of language? No concept can lie outside the language, which produced it, however dynamic and unstable language might be. Unlike other philosophic systems dismissed by Derrida as logocentric, language is the ground of being, the basic principle on which systems of thought are built, or made: and this language is also part of the structure, and is itself as evolving, ever changing and problematical, as the views or ideologies it produces. Hence, there cannot be any centre that controls or organises our thinking. Dismissal of the notion that the centre controls our thoughts is decentring. Derridean logic decentres Western philosophy that pins its faith on the centre. There are ever so many perspectives to view the world, and each perspective employs a kind of language peculiar to it. This is what is termed as *discourse*.

Language is neither the product of our experience, nor is it the medium for conveying our thoughts, but it is the very framework that produces our experience. Structuralists discovered that our world is created by our language and they believed that language is generated by the stable and innate structures of human consciousness.

But poststructuralism rejects this notion of an ordered vision of language and human experience. Language is the ground of being, and the world is the text, which is made of an infinite number of signifiers always at play. 'Language' says Derrida, 'bears within itself the necessity of its own critique.' Human beings are also in this system of language. Who is the human, and what is it to be a human being? This is the problem of *subjectivity*. We are produced by the language we speak. Language is always unstable and so are we. The stable image that we have of ourselves is an illusion produced by the culture we inhabit. Culture itself is not as stable as we presume, because it is inscribed in language. We have no identity as such. We are all divided selves full of conflicting beliefs and fragmented by fears, anxieties and unfulfilled hopes, etc. In the words of Arnold, 'each half lives a hundred different lives.' Through language, we internalise the conflicts and contradictions of our culture, little realising that we are the product of the fragmented language that constitutes our very being. We have invented our identity, which is determined by our culture.

Language, as we have seen in our discussion so far, is unstable, slippery, dynamic, always spreading likely meanings. Existence on this earth for us is not controlled by any centering agency; nor does it have any stable meaning. We choose and invent our own identity. From all this, it is the next step to conclude that literature, created by and composed in language, is unstable, dynamic and always equivocal. Meaning does not lie in the text for us to consume or uncover. In the act of reading, meaning is created by the reader, that is, meaning is generated by the play and interplay of language in the very process of reading. The meaning or meanings thus generated are not stable. These meanings constantly play with—and are in conflict with—one another: we have a multiplicity of endless possibilities of meaning, always overlapping with one another. All readings are the result of the culture and system of beliefs we possess. When an author constructs a text, he draws upon the cultural milieu he is familiar with. Even so, the reader constructs a text drawing on the cultural milieu he is raised in. Deconstruction helps us to get to know the undecidability of the text, and the complex ideologies the text is composed of. The undecidability of the text suggests that it has an array of possible, conflicting meanings, and, in the traditional sense of an unchanging meaning, it has none. Undecidability implies that the reader and the text are both caught in a maze; both are inextricably bound to each other within language which is always slippery. Particular meanings are just fleeting moments, passing fancies.

All texts, literary and non-literary, are made of language. Meanings always proliferate in endless ways. Normal traditional interpretations do not recognise the conflicting ideologies of the text. A deconstructive reading looks for meanings in the text that stand in conflict with what is held as the main theme in traditional interpretations. The text itself is not aware of these contradictions. And deconstruction does not resolve the tensions in them into a unity or harmony. Instead, it sustains and even promotes such tensions, because it is the nature of the language not to get resolved. Ideological conflicts and instabilities constitute the very fabric of language. We should be alive to this, if we wish to figure out how deconstruction can enrich our modes of thinking. In a strict sense, nobody ever deconstructs a text; it deconstructs itself. Meanings are always disseminated and any deconstructive reading of a text catches a fleeting moment of this dissemination.

Barbara Johnson describes the deconstructive act as follows:

> *Deconstruction* is not synonymous with destruction . . . It is in fact much closer to the original meaning of the word *analysis,* which etymologically means 'to undo' – a virtual synonym for 'to de-construct.' The de-construction of a text does not proceed by

> random doubt or arbitrary subversion, but by the careful teasing out of warring forces of signification within the text itself. If anything is destroyed in a deconstructive reading, it is not the text, but the claim to unequivocal domination of one mode of signifying over another (5).

And, here is Catherine Belsey:

> The object of deconstructing the text is to examine the *process of its production*—not as the private experience of the individual author, but the mode of production, the materials and their arrangement in the work. The aim is to locate the point of contradiction within the text, the point at which it transgresses the limits within which it is constructed, breaks free from the constraints imposed by its own realist form. Composed of contradictions, the text is no longer restricted to a single harmonious and authoritative reading. Instead, it becomes *plural*, open to re-reading, no longer an object of passive consumption but an object of work by the reader to produce meaning (104).

Gayatri Spivak, in her preface to *Of Grammatology*, illustrates the way deconstructors read a text:

> If in the process of deciphering a text in the traditional way we come across a word that seems to harbour an unresolvable contradiction, and by virtue of one word being made to work in one way and sometimes in another and thus is made to point away from the absence of a unified meaning, we shall catch at that word. If a metaphor seems to suppress its implications, we shall catch at that metaphor. We shall follow its adventures through the text and see that text coming undone as a structure of concealment, revealing its self-transgression, its undecidability (lxxv).

J. Hillis Miller, one of the most prominent practitioners of deconstruction defines it as follows:

> Deconstruction as a mode of interpretation works by a careful and circumspect entering of each textual labyrinth . . . The Deconstructive critic seeks to find, by this process of retracting, the element in the system studied which is alogical, the thread in the text in question which will unravel it all, or the loose stone which will pull down the whole building. The deconstruction, rather, annihilates the ground on which the building stands by showing that the text has already annihilated the ground, knowingly or unknowingly. Deconstruction is not a dismantling of the structure of a text but a demonstration that it has already dismantled itself.

By way of an example, let us choose Hillis Miller's deconstructive reading of a well-known passage from *Paradise Lost.*

> She as a veil down to her slender waist
> Her unadorned golden tresses wore
> Dishevelled, but in wanton ringlets waved
> As the vine curls her tendrils, which implied
> Subjection. . . . Book 4 (304–8)

These lines form part of a long passage of astonishing beauty which describes Satan's first view of the Garden of Eden and our first-born parents, Adam and Eve. Adam's locks do not fall below his shoulder but Eve's hair falls down as a veil to her waist. Milton's language goes against his intentions in the argument. Apparently Milton wants to fix Adam and Eve in the general economy of creation. They are 'not equal, as their sex not equal seemed.' 'He for God only, she for God in him.' Eve is made for subjection to Adam and through him to God. This is the main purpose of the argument. But the line, 'as the vine curls her tendrils,' is clearly and noticeably an echo of an earlier description of Eden, 'Of umbrageous grots and caves/ Of cool recesses o're which the mantling vine/ Lays forth her purple grape, and gently creeps/ Luxuriant.' This description places Eve 'in the general dishevelled and untameable luxuriance,' or 'wantonnes [sic] of Nature,' according to Miller. This, in effect, implies that Eve has already fallen when Satan sees her for the first time. Milton wants to suggest that the curling tendrils imply subjection. But the earlier image contradicts this suggestion, and places Eve outside the control of Adam. So within the phrase 'as the vine curls her tendrils,' there is the interference of figuration with theology. The two meanings are 'asymmetrical and irreconcilable.' The text contradicts itself. It says the very opposite of what it believes it says. This is exactly what Derrida means when he says, 'language bears within itself the necessity of its own critique.'

The ideas innate to the theory of Derridean deconstruction are disturbing, provocative and challenging. Derrida's precursors were Nietzsche, Freud, Heidegger and Husserl. There are stubbornly strong defenders of deconstruction, on the one hand, and aggressively hostile critics, on the other. M.H. Abrams, Gerard Graff, Wayne Booth and others vehemently attack and repudiate its claims, its suppositions, and criticise its method (or lack of it) of what is called rhetorical reading of texts. For Abrams, for example, deconstructive reading is 'plainly and simply parasitical on the obvious and univocal reading.' Some claim that while its theory is suspicious of everything that is assertive, in practice however, it is self-assured, confident and aggressive. They call deconstruction nihilistic, wholly concerned with language severed from its connections with the world of reality, ahistorical, appealing to chosen elitists, ignoring the presence of the 'common reader.' It is felt that it is a needless regression to irrationalism. Derrida's doctrines are seen to be a sort of *reductio ad absurdum.* They do not accept the Derridean theory that 'our use of language is never constrained by a non-linguistic world.' There is a whole body of analytical philosophy which holds the belief that there is some correspondence between language and reality. The case against the apparent novelty and the personal whims of fancies of deconstruction is eloquently put forward by John Ellis in his *Against Deconstruction* in the following words:

> The most enduring fault of literary criticism as a field has been its readiness to abandon the communal sense of a shared inquiry, in which individual perceptions are expected to be tested and sifted by others. A shared inquiry means a commitment to argument and dialogue, while a criticism that insists on the value of each individual critic's perspective, in effect, refuses to make that commitment (159).

Paul de Man, Hillis Miller and Geoffrey Hartman subscribe to the notion of deconstruction, and propagate it in their works of criticism. In the words of Paul de Man, 'Derrida's text, as he puts it so well, is the unmaking of a construct. However negative it may sound, deconstruction implies a possibility of a rebuilding.' In fact, it was given to Paul de Man to act as a mediator to introduce Derrida's thought. He found fault with the ahistorical and aphilosophical character of New Criticism, which had been blind to the European methods (*Blindness and Insight* 20). Literary texts had been placed without a historical and political context. This had resulted in blindness to 'the intentional structure of literary form.' De Man said that the New Critics themselves went against their doctrine of organic form when they accepted a plurality of meanings. 'In spite of itself, it pushes the interpretive process so far that the analogy between the organic world and the language of poetry finally explodes' (*Blindness* 280). For Hillis Miller, deconstruction provides exemplary acts of reading. It 'liberates a past text for present uses.' It encourages us to read actively, and prepares us for a better and more adventurous reading of literature. Scholars in women's studies, cultural studies, and minority discourses have profited from deconstructive reading of texts, and have acknowledged their indebtedness to it. It would be putting the clock far back, were we to revert to the conservative modes of reading the detractors of deconstruction wish to encourage. For Miller, 'appropriating, transforming, and, most of all, using performatively this insight of deconstruction is a chief task of the humanities today.' All practitioners of deconstruction are one in looking upon themselves as reformers and political activists. They do not accept literature in its traditional sense, as containing timeless, moral truths that are essentially human. For them literature is 'the persistent naming of the void.'

Those who attack this theory on philosophic grounds raise the most fundamental question: how can deconstruction find a place within an institution it seems to undermine and subvert? This question, however, remains unanswered and, yes, unanswerable!

Works Cited

Belsey, Catherine. *Critical Practice.* London: Methuen, 1980.

Culler, Jonathan. *On Deconstruction: Theory and Criticism after Structuralism.* London: Routledge and Kegan Paul, 1982.

De Man, Paul. *Blindness and Insight: Essays in the Rhetoric of Contemporary Criticism.* London: Methuen, 1983.

Derrida, Jacques. 'Structure, Sign and Play in the Discourse of the Human Sciences'. *Critical Theory and Practice since 1965.* Ed. Hazard Adams and Leroy Searle. Tallahassee: University of Florida Press, 1986.

Ellis, John. *Against Deconstruction.* Princeton: Princeton University Press, 1989.

Johnson, Barbara. *The Critical Difference.* Baltimore: Johns Hopkins University, 1980.

Ong, Walter S. *Orality and Literature*. Cambridge: Harvard University Press, 1982.

Spivak, Gayatri, trans. *Of Grammatology*. By Jacques Derrida. Baltimore: Johns Hopkins University Press, 1967.

Select Bibliography

Abrams, M.H. *Doing Things with Texts*. New York: W.W. Norton, 1991.

Atkins, G. Douglas. *Reading Deconstruction/Deconstructive Reading*. Lexington: University Press of Kentucky, 1983.

Barthes, Roland. *The Pleasure of the Text*. Trans. R. Miller. New York: Hill and Wang, 1975.

Belsey, Catherine. *Critical Practice*. London: Methuen, 1981.

Bloom, Harold. *The Anxiety of Influence: A Theory of Poetry*. London: Oxford University Press, 1973.

———. *A Map of Misreading*. New York: Oxford University Press, 1975.

Culler, Jonathan. *On Deconstruction: Theory and Criticism after Structuralism*. London: Routledge and Kegan Paul, 1982.

———, ed. *Critical Concepts in Literature and Cultural Studies*. London: Routledge, 2003.

De Man, Paul. *Blindness and Insight: Essays in the Rhetoric of Contemporary Criticism*. 2nd ed. London: Methuen, 1983.

———. *Allegories of Reading*. New Haven: Yale University Press, 1979.

———. *The Resistance to Theory*. Manchester: Manchester University Press, 1987.

Derrida, Jacques. *Speech and Phenomena*. Trans. David Allison. Evanston: Northwestern University Press, 1973.

———. *Of Grammatology*. Translated and introduced by Gayatri Spivak. Rev. ed. Baltimore: Johns Hopkins University Press, 1976.

———. *Writing and Difference*. Trans. Alan Bass. London: Routledge & Kegan Paul, 1978.

———. *Positions.* Trans. Alan Boss. Chicago: University of Chicago Press, 1981.

———. *Dissemination.* Trans. with Introduction by Barbara Johnson. Chicago: University of Chicago Press, 1982.

———. *Margins of Philosophy.* Trans. Alan Boss. Chicago: University of Chicago Press, 1982.

Eagleton, Terry. *Literary Theory: An Introduction.* Oxford: Blackwell, 1983.

———. *The Function of Criticism.* London: New Left Books, 1984.

Ellis, Frank. *Against Deconstruction.* Princeton, N.J.: Princeton University Press, 1989.

Felperin, Howard. *Beyond Deconstruction: The Uses and Abuses of Theory.* Oxford: Clarendon Press, 1985.

Harari, Josue V, ed. *Textual Strategies: Perspectives in Post-Structuralist Criticism.* Ithaca: Cornell University Press, 1971.

Hartman, Geoffrey. *Criticism in the Wilderness.* Baltimore: Johns Hopkins University Press, 1980.

Jefferson, Ann and D. Robey, eds. *Modern Literary Theory: A Comparative Introduction.* 2nd ed. London: Batsford, 1986.

Johnson, Barbara. *The Critical Difference: Essays in the Contemporary Rhetoric of Reading.* Baltimore: Johns Hopkins University Press, 1980.

Leitch, Vincent B. *Deconstructive Criticism: An Advanced Introduction.* London: Hutchinson, 1983.

Macksey, Richard, and Eugenio Donato, eds. *The Structuralist Controversy: The Languages of Criticism and the Sciences of Man.* Baltimore: Johns Hopkins University Press, 1970.

Miller, J. Hillis. *The Ethics of Reading.* New York: Columbia University Press, 1987.

Norris, Christopher. *Derrida.* London: Fontana, 1987.

———. *Deconstruction: Theory and Practice.* 2nd. ed. London: Routledge, 1991.

Reynolds, Jack and Jonathan Roffe. *Understanding Derrida.* New York: Continuum, 2004.

Royle, Nicholas, ed. *Deconstruction: A User's Guide.* Basingstoke: Macmillan, 2000.

Scholes, Robert. *Textual Power: Literary Theory and the Teaching of English.* New Haven: Yale University Press, 1985.

Young, Robert, ed. *Untying the Text: A Post-Structuralist Reader.* London: Routledge and Kegan Paul, 1981.

New Historicism and Cultural Criticism

Critical theories can overlap one another, and they quite often do. One critical theory can be pressed into the service of another. But each theory has its purpose and function, and remains distinct in terms of its goals and assumptions. Marxism is interested in examining the ways in which our socioeconomic system determines our life and experiences. Feminism tries to examine the ways in which patriarchal gender roles affect our experience. How repressed psychological conflicts are the source of our experience is studied by psychoanalytic criticism. Structuralism analyses how certain basic structures make it possible for us to understand the seemingly disorganised world. Reader-response theories are concerned with the operations involved in the readers' creating the text they read.

In the late 1970s and 1980s, the dominance of deconstruction was challenged by a new literary theory. While deconstruction was sceptical of the function of language to carry and convey meaning (language is not constitutive of reality), this new theory pinned its faith on the 'psychic and physical' reality of language, the primary purpose of which is to erect systems of thought ('discourse'). While the American theorists gave it the name 'New Historicism' to distinguish it from its earlier manifestation, old historicism, the Marxist-oriented British counterparts, Jonathan Dollimore, Alan Sinfield, Catherine Belsey among others, called it cultural poetics. They were directly influenced by Raymond Williams (who put in circulation the term 'cultural materialism'), Michel Foucault, and Louis Althusser. New historicism and cultural poetics share a common ground, and only thin partitions divide their boundaries.

Traditional historians, and new historicists approach history in different ways. They have different views of history and what it constitutes. Old historicists ask the question, 'What happened and what do we learn about the event that happened?' New historicists would ask, 'How has the event that happened been interpreted, and what do these tell us now?' And the traditional conception of history is that it is an objective record of events, represented in a linear fashion, with causal relationships determining the events. The historians also believed that it was possible to record objectively the past events as they happened. The events of the past disclose to us the spirit and the world view of those bygone ages. Traditional approaches have brought to light concepts to understand the *weltanschauung* of the different ages, such as the belief in the Great Chain of Being, held during the Renaissance. This was used to read and interpret Elizabethan culture. Events of the past were seen in the background of the *zeitgeist* of the times. Even the study of literature is classified period-wise such as neoclassical, romantic, etc. Old historicists believed in the progressive nature of history, in the perfectibility of man, and in the growth and improvement in the civilisation of the world. Usually, E.M.W. Tillyard's *The Elizabethan World Picture* (1943), and *Shakespeare's History Plays* (1944) are cited as the best representative examples of old historicism. Tillyard portrayed the Elizabethan world based on a belief in the divinely ordered world. In such a unified cosmos, 'disorder' has no place. Literary texts are treated as transcendental and sublime expressions of a stable and ordered world of values. Such a monological, deterministic view of history went unchallenged for centuries.

New historicists, on the other hand, believe that we can at best only have access to facts of the past. What we do is to interpret these facts from our own point of view, and create a history. There are only different interpretations of facts, and one interpretation is as reliable or not as another. Objective analysis of the facts is impossible. Progressive notions of history often misrepresented ancient cultures, which were highly developed, as barbaric and anarchic. History does not progress in any linear fashion, as the old historians often believe. It does not proceed towards any set goal. New historicism dismisses the eschatological, or teleological connotations of traditional historians. New historicism is, therefore, historicist rather than historical. It is interested in history-as-text, that is, history as recorded and represented in different documents, which form its texts. There are no single causes that lead to events in a predictable way. Our *subjectivity* too is shaped by, and shapes, culture. One constitutes the other. Social formation and individual identity influence each other. Our subjectivity exists and extends all through our life, figuring out the way to live in the context of the freedom offered to us amidst the restrictions or constraints involved.

Again, there is the problem of power. It does not flow from any outward agency one-way, controlling all below it. Power is what circulates at all levels. It helps in the exchange, and the give and take of objects, institutions and discourses. Any discourse is a social language created for a way of understanding the experience of an institution. Discourses all the time are dynamic, one trying to exchange with the other by laws of supply and demand, and negotiate with the other. Discourses do not exist on a permanent basis. Discursive practices are often linked to the exercise of power. Forms of discourse ensure the reproduction of a social system through 'selection, exclusion and domination'. They wield power, but also undermine it. Power always circulates through various discourses, as religion, science, fashion, law, and so forth. According to Foucault, all discourses are social constructs by which power is maintained. In one of his cardinal essays, 'The Order of Discourse,' Foucault maintains, 'In every society, the production of discourse is controlled, organised, redistributed by a certain number of procedures whose role is to ward off its powers and dangers, to gain mastery over its chance events, to evade its materiality.' We accept them as natural, or right, or normal. In the same way, all history is narrative written according to the point of view held by the historians. Historians are not aware of their leanings, and do often think that their history is objective. Therefore, historical events cannot be understood as they are represented in the discourses of those who have written them. They carry with them the prevailing ideology of their time. New historicism deconstructs the traditional distinction between history (thought to be factual) and literature (thought to be fictional). History is another text even as literature is: literature is another cultural artefact, even as history is, and it can tell us something about the social life of the times when they were written. Louis Montrose's famous definition of new historicism is that it centres upon both the historicity of the text, and the textuality of history.

Traditional historians use other texts which are only forms of narrative, and new historicism helps in deconstructing the dominant and oppressive narratives. That is to say that *master* or *grand narratives* have come into question with new historicism. In this way, histories of marginalised groups assume some importance because of the plurality of historical voices. There is no history in the traditional sense; there are only representations of history. New historicists use *thick descriptions,* which examine a cultural production in order to discover the meanings of the cultural production as well as the social conventions that were responsible for them. It is a search for meanings, not facts. Thus personal and small private issues are foregrounded. Every historical analysis is subjective: it views historical issues through a human 'lens'. This is described as *self-positioning.* Personal investments are unavoidable in any representation, which is not to say that every representation is self-indulgent. The basic propositions of new historicism are as follows:

- History is always narrated. History is a matter of interpretation; all historical writings are narratives to be analysed like literary texts.
- History is neither progressive nor linear.
- Power does not flow one way. It circulates through exchange of ideas and discourses.
- The eschatological (doctrine of the final things such as death, state after death, etc.) or teleological (doctrine of the final causes of things) connotations of history have to be eschewed. There is no unified, monolithic spirit of an age. Historical periods are not unified entities. There are no totalising explanations of history. There is no single history; there are only contradictory and conflicting histories. In other words, there is only a play of discourses which contradict, destabilise and modify each other.
- The past is something that we construct. It is an ideological construct. Personal identity shapes, and is, in turn, shaped by the culture in which it exists. Cultural categories such as insanity, or madness are a matter of definition.
- All historical analysis is subjective. Historians only position themselves to interpret history.

- From all these, it follows that the relationship between history and literature must be redefined.

Old historicism which was in vogue in the nineteenth and early twentieth centuries limited itself either to studies about the life of the author in order to know his intentions, or to historical periods, to know the spirit of the age in which the work was written. The outer world of ordinary history served only as the background. The inner world of gifted and great writers was privileged and legitimised. New criticism rejected this approach to literature because it viewed literary works as autonomous, timeless, and existing in a realm transcending history. Emerging in the 1970s, new historicism rejects both old historicism's marginalisation of history and New Criticism's fetishisation of literature as timeless beyond the realm of history. Literary texts are cultural artefacts like other artefacts which reveal to us the different social systems that operated when the texts were written. Literary text is one social discourse. Text and context are mutually constitutive. Literary texts shape, and are in turn shaped, by historical contexts. Louis Montrose describes the practice of new historicism in a telling phrase: 'a reciprocal concern with the historicity of texts and the textuality of history.'

New historicism is based on a parallel reading of literary and non-literary texts (chosen from the archive) both of which belong roughly to the same historical period. It does not privilege the literary text. It does not attempt to 'foreground' the literary text and treat history as its 'background.' Literary and its parallel non-literary texts are given equal importance: the one is used to read and interpret the other. The two are seen mutually to interrogate, contradict, modify, and thus inform each other. New historicism draws from Derrida's view that every aspect and feature of reality is textualised. There is nothing outside the text. It draws upon Foucault's belief that social structures are determined by dominant 'discursive practices'. It was the American critic Stephen Greenblatt who gave wide currency to the term in the early eighties. The journal, *Representations,* became its organ, promoting essays that gave a new historicist reading of the literature of the Renaissance. In his essay, 'Towards a Poetics of Culture', Greenblatt developed his hypothesis of what he called the poetics of new historicism. For him it is a practice, not a doctrine.

> The work of art is the product of a negotiation between a creator or class of creators, equipped with a complex, communally shared repertoire of conventions, and the institutions and practices of society. In order to achieve the negotiation, artists need to create a currency that is valid for a meaningful, mutually profitable exchange. It is important to emphasise that the process involves not simply appropriation but exchange, since the existence of art always implies a return, a return normally measured in pleasure and interest (12).

In the literary scene in our country, new historicism as a cultural theory and reading strategy will have an impact with far-reaching consequences. Many of us, time and again, voice our scepticism as regards the applicability of Western theoretical concepts, such as deconstruction, as tools of enquiry to read and interpret our vast and varied literature. The variety and diversity of Indian culture, with its vast storehouse of writings, affords ample nourishment to a new historicist treatment of texts as a product of 'collective negotiations and exchange'.

CULTURAL MATERIALISM

Cultural materialism (also called cultural criticism) as a critical method of enquiry gained currency, when it was put to use in the mid-1980s by Jonathan Dollimore, and Alan Sinfield in their book of essays, *Political Shakespeare.* These essays on religion, ideology and power in the drama of Shakespeare and his contemporaries provided a reading based on political commitment. This served as an alternative to the conventional, Christian framework of Shakespeare criticism which had run its course for more than four hundred years. Cultural materialism and new historicism have several affinities. The former is overtly British, and the other overtly American. The two movements belong to the same family, as it were, and the quarrel between them is said to be a family quarrel. Both draw upon the same sources, and in many ways, they are indistinguishable from each other.

Cultural criticism is an outgrowth of Marxism. The term 'culture' does not merely mean high 'art'. It includes all forms of culture, high, and what is considered low, such as popular art, fiction and television. In his *Notes towards the Definition of Culture,* Eliot describes culture as that which makes life worth living. It includes all the characteristic activities of a people. Cultural materialism is apparently Marxist, according to which culture can never transcend material forces and relations of production. The most widely known British left-wing critic Raymond Williams, who was the 'pied piper' of his generation, gave it its name. Its prime argument is that the culture of the working classes is never taken into consideration in highbrow criticism of literature. It is considered inferior culture. All cultural productions reveal the role of culture in the circulation of power. And what is considered low by the dominant ruling culture often produces forms of art which transform and affect the whole culture. Raymond Williams used the phrase 'structures of feeling' to refer to the systems of beliefs and values which are felt by people in their bones and experienced by them in their daily existence. These are at variance with, and antagonistic to, the dominant (aristocratic) ideologies which prevail in any society. Complex operations are at stake in this mechanism. Culture is a process, and not a fixed entity. Many factors interact in this complex process. Race, gender, socioeconomic factors, ethnicity, sexual differences—all these are involved in culture. The ever-dynamic oppositional values of culture help in challenging—even changing—the dominant ideology. Cultural criticism differs from new historicism in the following practices:

- It is overtly political in questioning the dominant forces, and supporting the oppressed groups. Its conviction is that it can resist and transform dominant power structures.
- It draws on Marxist and feminist ideologies.
- It is concerned mostly with popular forms of art and culture, but not always.

Though new historicism and cultural materialism have several factors in common, there are some features which distinguish one from the other. New historicism focuses on the collusion of beliefs, 'power of social and ideological structures'. Non-literary documents and literary texts are seen to be those which appropriate, through a process of negotiation, systems of thought prevalent in them. Cultural materialism, on the other hand, subverts and undermines the power grid. 'The result,' in the words of Peter Barry in *Beginning Theory* 'is a contrast between political optimism (cultural materialism) and political pessimism (new historicism)' (185). And then, 'the New Historicist situates the text in the political situation of his own day, while the Cultural Materialist situates it within that of ours' (Barry 186).

By way of an example, let us juxtapose the readings of Greenblatt and Dollimore of *King Lear.* In his essay, 'Shakespeare and the Exorcists', Greenblatt makes a comparative study of *King Lear* in relation to an unnoticed social document, *A Declaration of Egregious Popish Impostures* written by one Harsnett, in 1603, two years before Shakespeare's play made its first appearance. Harsnett demystifies exorcism, exposes the exorcists as frauds, and persuades the state to punish them. Greenblatt proves, with textual evidences, that Shakespeare uses the theatre for a similar purpose of ritual demystification of the supernatural. '*King Lear*'s relation to Harsnett's book,' Greenblatt adds, 'is essentially one of reiteration that signals a deeper and unexpressed institutional exchange.' Dollimore, on the other hand, interprets the play as questioning the values of Tudor monarchy. Dollimore writes:

> *King Lear* is above all, a play about power, prosperity and inheritance. . . A catastrophic redistribution of power and property—and, eventually a civil war—disclose the awful truth that these two things are somehow prior to the laws of human kindness rather than vice-versa. Human values are not antecedent to these material realities but are, on the contrary informed by them (*Radical Tragedy* 197).

Dollimore concludes the discussion of the play with the view that the materialist conception challenges all forms of literary criticism premised on essentialist humanism and idealist culture. More importantly, it invites a positive and explicit engagement with the historical, social and political realities with which literary criticism is basically concerned. While Greenblatt emphasises containment and consolidation, Dollimore discovers resistance and subversion.

New historicism and cultural criticism help us in many ways in strengthening our understanding of literature. They help us to see how literary texts participate in the circulation of discourses; how they are shaped, and, in turn, shape the cultures in which they exist; how the circulation of discourses and power structures affect our lives, and finally, how our own positioning (self-fashioning) determines and influences our interpretation of literary and non-literary texts.

Works Cited

Barry, Peter. *Beginning Theory: An Introduction to Literary Theory and Criticism.* Manchester: Manchester University Press, 1995.

Dollimore, Jonathan. *Radical Tragedy.* Sussex: The Harvester Press, 1984.

Greenblatt, Stephen. 'Towards a Poetics of Culture.' *The New Historicism*. Ed. H. Aram Veeser. London: Routledge, 1989.

Select Bibliography

Belsey, Catherine. *Critical Practice.* London: Routledge, 1980.

Dollimore, Jonathan. *Radical Tragedy.* Chicago: University of Chicago Press, 1984.

———. *Sex, Literature and Censorship.* Cambridge: Blackwell, 2001.

Dollimore, Jonathan and Alan Sinfield. *Political Shakespeare: New Essays in Cultural Materialism*. Ithaca, N.Y.: Cornell University Press, 1985.

Drakakis, John, ed. *Shakespearean Tragedy.* London: Longman, 1981.

———. ed. *Alternative Shakespeare,* London: Methuen, 1985.

Foucault, Michel. *The Foucault Reader.* Ed. Paul Rabinov. London: Penguin Books, 1991.

Greenblatt, Stephen. *Renaissance Self-Fashioning: from More to Shakespeare*. Chicago: University of Chicago Press, 1980.

———, ed. *Representing the English Renaissance.* Berkeley: California University Press, 1988.

———. *Shakespearean Negotiations: The Circulation of Social Energy in Renaissance England*. Berkeley: University of California Press, 1988.

———. *Will in the World: How Shakespeare became Shakespeare.* New York: W.W. Norton, 2004.

Greenblatt, Stephen and Catherine Gallagher. *Practicing New Historicism.* Chicago: University of Chicago Press, 2000.

Howard, Jean E. and O'Connor, Marion F, eds. *Shakespeare Reproduced: The Text in History and Ideology.* New York: Methuen, 1987.

Lyotard, Jean-Francois. *The Postmodern Condition: A Report on Knowledge.* Minneapolis: University of Minnesota Press, 1984.

Miller, J. Hillis. 'The Triumph of Theory.' *PMLA*, 102 (1987): 281–91.

Sinfield, Alan. *Literature, Politics and Culture in Postwar Britain.* Oxford: Blackwell, 1989.

———. *Cultural Politics: Queer Reading.* Philadelphia: University of Philadelphia Press, 1994.

———. *On Sexuality and Power.* New York: Columbia University Press, 2004.

Veeser, H. Aram, ed. *The New Historicism.* London: Routledge, 1989.

POSTCOLONIAL CRITICISM

> The island's mine, by Sycorax my mother,
> Which thou tak'st from me. When thou cam'st first
> Thou strok'st me, and made much of me; wouldst give me
> Water with berries in't; and teach me how
> To name the bigger light, and how the less,
> That burn by day and night: and then I lov'd thee,
> And show'd thee all the qualities o'th'isle,
> The fresh springs, brine-pits, barren place and fertile:
> Curs'd be I that did so! All the charms
> Of Sycorax, toads, beetles, bats, light on you!
> For I am all the subjects that you have,
> Which first was mine own king: and here you sty me
> In this hard rock, whiles you keep from me
> The rest o'th'island.
>
> William Shakespeare, *The Tempest*

Europe's dominance over the rest of the world began in the fifteenth century. The countries of Europe, England primarily, and to a lesser extent, France, Spain, Portugal and the Netherlands colonised many other countries and states, and the European empire extended over a large territory of the world. Great Britain was the single largest imperial power ruling over a quarter of the world by the end of the nineteenth century. India, Australia, New Zealand, Canada, many states of Africa, the West Indies, the Middle East and Southeast Asia came under British colonial rule which gradually came to an end at different times in the twentieth century. For India, the end of the British rule came after World War II when India attained independence in 1947. By 1980, England had lost almost all its colonial possessions. The concept of one nation ruling the other has become almost unthinkable in the present day.

As a discipline in literary studies, however, postcolonialism emerged during the late1980s or rather in the early 1990s of the last century. This discipline has now attained wide currency on account of the influence of such works as Frantz Fanon's *The Wretched of the Earth* (1961), Edward Said's *Orientalism* (1978), Homi Bhabha's *Nation and Narration* (1980), and Helen Tiffin and Bill Ashcroft's *The Empire Writes Back* (1989). But long before that there were anti-colonial political movements, which were responsible for getting independence and local self-governance for those countries that had been subject to an alien rule. The nomenclature 'postcolonialism' is used to refer 'to all the culture affected by the imperial process from the moment of colonisation to the present day.' Postcolonialism examines and analyses the aftermath of colonisation, and the effects of colonial oppression. In other words, it analyses the literature that was affected by the imperial process, the literature that grew in response to colonial domination, right from the time of contact between the coloniser and the colonised down to the contemporary situation. Its theoretical framework is different, however, from the criticism of other literature, such as British or American. It tries to unearth the operations and ideologies, political, economic, etc., at work during the period of colonisation. Colluding with the values of the colonisers, or resisting and challenging these are the essential part of the programme of the methodology employed in postcolonial criticism.

There is an inherent clash between the native, indigenous precolonial cultures, and the culture imposed on the natives by the imperial forces. Cultural colonisation still exists, and there has been no complete decolonisation. Much of postcolonial criticism is concerned with the loss of postcolonial identity. Colonialist discourse represents the language in which the colonisers expressed their superiority over the natives. The natives were uncivilised, lacking morals, and the Anglo-Europeans must educate them, because they were advanced in life. The whole native culture must be set aside. The colonisers were the centre, 'the self', and the colonised were the margins, 'the other'. This is the practice of 'othering' going by names such as 'the demonic other,' or the 'exotic other'. It is the result of the long-held arrogant and supercilious belief in the racial superiority of the Caucasian over the Asiatic. This attitude, of raising the European culture as the ultimate standard by which to measure the other cultures, is designated Eurocentrism which employs what is called the philosophy of 'universalism'. European ideas and experiences were universal, the standard for all others to follow. Eurocentric discourse is seen even in the division of the world: *First World* refers to Britain, Europe, and the USA; *Second World* to the white population of Canada, Australia, New Zealand, southern Africa, and the former Soviet Russia; *Third World*, the developing countries such as India, and countries in Africa, Central and South America, and Southeast Asia; *Fourth World*, the native populations subjugated by the white settlers, and governed by the majority culture that surrounds them: the native Americans, the aboriginal Australians, or non-white population with a minority status in First World countries, such as African-Americans in the USA. World history itself is organised in terms of the conquest by Europe, and not by the normal sense of past culture or history. How sad it ignores the existence of the earlier worlds such as Greece, Egypt, Africa, etc.! The term 'world war' is used to stand for the war between England and Germany, or between the US and Japan. The rest of the countries of the world—all of them far bigger in area and population—were not involved in the so-called world wars. What an irony!

Edward Said's *Orientalism* defines this Eurocentrism as practised in England, Europe, and the USA. Said was drawn to Foucaultian analysis of literature and culture as sites of political, and ideological struggle. 'Orientalism' is the discourse of the West about the East, a huge body of texts—literary, topographical, anthropological, historical, and sociological—that have been accumulating since the Renaissance. Said is concerned to show how this discourse is at once self-validating, constructing certain stereotypes which become accepted as self-evident facts . . . in collusion with political, and economic imperialism. Orientalism is a western style for dominating, restructuring, and having authority over the orient. It is the result of the arrogant and overbearing attitude of the nineteenth, and the early twentieth century European imperialism. Orientalism is a style of thought based upon an ontological and epistemological distinction between the orient and the occident. Without examining orientalism as a discourse, one cannot understand how European culture was able to manage its control over its colonies during the post-Enlightenment period. European culture gained in strength and identity by setting itself against the orient as a sort of surrogate self. The east is seen as a career, a place of business. One does not fail to notice that in the so-called cultural humanism of the high priests of culture from England—Arnold, Ruskin, Carlyle, Newman and even Eliot—the 'outsider' is totally banished. Culture stands for the whole edifice of knowledge and learning built by the Europeans, the true custodians of culture. Western historicism has homogenised world history from a privileged—and supposedly superior—position which culminates in Eurocentrism. It (orientalism) is an invention of the west, when it defines itself in positive terms, and throws all the mud on the countries which it had been able to conquer and subdue.

This colonialist ideology created colonial subjects who behaved in the way the coloniser had programmed. They willingly accepted the superiority of the British, and their own inferiority. It produced a 'cultural cringe,' so to speak. This phenomenon of imitating the West is called 'mimicry.' They (the colonial subjects) developed what is called a 'double consciousness,' that is, perceiving the world through the consciousness of the coloniser as well as through their own vision provided by their native culture. This is also termed unstable or double identity. The other term to refer to the divided self of the colonised is, to be 'unhomed' (not the same as homeless), or 'unhomeliness'. Enforced migrations, rootlessness and similar factors have caused an identity crisis. Alas! one becomes a psychological refugee, in not being able to feel at home even in one's own home. Many of those who live in decolonised nations now experience double consciousness and unhomeliness! How do we reclaim the pre-colonial past and how do we overcome the colonial ideology? These are the problems that postcolonial critics face. Some authors resort to writing in their own native language: Ngugi, the Kenyan writer, for instance. But they have to face the publishing industry, which is controlled by English publishers. It is not easy to recover the pre-colonial past which was lost many generations ago. Amnesia sets in. Culture always changes, and does not exist in the same pristine form. Change is the condition of art remaining as art. Nowadays, one notices that there has been an ongoing process of globalisation, resulting in a merger of these two cultures—the endemic and the alien. There are proponents arguing for each side, and the debate goes on endlessly. On the one side, there are those like Wole Soyinka, who plead for decolonisation. They maintain that we must assert the tradition of our native culture, recover and rejuvenate our past. There are those like Derek Walcott, who believe in hybridity, in encouraging cultural transplantation, and cross-pollination. Some argue positively that postcolonial identity is hybrid and constantly evolves by being in contact with newer forms. In the context of globalisation, this hybridity or syncretism is good. Rushdie, in his *Imaginary Homelands,* raises this existential question: 'What does it mean to be an "Indian" outside India?' and adds, 'To forget that there is a world beyond the community to which we belong, to confine ourselves within a narrowly defined cultural frontier would be to go voluntarily into that form of internal exile which in South Africa is called the "homeland" ' (15–17). Some ex-colonials feel the need to re-juvenate, and assert their native cultures in order not to be wholly consumed or inundated by foreign culture. This extreme form of adherence to the past, and the revival of the indigenous culture is called 'nativism' or 'nationalism'.

Postcolonial, or third world literatures follow a transition or periodisation of three phases which can be termed as 'adopt,' 'adapt', and 'adept' (as used by Helen Tiffin, and others). The phase of 'adopt' is that in which the European models are imitated, as these are supposed to be the best models universally acclaimed. The second stage of 'adapt' begins when the European form is modified to suit indigenous requirements. The third is the 'adept' phase in which the new literature breaks away from all the previous norms and conventions, and strikes a path creating a literature that is one's own. It is to this end, and towards such an attainment, contemporary literature of the third world moves. One cannot but notice such a movement in the history of Indian Writing in English, say from 1830 to the present day. K.R. Srinivasa Iyengar's *Indian Writing in English* strictly adheres to this pattern. It is only by invoking the absent European ethos and values, the true native reality could acquire legitimacy as a subject. That is why questions about sincerity and authenticity of experience are raised in any discussion of contemporary literature. We use Rushdie's phrase 'writing back to the centre' to describe this phenomenon. The centre has pushed the consciousness of the colonies. Every action has an equal and opposite reaction. 'The alienating process which initially served to relegate the post-colonial world to the "margin" turned upon itself and acted to push that world through a kind of mental barrier into a position from which all experience could be viewed as uncentred, pluralistic and multifarious. Marginality thus became an unprecedented source of creative energy' (Bill Ashcroft 12). This is what is known as decentring monocentrism, or better still, decentring Eurocentrism. The result of such writing back to the centre can be witnessed in a diaspora of writings that keep emerging in large numbers from the erstwhile commonwealth countries, the modern name for which is third world nations. Milan Kundera, the Czech novelist, predicts in his *Testaments Betrayed* (1995) that the future of the novel lies with the countries of the third world.

There is a lot of parallel between postcolonial criticism and feminism. A critic, Anne McClintock, observes in the book *Colonial Discourse and Postcolonial Theory*, 'In a world where women do two-thirds of the world's work, earn 10% of the world's income, and own less than 1% of the world's property, the promise of postcolonialism has been a history of hopes postponed' (298). In any discussion of postcolonial criticism some distinction has to be maintained between invader colonies that are colonies established among non-whites through force such as in India, and white settler colonies such as in Canada, Australia, New Zealand and southern Africa. The USA and Ireland are not generally termed postcolonial nations. White settler colonies share many common features with England, which is viewed as a mother country, and not as an invader. Racially, they are one, and on that score there is no reason for subjugation. But we cannot ignore the fact that the white colonial subjects too have faced cultural onslaught in the hands of the settler whites. Theirs is also a literature of resistance and protest. The voice of protest comes off most eloquently in the concluding stanza of A.D. Hope's poem, 'Australia'.

> Such savage and scarlet as no green hills dare
> Springs in that waste, some spirit which escapes
> The learned doubt, the chatter of cultured apes
> Which is called civilization over there.

Colonialism cannot be treated as a matter of the past. More subtle form of control emerges in what may be termed *neo-colonialism,* where the big powers hold the purse strings, and control the fate of the developing nations. Cultural imperialism of the USA, for instance, slowly destroys by cutting at the roots of indigenous cultures. Economically powerful nations dominate the weaker, and less powerful nations. Ironically, postcolonial criticism is itself a form of cultural imperialism. Imperial domination shapes the way we think of ourselves. Most of these critics, educated abroad, have nothing in common with the poor exploited beings of the countries they talk about. And the forms of analyses, and the theories of criticism they practise (deconstruction, for example) are a product of the metropolitan universities of the First World countries. Sometimes postcolonial criticism is used as just another way of (revisionist) reading the Western canon. Postcolonial literature may face the danger of being 'colonised' by the imperialism that dominates literary criticism and education the world over. Indian critics, such as Aijaz Ahmed, raise their voice of protest against such an attitude of parasitic intellectual dependence.

Themes advanced by postcolonial critics, in their readings and interpretations, can be summed up in the following terms: colonial encounter, and the disintegration of indigenous culture (*Things Fall Apart*), the journey of Europeans with native guides, colonial oppression, mimicry, exile, disillusionment, cultural identity, double consciousness, hybridity, unhomeliness and alienation. The analysis is generally to see how far a text is colonist or anticolonist. Achebe's 'An Image of Africa,' in *Research in African Literature,* uncovers the sub-text of Conrad's 'offensive and totally deplorable' novel *The Heart of Darkness* (acclaimed by the high-priest of criticism F.R. Leavis, as one among the greatest short novels in the English language). Achebe argues that the Africans are represented as barbaric, in contrast to the Europeans, despite the overt theme of anticolonialism. The Europeans conducting slave trade in Congo are heartless and greedy. Here is Achebe:

> . . . Conrad was a bloody racist. That this simple truth is glossed over in criticisms of his work is due to the fact that white racism against Africa is such a normal way of thinking that its manifestations go completely undetected . . . Africa as setting and backdrop which eliminates the African as human factor. Africa as a metaphysical battlefield devoid of all recognizable humanity . . . The real question is the dehumanization of Africa and Africans which this age-long attitude has fostered and continues to foster in the world. And the question is whether a novel which celebrates this dehumanization, which depersonalizes a portion of the human race, can be called a great work of art (9).

Homi Bhabha offers newer ways by suggesting that world literature might be studied in terms of the historical trauma people have suffered—'a focus on . . . the unspoken, unrepresented pasts that haunt the historical present.' Historical reality can be seen as affecting personal lives of people, rather than as happening on a large national scale. Helen Tiffin suggests a 're-reading and re-writing of the European historical and fictional record.' She suggests the use of 'colonial counter discourse' in which 'a postcolonial writer takes up a character or characters or the basic assumptions of a British canonical text, and unveils its assumptions, subverting the text for post-colonial purposes.' *Jane Eyre, Robinson Crusoe,* and *The Tempest* are studied through this method. Edward Said rereads *Mansfield Park* in a similar way moving the margins of a work to the centre.

Any discussion of postcolonialism cannot afford to bypass some of the following basic issues: the conception and representation of the empire, nationalisation and globalisation, its relationship with postmodernism and feminism, the play and place of language, material practices and control of production. All these issues are implied in the experience of postcoloniality.

Works Cited

Achebe, Chinua. 'The Image of Africa.' *Research in African Literature.* 9.1 (Spring 1978).

Ashcroft, Bill, Gareth Griffiths and Helen Tiffin, eds. *The Empire Writes Back.* London: Routledge, 1989.

Rushdie, Salman. *Imaginary Homelands.* London: Granta Books, 1971.

Williams, Patrick and Laura Chrisma, eds. *Colonial Discourse and Postcolonial Theory.* New York: Columbia UP, 1994.

Select Bibliography

Aijaz, Ahmad. *In Theory: Classes, Nations, Literatures.* London: Verso, 1992.

Ashcroft, Bill, Griffiths, Gareth and Helen Tiffin, eds. *The Empire Writes Back: Theory and Practice in Post-Colonial Literature.* London: Routledge, 1989.

———, eds. *The Post-Colonial Studies Reader.* London: Routledge, 1995.

Bhabha, Homi. *Nation and Narration.* London: Routledge, 1990.

———. *Location of Culture.* 1994. London: Routledge, 2004.

Bhabha, Homi and W.J.T. Mitchell, eds. *Edward Said: Continuing the Conversation.* Chicago: University of Chicago Press, 2005.

Fanon, Frantz. *The Wretched of the Earth.* Trans. C. Farrington. Harmondsworth: Penguin, 1961.

———. *Black Skin White Masks.* London: Paladin, 1970.

Gates, Henry Louis Jr., ed. *Black Literature and Literary Theory.* London and New York: Methuen, 1984.

———. *The Signifying Monkey: A Theory of Afro-American Criticism.* New York: Oxford University Press, 1988.

Greenblatt, Stephen and Catherine Gallagher. *Practicing New Historicism.* Chicago; University of Chicago Press, 2000.

Griffiths, Gareth. *A Double Exile: African and West Indian Writing between Two Cultures.* London: Marion Boyars, 1978.

JanMohammed, Abdul. *Manichean Aesthetics: The Politics of Literature in Colonial Africa*. Amherst: University of Massachusetts Press, 1983.

King, Bruce. *The New Literatures in English*. London: Macmillan, 1980.

Lamming, George. *The Pleasures of Exile*. London: Allison and Busby, 1960.

Matthews, John. P. *Tradition in Exile*. Toronto: University of Toronto Press, 1962.

Ngugi wa Thiong'o. *Decolonising the Mind: The Politics of Language in African Literature*. London: Curry, 1986.

Said, Edward. *Orientalism*. London: Routledge, 1978.

———. *The World, the Text and the Critic*. Cambridge, Mass: Harvard University Press, 1983.

———. *Culture and Imperialism*. London: Chatto and Windus, 1993.

———. *Humanism and Democratic Criticism*. New York: Columbia University Press, 2004.

Soyinka, Wole. *Myth, Literature and the African World*. Cambridge: Cambridge University Press, 1976.

Spivak, Gayatri Chakravorty. *In Other Worlds: Essays in Cultural Politics*: London: Routledge, 1987.

———, ed. *The Post-Colonial Critic: Interviews, Strategies, Dialogues*. London: Routledge, 1990.

Viswanathan, Gauri. *Masks of Conquest: Literary Studies and British Rule in India*. New York: Columbia University Press, 1989.

———, ed. *Power, Politics, and Culture: Interviews with Edward Said*. New York: Pantheon Books, 2001.

Young, Robert. *White Mythologies: Writing, History and the West*. London: Routledge, 1990.

READER-RESPONSE CRITICISM

Way back in the 1920s, I.A. Richards said that arts are the storehouses of wisdom, implying that they affect us by playing upon our emotions. They satisfy our 'appetencies,' and enlarge our potentialities, leading to a richer and fuller life. One is never the same before and after reading a book. In a vague sense, Richards can be called the forerunner of reader-response (also called audience-oriented) criticism. Based on philosophic grounds, there can be another route to reader-response criticism through phenomenology. The Greek origin of this word means, 'to bring to light'. In the twentieth century, phenomenology gained ground as a major subject of study. The German philosopher Kant uses the term to make a distinction between the study of essences (from which New Criticism is derived), and the study of the phenomena or appearances (from which reader-response criticism derives). Hegel uses the term to denote the study of the appearance of consciousness. In literary study, two tendencies, both of which are the outcome of Phenomenology, are noticeable. The Polish philosopher, Roman Ingarden (1895–1970) developed the theory of aesthetics as applied to the mode of existence of a work of literature. The other is usually associated with the 'Geneva school' which is concerned with the practice of criticism, and not with its mode of existence. The critics of the Geneva school conceived of literature as a manifestation of the author's consciousness which the critic tries to appropriate. This view is also held by Indian aestheticians. In the words of Hillis Miller, criticism becomes 'primarily consciousness of the consciousness of another, the transportation of the mental universe of an author into the interior space of the critic's mind.'

The title 'reader-response criticism' justifies what this criticism means, but the fact is that it is not just the response that matters (as in the case of Richards): it is the analysis of *how* we respond to a given text that matters. And that is what accounts for its success or the lack thereof. In the context of literary studies, it is still evolving, and it helps us to understand our own reading processes. As a pedagogic tool it is most helpful, and most frequently resorted to in classroom situations. Do we not hear teachers say, 'Do not worry about what critics say. What is your response?' The idea that the process of reading requires special attention took root as early as the 1930s as a reaction to, and rejection of the tendency propagated by New Criticism that the role of the reader does not matter at all. The meaning of a text is contained in the text, and it is not the product of the author or the reader. Witness, for example, the twin essays, 'The Intentional Fallacy', and 'The Affective Fallacy' which are two of the most uncompromising texts forwarded by the proponents of the school. As Wimsatt and Beardsley put it:

> The Intentional Fallacy is confusion between the poem and its origins . . . It begins by trying to derive the standard of criticism from the psychological *causes* of the poem and ends in biography and relativism. The Affective Fallacy is a confusion between the poem and its *results* (what it *is* and what it *does*). . . . It begins by trying to derive the standard of criticism from the psychological effects of the poem and ends in impressionism and relativism. The outcome of either Fallacy, the Intentional or the Affective, is that the poem itself, as an object of specifically critical judgment, tends to disappear (345).

Against this apotheosis of the physical text, reader-response critics react vigorously. They hold the view diametrically opposite. 'Objectivity of the text is an illusion,' as Stanley Fish would say. A work is not an achieved structure of meanings. Far from it, it is the result or the outcome of the evolving process of reading. The work has no independent existence. Rather, it is the experience of the reader who opens it up (even in the literal sense). For the reader-response critics, what the text *does* is what matters; not so much what the text *is*. They are sure of their ground that the

- readers do not merely consume the texts passively; instead they are actively involved in constructing a meaning out of it.
- the part played by the reader can by no means be ignored in any literary understanding.

Before getting into a discussion of the process of reading, should we not know about the agent who performs the activity—the Reader, with capital R. Who is the reader? Anyone who reads? Not as simple as that. For the New Critics, a literary text is a structure of stratified norms. It exists for its own sake. For reader-response critics, a literary text (or any text for that matter) cannot have an independent existence. It comes into existence, and acquires life only when a reader reads. The reader is absent when the writer writes, and the writer is normally absent when the reader reads. Readers can be classified broadly into two classes: the ideal (or the hypothetical), and the actual (or the real or the empirical). The usual tendency on our part is to ignore the actual reader, and then idealise readers. Kenneth Burke's essay 'Psychology and Form' is a good starting point for a discussion on readers and reading. He treats the reader as a variable, depending on the work concerned and not as an abstraction. Different readers have different expectations from a work: they ask different questions. Have we not heard of such terms as the feminist reader, or *Paradise Lost* and the seventeenth century reader? Sometimes the word 'narratee' (mostly in discussions in narratology) is used to designate the ideal reader. The narratee is the one whom the narrator addresses. Often the narratee is conceived as someone, who is part of the narration, an imagined character, as it were. The dramatic monologue is addressed to the narratee.

Wolfgang Iser uses the term 'implied reader' to refer to the reader who will respond in full measure to the demands made by the text. It is the reader whom the text addresses. We are reminded of Wayne Booth's term 'implied author' to refer to the intelligence or faculty that superintends the work, as different from the biographical author, the corporeal being who lives, who has a local habitation and a name. Iser develops the idea of the 'implied reader' as both a textual entity and a process of meaning production. It encompasses the prestructuring and the potential meaning as well as the reader's concretisation of the meaning. It is at once textual and imbued with consciousness. Hence, he is a phenomenological reader, a transcendental model, not empirical as an 'informed reader'. There is the 'intended reader', whom the author has in mind when he writes the work. Technical writings and social documents are meant for particular audiences. Jonathan Culler develops the term 'competent reader': one who has learnt or mastered the skills required to understand or interpret a text. The academy of English studies, for example, exposes students to terms such as the metaphor, the simile, etc., knowledge of which is a requirement for literary understanding. All these readers mentioned so far are mental constructs. The actual reader is a living being who brings to bear upon the text he reads, his accumulated knowledge of the world, with his personal predilections. Of the actual readers, the 'informed reader' is not a Tom, Dick, or Harry; but one who is educated, whose understanding and experience of the world is so comprehensive, that it can be relied upon, and accepted by a majority. He/she has the competence to experience the text in all its linguistic and literary complexity, and the ability to suppress personal responses. Indian aestheticians use the much-loaded term *sahrudaya.* This person is a perceptive reader—at once responsive and responsible—who is capable of a total identification with the art and the artist. There is far too much in this seemingly little term. He is not the result of a sudden spurt of education. There is a long process of *samskara* involved. He is not a unit but part of continuity. Indian aestheticians employ the metaphor of a rock that subsides into dust which is swept down in a river to describe the process of the emergence of a *sahrudaya* from constant and continuous immersions in the flow of poetry. He is the result of an unremitting refinement acquired through several births. There is a participatory communion between him and the work. He is no more an individual, but an all-man in the metaphysical experience, an overpowering experience, neither painful nor pleasurable—that is *ananda.* The duality between the text and the reader merges, and there is total identity between 'being' and 'becoming'. The Western mind has not conceived of this term in such a profound Vedic sense!

Not only do different readers read one and the same text differently but the same reader may read one and the same text differently on different occasions. A text is not a physical object alone, but it is something like an event, and an interaction with the reader creates the text. Birds of the same feather fly together. This is not true of the reader-response critics. Feminists and deconstructionists have more similarities than differences. Reader-response critics share the same assumptions; but they do not have a shared methodology in their approaches to a work. Reader-oriented theories are not necessarily united by a single, uniform methodology, though they may have a common goal in view. 'It is not one field but many, not a single widely trodden path but a multiplicity of crisscrossing, often divergent tracks.' But they are one in their belief that writing and reading are two names for the same activity, and it is not possible to separate the perceiver from the perceived, or the subject from the object. Their disagreements with which we are concerned centre on questions such as these: What is the act of reading? What is the source for the authority of interpretation? Does reading refer to the product, or the process? Is reading a completed, finished act or is it a temporal activity? The general theory of the school is usually classified into four sections:

1. transactional reader-response theory
2. affective stylistics
3. subjective reader-response theory
4. psychological reader-response theory

Transactional Reader-response Theory: This theory was originally formulated by Louise Rosenblatt. The literary work is the result of the transaction between the text and the reader. As we read on, the text corrects our interpretations. Our approach should be aesthetic, and not merely focussing on the facts contained in the text. There are what are called the determinate meanings which refer to the facts in the text, and there are indeterminate meanings which refer to the 'gaps' in the text that force the readers to create the meanings. An example, usually used in this context, is one of Wordsworth's 'Lucy' poems. This is a poem which is a focal point of critical enterprise, like Hopkins's 'The Windhover', or Edgar Allan Poe's 'The Purloined Letter' or Henry James's 'The Figure in the Carpet'. This short lyric, in two stanzas, comes in handy as it serves our purpose.

> A slumber did my spirit seal:
> I had no human fears;
> She seemed a thing that could not feel
> The touch of earthly years.
>
> No motion has she now, no force;
> She neither hears nor sees;
> Rolled round in earth's diurnal course,
> With words, and stones, and trees.

The poem contains two statements, one in each of the stanzas. The 'I' of the poem is known to us as the narrator of Wordsworth's poem, whereas the 'she' who is the protagonist is an unknown being, assumed to be Lucy. Stanza one says that the poet thought that she (Lucy) could not die, whereas stanza two contradicts this view saying, or implying, that she is dead. The space between the two stanzas is filled in by the reader, depending on the reader's background, belief and upbringing. The reader does this by bringing to bear upon the poem, his/her reading of the poem. Lucy is dead. Her physical body has ceased to exist. But she has merged and become one with the natural world. Thus she has attained immortality. There can be no more deaths for her. In the first stanza, she is a 'thing', and so was immortal, and in the second she has achieved immortality by becoming a part of the diurnal motion of the earth. The poem is a lament on the death of an innocent girl. She was a mortal. Her death is an occasion for rejoicing and celebrating, as she has returned to the world of nature, thus achieving immortality. Wordsworth, incidentally, was a pantheist who believed in nature worship. The continuous interplay between these two meanings (the determinate and the indeterminate) is what constitutes reading; and this process of reading involves retrospection, anticipation, fulfilment, revision, and so on. Determinate meanings may become indeterminate as our focus shifts, and our point of view varies.

The widely known German critic Wolfgang Iser develops, after Roman Ingarden, the phenomenological approach to the reading process. For him, meaning is not contained in the text itself, but generated in the reading process. Meaning is the result of an interaction between the text and the reader. By filling the gaps or the indeterminacies in the text, the reader completes the work, and participates in the production of its meaning. All art objects have an infinite number of determinants, and no single act of cognition can take into account all these determinants. Hence, the indeterminacy in a literary work. It could be limited by context, but not entirely eliminated. Filling of the indeterminacies is called concretisation. For Iser, the reality of a text is not the reflection of the real world that exists prior to, and outside of, the text, but rather, a reaction to the world constituted in a textual universe. Our encounter with the world is real, but with the text it is fictional. Literary texts have a greater pedagogical value than other textual experiences. Iser distinguishes between the text, its concretisation, and the work of art. The first is what is given to us by the author, the second is the reader's activity of producing the text, and the work of art lies between these two. It lies at the point where the text and the reader converge. 'The wandering viewpoint' is that which describes the reader from within the text. The reading process involves a dialectical process of change and self-realisation for the reader. He constructs himself in the process of reading. According to Iser, the reading activity through which our meaning is constructed is prestructured in the text. The text contains, and controls the responses of the reader. Though the reader creates the meaning, the text guides him through this construction. Every reading is a collaborative effort between the text (the given object) and the reader (the producing subject). The text proposes; the reader disposes. The text allows for a wide range of meanings, and supports them. But not all readings are acceptable. Even the author's meaning is no exception. The authority of the text must be relied upon.

Iser's work has come in for a good deal of discussion. Stanley Fish, for example, raises objections to his refusal to take a firm stand, and his compromise on several issues. On the question of determinacy, Fish says that the blanks in a text do not exist independent of the reader; nor do they exist prior to the act of interpretation. Interacting with the text and interacting with the world are activities which are mediated. In the same way, there is nothing totally indeterminate, since all the time the reader operates within an interpretative framework. There is no such thing as something being given, and something being supplied. The whole activity is fluid. Interpretation takes place between the textual givens, and the reader's contribution. But each interpretative strategy is valid only within a particular system of intelligibility.

Affective Stylistics: This theory is usually associated with Stanley Fish. It is also based on the assumption that the literary text is not just an object that exists, but takes its existence from the act of reading. In his essay 'Affective Stylistics', he attacks the notion that reading is a finished activity, and substitutes a temporal view in place of a spatial view. The text is put to a close examination to know how stylistically it affects the reader, or rather how the sequence of words on a printed page gets converted to a felt experience. Sure enough, there is focus on the text, but it is not an autonomous entity (the departure from transactional theory). The results occur within the reader. The attention is focused on what sentences *do* rather than on what they mean or what they propose. A sentence for him is 'an action made upon a reader rather than a container from which a reader extracts a message'. Stanley Fish describes the process of the structure of the text as it occurs from moment to moment, when it undergoes the process of being read. It should not be mistaken for the impressionistic responses of the reader, but should be understood as the cognitive analysis of the reading process, resulting from specific and particular elements in the text. The process is described in 'slow-motion'; it is a word-by-word, or phrase-by-phrase, analysis of the response of the reader. The reader travels from one word to another, even as one eats food spoon after spoon, or morsel after morsel. At every convenient point, there is a pause in order to make sense of what is read, and to get ready to adjust to what is to be expected or anticipated. These expectations may or may not be fulfilled. Often, they are not. The mistakes in expectations, and later corrections are inherent in any reading process, and are inevitable to it. There is always a continuous adjustment of perceptions. To quote Fish, 'Meaning is an *event*, something that happens, not on the page, where we are often accustomed to look for it, but in the interaction between the flow of print (or sound) and the actively mediating consciousness of a reader-hearer.' Hence, the meaning of the text is not the outcome of what the text says; rather the meaning is the experience of what the text does to one as one reads it. Generally, other evidences (such as thematic) are used to support and corroborate the claim that the text is the experience of reading. This is done to justify the validity of the reading. It is the text which plays the most significant role in establishing the experience of the reader.

In the later criticism of Fish, there is a shift of focus from reading as an individual experience to reading as a collective endeavour. Reading, for him, always takes place within what he calls 'interpretive communities'. All of us who are readers belong to an interpretive community, which is to say that we share the strategies of interpretation that we employ when we read texts. These are the outcome of assumptions about literature and reading practices that are institutionalised by cultural attitudes and philosophies. For example, music critics, and film critics belong to two different interpretive communities, each with its own tools and modes of understanding, with its own well-developed epistemology. Interpretive communities evolve all the time. We do not interpret poems, but we create them in this sense. Interpretive strategies are limited, and these control the interpretations. In order to monitor the waywardness, and excesses that might result in any individual reader, Fish developed this concept. Every reading is bound by its own laws. We would rather give it the name social reader-response criticism. It does not offer newer or more startling ways of reading texts: nor does it take side with any one method of interpretation. There is a lot of controversy associated with the microscopic examination of the reading process, as described by Fish. The reader's response, in Fish's theory, is arbitrary and ungrounded. The reader seems to start every sentence afresh without any history of reading. He 'never learns anything from his reading'. And retrospective reflection on a text's overall meaning and coherence is simply banished from the realm of reading. Fish's unified reader cannot account for many complex responses. His interpretive communities are concerned with the specification on the grounds of possibility that makes interpretation possible.

Subjective Reader-response Theory: David Bleich is the major spokesman of this theory. It shows a radical departure from the two theories we have mentioned. In them, we learnt that the text guides and controls the reader in the reading process. The text serves as the base. Bleich's theory is that our response is not determined by the text. According to him, reading is wholly a subjective matter, and the nature of what is perceived is determined solely by the perceiver. The reader's interpretations create the literary text. He talks about real and symbolic objects. The act of reading creates a conceptual, symbolic world. Reading is symbolisation. We interpret the meaning of this symbolisation. When we wish to explain our experience we resymbolise. The text is there in our mind. The text, therefore, is the written response of the readers. How are we to arrive at knowledge from out of our experience of reading? The objective is self-understanding. This method instils a way or mode of critical thinking, since knowledge is created and that is the main concern of this theory.

Psychological Reader-response Theory: Norman Holland advanced this theory. What we do when we read a literary text is not in any sense different from what we do in a real-life situation, psychologically speaking. He has Freudian leanings in his use of concepts. A work of literature projects fantasies, and our interpretations of literary texts fulfil our psychological needs. The source of pleasure for a reader lies in the transformation of the unconscious wishes through a literary work. The individual's subjective response is a close encounter with the fantasies created by the work. The strategies by which we cope with our psychological conflicts are called the identity theme. We project this into the text which we read, and unconsciously create the text. Our interpretations are the result of the desire, fears, etc., which we read into the text. It is a psychological process. This is divided into a defence mode when our psychological defences are raised by the text, a fantasy mode which discovers ways of tranquillising the defences, and a transforming mode which uses these two for interpreting the work.

Reader-response criticism, as pointed out earlier, is not the analysis of a literary text, but the analysis of the response of readers to the text. It has gone a long way in changing the traditional methods in teaching and learning pedagogy. It has helped in close, slow, and deliberate reading of texts. The travel is what matters; reaching the destination in great haste is not the end in view. Judgments and evaluation have never been its aims. For the most part, it remained an academic enterprise focused on the classroom, on the canon established so fervently by New Criticism. In recent times, reader-response critics have tried to place texts in a historical/cultural setting in order to prove that reading is determined by the prevailing ideology of the times as well as by race and gender and class considerations. Feminist and postcolonial criticism encourage this practice. The impact can be seen in the formation of the canon in literary studies, and the debate on what constitutes it. Traditionalists raise the question whether all these theories about the practice of reading will undermine and dehumanise all our views about literature and its meaning. Reader-response theory is not a movement in the strict sense. The turn towards the reader has had an enormous impact on literary studies, by reorienting critical discussions and debate. In the post-war era, the return to the reader—with a bang—is a major shift in critical perspective

Reception Theory: It is also called the 'aesthetics of reception', meaning thereby the ways in which a text has met with its reception over a historical period of time. If reader-response theory is concerned with the microcosm of response, reception theory is concerned with the macrocosm of response.

In 1967, Robert Jauss, Professor of Romance Languages, University of Constance, Germany delivered a lecture on 'Literary History as a Provocation to Literary Scholarship', which created a stir by way of altering (and revitalising) prevailing notions on literary studies and literary history, in particular. He proposed a shift in the study of literature from a preoccupation with authors and texts to a concern with reading and reception, in general. He rejected the aesthetics that valorises the synchronic over the diachronic. He said, 'A literary work is not an object which stands by itself and which offers the same face to each reader in each period. It is not a monument which reveals its timeless essence in a monologue' (14). The focus should be on the altering response of the general audience, the public at large. Historically, readers who come at a later point of time have an access to the response of the earlier generation of readers. Thus, out of a cumulative response, there grows an evolving, modifying historical tradition. And this helps in rewriting literary histories. *Hamlet*, for example has a four-hundred-year-old history, ever since the play was first produced in 1601. A contemporary reader of the play has an accumulated knowledge of the play, as a result of its theatre and interpretative history, which an Elizabethan reader could not have had. Literary works are situated in a larger continuum of events. Works of the past are affected (and even conditioned) by current events and writings. 'Literature can only be meaningful for us, in so far as it can be understood as the prehistory of a present experience. Past meanings are thus understood as an integral part of the present practices, and literature acquires meaning as one important source of mediation.' A work of literature is not just a reflection of past social order. It alters our social concerns, here and now. Thus, literary history helps us in conceiving of our literary heritage in newer, and, yet newer ways.

Works Cited

Jauss, Hans Robert. 'Literary History as a Challenge to Literary Theory.' *New Directions in Literary History*. Ed. Ralph Cohen. London: Routledge and Kegan Paul, 1974.

Wimsatt, William K and Munroe C. Beardsley. 'The Affective Fallacy.' *Twentieth Century Literary Criticism.* Ed. David Lodge. London: Longman, 1972.

Select Bibliography

Bleich, David. *Subjective Criticism.* Baltimore: Johns Hopkins University Press, 1978.

Eco, Umberto. *The Role of the Reader: Explorations in the Semiotics of Texts.* Bloomington: Indiana University Press, 1979.

Fetterley, Judith. *The Resisting Reader: A Feminist Approach to American Fiction.* Bloomington: Indiana University Press, 1978.

Fish, Stanley. *Is There a Text in this Class? The Authority of Interpretive Communities.* Cambridge, Mass: Harvard University Press, 1980.

———. *Professional Correctness: Literary Studies and Political Change.* New York: Clarendon Press, 1995.

———. *How Milton Works.* Cambridge, Mass.: Harvard University Press, 2001.

Holland, Norman. *The Dynamics of Literary Response.* New York: Oxford University Press,1968.

———. *5 Readers Reading.* New Haven: Yale University Press, 1975.

Ingarden, Roman. *The Literary Work of Art.* Evanston, IL: Northwestern University, 1973.

Iser, Wolfgang. *The Implied Reader.* Baltimore: The Johns Hopkins University Press, 1974.

———. *The Act of Reading: A Theory of Aesthetic Response.* Baltimore: Johns Hopkins University Press, 1978.

———. *The Range of Interpretation.* New York: Columbia University Press, 2000.

Jauss, Hans-Robert. *Toward an Aesthetic Reception.* Minneapolis: University of Minnesota Press. 1982.

Rosenblatt Louise. *The Reader, the Text, the Poem: The Transactional Theory of the Literary Work.* Carbondale: Southern Illinois University Press, 1978.

Suleiman, Susan and Inge Crosman, eds. *The Reader in the Text: Essays on Audience and Interpretation.* Princeton, N.J.: Princeton University Press, 1980.

Tompkins, Jane P. Ed. *Reader-Response Criticism: From Formalism to Post-Structuralism.* Baltimore: Johns Hopkins University Press, 1980.

FEMINIST CRITICISM

> I myself have never been able to find out precisely what Feminism is: I only know that other people call me a feminist whenever I express sentiments that differentiate me from a doormat or a prostitute.
>
> *Rebecca West*

> Feminism is the place where in the most natural, organic way subjectivity and politics have to come together.
>
> *Adrienne Rich*

The complaint lodged by women is that literary criticism, since the days of Aristotle, has consistently excluded their achievements. By way of redressing the balance, feminist criticism seeks to challenge traditional notions and establish, instead, the perspectives and experiences of women which had been marginalised for ages and ages. The two axioms on which feminism is built are 1. gender difference is the foundation for structural inequality between men and women by which women suffer sympathetic social injustice, and 2. the inequality between the sexes is not the result of biological necessity, but is produced by cultural construction of gender differences.

The agenda of feminism, therefore, is to understand the social and psychic mechanism that constructs and perpetuates gender inequality, and change it, as much as possible. Feminist literary criticism aims to study the ways in which cultural representations, like literature, undermine and reinforce the economic, social, political, and psychological suppression and oppression of women in society. In fact, it would be proper to call the field *feminisms*, if a plural of an abstract noun may be permitted. Feminism is conspicuous by its diaspora. The feminist movement, women's liberation movement, etc., are active social bodies and institutions which fight for women's rights. This has even become a global issue these days. There are platforms and media support for these women empowerment movements. We are not concerned here with such social and political movements. We are concerned with feminism as an academic discipline, an intellectual inquiry that goes by the name of 'women's studies'. This academic discipline, as it prevails today as a self-conscious movement, should be understood as the direct product of the 'women's movement' of the 1960s. It is to be seen as one of the practical ways by which to spread its ideals of freedom and equality, and transform patriarchal notions. Literary study is, perhaps, the most powerful medium to stimulate public minds.

Up until the nineteenth century, women were scarcely an influential presence in public life, even in the so-called advanced countries. They were powerless to counter the prevailing view of male supremacy. They felt that male supremacy was even desirable. A woman's place was supposed to be in the home. She was the 'angel of the home', as the poet Coventry Patmore called her. John Ruskin, the political philosopher, in his essay 'Lilies: Of Queens' Gardens' says, 'The man's work for his own home is, to secure its maintenance, progress, and defence; the woman's, to secure its order, comfort and loveliness' (75). It still operates the same way in many countries of the world, where woman is meant for bearing and rearing children. In the western world, women were largely preoccupied with getting access to the ballot box, family support and preservation. They were content with the private world of family and domesticity. They were wives, mothers, caretakers, nurturers, and homemakers. The cultural anthropologist, Levi-Strauss, considers that women have always been passive objects in the final decisions of marriage. Brides were—and still are—chosen by men. Aristotle, Aquinas, and Donne—all held the view that form is masculine, while matter is feminine. The mother was supposed to be no parent at all in Greek mythology. Milton wrote in his *Paradise Lost,* 'He (Adam) for God only: she (Eve) for God in him.'

In the past, we have had some landmark studies on this subject. Shelley's mother-in-law Mary Wollstonecraft's book *A Vindication of the Rights of Woman* (1792), and John Stuart Mill's *The Subjection of Women* (1879), deserve special mention. At a time when male supremacy was taken for granted (political power, property rights and reputation rested with men), and it was an unwritten convention that woman should obey man, these works articulated, in no uncertain terms, the sense of discrimination created by such an inequality between the sexes. Since then feminism has sought to offset the complacent certainties of patriarchal culture, assert sexual equality, and eradicate sexist domination – the sperm versus ovum nexus. Women writers have always had to work 'against the grain', so to say. Feminist criticism seeks to free itself from time-honoured and naturalised patriarchal notions by subverting them. The goal is to expose the misogyny involved in the literary production and practice of the past. To do this, there is no one method, but a plurality of methods. A conjoined effort was seen to be necessary. It is even fashionable these days to term it 'cultural politics', rather than 'feminist theory'.

In the twentieth century, continuing the efforts of the previous century, some highly reputed women writers have articulated their views, and raised fundamental issues. Virginia Woolf's *A Room of One's Own* (1929), Simone de Beauvoir's *The Second Sex* (1949), Kate Millet's *Sexual Politics* (1969) are invaluable studies, indispensable to an understanding of the case for feminism. Since the 1970s, there has been a proliferation of feminist writings, the world over. Some of the basic issues raised by feminist literary criticism can be classified thus:

- Western society is entrenched in patriarchal ideology and controlled by it: in consequence, women are kept in subjugation.
- Men always establish norms, and women are defined as the 'other' with reference to these norms.
- Sex and gender are entirely different from each other, and need to be distinguished. Sex is biologically determined, while gender is created by society/culture.
- The be-all and end-all of feminist criticism is to promote gender equality.

We may now examine some of these issues. Feminist theory, broadly, chooses two areas to tackle these issues and develop what critics call a 'criticism of their own'—woman as reader, and woman as writer. The first task is to scrutinise the literature of the past with a view to exposing the notorious patriarchal ideology inscribed in it, and subject it to a re-visionary, re-reading from the perspective of the woman. This task has involved a re-interpretation of the classics. The curriculum of women's studies begins with a project that encourages students to read literature afresh. Feminist critics quote from the Scripture: 'the Lord God formed every beast of the field and every fowl of the air, and brought them unto the man to see what he would call them; and whatsoever the man called every living creature, that was the name thereof' (Genesis 2: 19), and often use this as a paradigm for patriarchal supremacy. Language is man-made. Freud's formulation of the theory of the 'Oedipus complex' keeps out of consideration all the women in the world, which is one-half of the human race. If this is not patriarchy, what else is? Hence, they would examine female characters in male-authored works as well as in the works by women in order to show which of the images of women are more authentic. This is done with a view to exposing the misogyny even in famous works of literature. Male authors may depict strong women characters that support family values, and female authors may create stereotypes of women. Judith Fetterly's *Resisting Reader* has proved most influential in its attempt to re-read classics. In the American classic *Rip Van Winkle,* for example, the woman reader is drawn to identify herself not with the dame, the woman of the house who represents family, community, etc., but with the male Rip and his adventures in the woods and his drinking at the inn. A woman is coerced into identifying against herself, against the virtues womanhood has stood for.

Wordsworth's 'Lucy' is usually used as a standard example for such readings, since the poem lends itself to such a treatment. Here is the poem:

> She dwelt among the untrodden ways
> Beside the springs of Dove,
> A maid whom there were none to praise
> And very few to love.
>
> A violet by a mossy stone
> Half-hidden from the eye!
> —Fair as a star, when only one
> Is shining in the sky!
>
> She lived unknown, and few could know
> When Lucy ceased to be,

But she is in her Grave, and Oh!
The difference to me.

From the feminist point of view, the poem has precious little to convey the inner life of Lucy, though overtly the poem is all about her. Lucy as a living being, with her own feelings, does not come through. As a quiet, humble, and passive being, she is only the object of Wordsworth's sympathetic condescending consideration. As is so often remarked in references to phallocentrism, 'to be male is to be human, to be female is to be the other.' And this short lyric exemplifies it in full measure. The poem is all about Wordsworth, the great poet, and not at all about Lucy, the poor girl!

There are many such instances of feminist re-reading. Harriet Beecher Stowe's *Uncle Tom's Cabin,* which was once dismissed as a trashy and sentimental novel of slavery, is now read as an early novel that glorifies virtues of family life and motherhood. Works of male authors such as D.H. Lawrence, Ernest Hemingway, and works such as *Jane Eyre* and *Mill on the Floss* by women writers have come in for re-interpretations. Even Shakespeare's tragedies have not escaped the attention of feminist readings. The great tragedies are read as androcentric, 'masculine dramas of self-definition', privileging male experience and portraying it as universal. The grand soliloquies of the tragic heroes, lapped up by ravenous generations, bear witness to this view. Ruskin, whom we quoted earlier, however, holds a different view. For him, 'Shakespeare has no heroes; he has only heroines . . . He represents them as infallibly faithful and wise counsellors—incorruptibly just and pure examples—strong always to sanctify, even when they cannot save' (55).

The second on the agenda of feminism is woman as writer. Here again, two factors are involved. The first is to unearth forgotten women talents, bring to light those women writers of the past who are unheard of. The second function is to create a whole body of literature by women and of women. Elaine Showalter gives the name *gynocriticism* to stand for the dual function. The focal elements of *gynocriticism*, according to her, are:

- Biology: To question biological essentialism, that is, the premise of patriarchy that a woman is a womb, a receptacle for male domination. To use the very attributes in women's biological features (childbirth, rearing of children, etc.) as a motif in writings with a view to celebrating it.

- Experience: To portray woman as a source of immense values in life as well as in art. There lie vast areas of delicate emotions and perceptions of women (subjectivity) that are specific to women's experiences, not available to men.
- Discourse: Women are caught up in a prison-house of language that is male-specific. Contest this and create woman's language (WL) which will be distinctively feminine in its style and structure.
- The unconscious: The female principle is to lie outside the definition of the male.
- Social and economic conditions: In writings reject notions of universal feminism. Encourage plurality and the concept of the diaspora.

Quite a few works have successfully implemented this. Elaine Showalter's *A Literature of Their Own* (1977), and Sandra Gilbert and Susan Gubar's *The Madwoman in the Attic* (1979) are two excellent works which have accomplished the task of rediscovering neglected women's talents. Less known authors like Elizabeth Barrett Browning, Elizabeth Gaskell, Christina Rossetti, and authors who have been overlooked or elbowed out by literary historians have been brought to a clearer focus. The existing order is sought to be altered. To accomplish this, they redefine the literary canon, jettisoning the unwanted baggage of male writers, and planting a newer one in place of the old. Ring out the old, and ring in the new, seems to be the motto. Promote scholarship pertaining to women's studies: rewrite literary history with this view in mind, the view of transforming the existing literary study, and creating a distinctive female literary tradition. By way of an example, the tradition and the emergence of modernism can be approached from the feminist point of view. Traditional historians define the movement in various ways: as a reaction to Victorianism, the after-effects of World War I, the ills of industrialisation, etc. The conventional view is that modernism, in art and literature, was born to work against the tendencies of the age. From the feminist perspective, on the other hand, modernism can be interpreted as an outward expression of women's movements fighting for suffrage and equal rights; and reflecting the changes in the relationship between men and women in a growing, permissive society. Evidence can be shown in the emergence of experimental literature in fiction. Women writers (especially the French) suggest, begin at the very beginning. Get back to the earliest stage of the pre-verbal relationship between the mother and the child and create WL, woman's language (*ecriture feminine*). Such a language has its own structure ('divine liquidness of diction and divine fluidity of movement', in the words of Arnold, referring to Chaucer's poetry) marked by associations, free play, and fluidity which can be differentiated from the logical, and linear, phallocentric writings of men. Reputed writers like Toni Morrison, Adrienne Rich, and *avant-garde* writers have given a lead in this direction, by creating such a distinctive style. While most feminist critics are wary of the frameworks in theory built by patriarchy, they are quick to seize upon those elements which suit them, like the psychoanalytic, Marxist and deconstructionist theories.

Feminism is multicultural and diasporic. It is a proven fact that women, in general, are subjected to patriarchal oppression. Also patriarchy operates in different ways in different countries. It is also true that women's problems are shaped by their class, race, nationality, religion and many other factors. It is a complex issue involving implications at various levels. The woman being treated as 'the angel in the house', and the woman being placed on the 'pedestal' are some of them. Feminist critics try to go against the grain in exploring/exposing the patriarchal ideology of literary texts. It is wide in its range, because it accommodates several issues—cultural, social, political, and psychological. Its goal is to widen our understanding of women's experience of the world, and their value in the world. As a critical movement, feminism is of recent origin, comparatively speaking. Yet, its growth is phenomenal in terms of the volume of books and articles written about it. Specialised journals promote critical reassessments. Feminism has become a productive industry that has an enormous impact on the centres of teaching and learning.

In recent times, especially in the advanced countries of the world like France, feminism has led to some radical offshoots, such as lesbian, gay and queer critical theories. Marriage is no longer restricted to men with women. Marriages of lesbian and gay couples have come to be legalised. Denying license to same-sex couples is held discriminatory in several countries. The traditional view of marriage as a social institution designed to promote childbearing and child rearing, has been redefined. Marriage, after all, is an enduring commitment, and a shared journey through life. Why should sex and gender be impediments to this? There should be no social stigma attached to being thought of as a lesbian or a gay. Hence, a good deal of works by lesbian or gay writers is included in the curriculum. Lesbian and gay theory emerged as a distinctive field during the 1990s. If gender is the fundamental category of analysis and understanding in feminist theories, sex and sexual orientation is the fundamental category in gay/lesbian theories. The charge against feminism is that it did not accommodate differences in the experience of women. It did not take into proper consideration the cultural, racial, and sexual differences: on the contrary, it universalised the experience by using the experience of white, middle-class, urban, heterosexual women as the yardstick. It failed to see the diasporic nature of female experience. This essentialism has come to be questioned by lesbianism which turns its attention away from patriarchal exploitation. The main issue is to establish firm relationships among women. By doing so, they can show their resistance to existing forms of social relationships. Men do not come into the picture at all!

There are some terms in the critical vocabulary of the radical feminists with which one needs to become familiar. *Homophobia* means fear of same-sex love, and this gets institutionalised in nations; *internalised homophobia* refers to the hatred and fear of the experience of gay people. They are even ostracised in some communities. *Heterosexism* privileges heterosexuality, and accepts it as a virtue to be practised; *heterocentrism* is a prejudice against the gay. *Biological essentialism* maintains that certain sections of the people are naturally gay. Opposed to this is the notion that homo or heterosexuality is the product of social and not biological forces, and this goes by the term *social constructionism*. There are minoritising and universalising views on this. There are *homoerotic* and *homosocial* depictions. These can occur in literature, films, painting, photography, etc. The former refers to the same-sex attraction, and the latter to the same-sex bond or friendship.

Lesbian criticism has become an exciting field of enquiry. Lesbians have felt that the feminists, who have embraced heterosexuality, have marginalised them. One can find lesbians even within heterosexual marriages. For lesbians, heterosexuality and patriarchy collude with each other. A lesbian text is that which expresses the feelings of a 'woman-identified woman'. Lesbian critics determine what makes for lesbian poetics and they analyse the sexual politics of texts, and make corrective readings of heterosexual interpretations of literature which ignore the lesbian dimensions of works.

In a similar manner, gay criticism (the counterpart of lesbian criticism) talks of gay sensibility, which means the manner in which the experiences of gays find expression in arts and literature. Among its important areas, *drag, camp* and AIDS are found in gay sensibility. *Drag* (known in common parlance as transvestism) is a practice of dressing in women's clothing as sexual stimulus. It is a way of challenging gender roles. *Camp* is irreverence, and exaggeration in conduct. It is a method of expressing one's difference from heterosexual culture, and a way of transforming oneself from being a victim to becoming a victor. Gay critics try to launch their poetics and establish a gay tradition. They reinterpret texts by exposing sexual politics involved in man–woman relationships.

Within the sphere of lesbianism, there emerged during the 1990s a less essentialist notion which has come to be called *queer* theory. Gay critics and lesbian critics call themselves *queer* critics. They deliberately adopt and use the homophobic term 'queer.' It is not a term of insult, but a term which asserts compellingly, with a vengeance, the identity of the homosexuals. For them, it is an inclusive term that offers them a collective identity, and it can, therefore, include all 'non-straight' people. Instead of being woman-centred, as lesbian feminism is, queer theory rejects female separatism, and seeks an alliance with gay men. For queer critics, sexuality is fragmented, dynamic, and fluid: it is not simply controlled by our biological needs or gender roles. Sexuality is socially constructed for *queer* theory. In relation to sexual identity, it is anti-essentialist. It aims to interpret literature from a non-straight perspective. It tries to reveal the problematic quality of representations of sexual categories, and to show the ranges of complexity. Sex and gender categorisation break down easily. Some clues as the following are identified in any queer criticism: homosocial bonding, gay or lesbian 'signs', same-sex 'doubles', transgressive quality, and so on.

Work Cited

Ruskin, John. *Sesame and Lilies*. Ed. G.E. Hollingworth. London: University Tutorial Press Ltd.

Select Bibliography

Beauvoir, Simone de. *The Second Sex*. 1949. Harmondsworth: Penguin, 1972.

Donovan, Josephine. *Feminist Literary Criticism*. 1975. Lexington: University Press of Kentucky, 1989.

Eagleton, Mary, ed. *Feminist Literary Criticism*. London: Longman, 1991.

———. *Working with Feminist Criticism*. Oxford: Blackwell, 1996.

———, ed. *A Concise Companion to Feminist Theory*. Oxford: Blackwell, 2003.

Ellman, Mary. *Thinking about Women*. London: Macmillan, 1968.

Fetterley, Judith. *The Resisting Reader: A Feminist Approach to American Fiction*. Bloomington: Indiana University Press, 1978.

Fetterley, Judith and Marjorie Pryse. *Writing out of Place: Regionalism, Women and American Literary Culture*. Urbana: University of Illinois Press, 2003.

Gilbert, Sandra M., and Susan Gubar. *The Madwoman in the Attic: The Woman Writer and the Nineteenth Century Imagination*. New Haven, Conn.: Yale University Press, 1979.

———. *The Norton Anthology of Literature by Women*. New York: Norton, 1985.

Gubar, Susan. *Critical Condition: Feminism at the Turn of the Century*. New York: Columbia University Press, 2000.

Irigaray, Luce. *Speculum of the Other Woman*. Trans. Gillian C. Gill. Ithaca, NY: Cornell University Press, 1985.

———. *An Ethics of Sexual Difference*. Ithaca, N.Y.: Cornell University Press, 1993.

Millett, Kate. *Sexual Politics*. Garden City, NY: Doubleday, 1970.

Moi, Toril. *Textual/Sexual Politics: Feminist Literary Theory*. London: Methuen, 1985.

———. *What is a Woman? And other Essays*. Oxford: Oxford University Press, 1999.

———. *Sex, Gender and Body*. Oxford: Oxford University Press, 2005.

Ruthven, K.K. *Feminist Literary Studies: An Introduction*. Cambridge: Cambridge University Press, 1984.

Schweickart, Patrocinio P. 'Reading Ourselves: Toward a Feminist Theory of Reading'. *Modern Criticism and Theory: A Reader*. Rev. ed. Nigel Wood. London: Longman, 1998.

Showalter, Elaine. *A Literature of their Own: British Women Novelists from Bronte to Lessing*. Princeton, N.J.: Princeton University Press, 1977.

———. *The New Feminist Criticism: Essays on Women, Literature and Theory*. New York: Pantheon Books, 1982.

———. *Inventing Herself: Claiming a Feminist Intellectual Heritage*, New York: Scribner, 2001.

———. *Faculty Towers: The Academic Novel and its Discontents*. Philadelphia: University of Philadelphia Press, 2005.

Spacks, Patricia Meyer. *The Female Imagination*. New York: Knopf, 1975.

Walker, Alice. *In Search of our Mothers' Gardens: Womanist Prose*. New York: Harcourt Brace, Jovanovich, 1973.

Warhol Robin, R. and Diane Price Herndl, eds. *Feminisms: An Anthology of Literary Theory and Criticism*. New Brunswick, New Jersey: Rutgers University Press, 1991.

PSYCHOANALYTIC CRITICISM

Psychoanalysis is a theory about the human mind. Psychoanalytic concepts are prevalent in our everyday life, and criticism related to these is psychoanalytic criticism. It came into being during the 1920s. This criticism can be understood as emerging from the romantic view that literature is an expression of its author's persona. The psychoanalytic view of human behaviour is relevant to our experience of literature. Psychoanalysis is defined as a form of mental therapy which aims to cure mental disorders 'by investigating the interaction of the conscious and unconscious elements of the mind.'

Many of the principles of such a therapy are derived from the works of the Austrian medical practitioner, Sigmund Freud (1856–1939), whose ideas about psychoanalysis evolved over a period of time. It was he who gave his ideas the name, psychoanalysis, in 1896. He said that people are motivated by desires, fears, and conflicts of which they are unaware. They are unconscious of these forces. These forces are stored in our memory, and are repressed. This is the unconscious mind. This is a part, or section, a sub-system of the mind, but lying below the level of consciousness, and it organises our current experiences and emotions. The unconscious is dynamic, and is always at work, controlling us from the very depths of our being. There are many *defences* by which we keep the unconscious under check. *Transference* and *projection* are two of these defences. There is also what is called *regression*, a short return to the past experience which is relived. It is a good therapeutic tool for cure. When some of these defences break down, we have *anxiety*. We have partial access to the unconscious through our dreams, and creative activities. During our dreams the unconscious is free to express itself. The dream becomes a nightmare, when it is too fearful or threatening. It may lead to trauma when the conscious defence breaks down. Death and sexuality are fascinating themes for study in psychoanalysis. Critics of this persuasion have varied notions on how these concepts can be fruitfully applied to literary criticism.

Freud uses the term *dream work* to refer to the ways by which real events are transformed into dream images. These are called *displacement* and *condensation*. Events are represented in a dream very much like they are represented in literary works. Abstract ideas and feelings are concretised. Dreams show or reveal things as literature does. Dreams are like literature. The purpose of a work of art, like the purpose of the dream, is the secret gratification of a forbidden infantile wish. That is the reason why literary critics have great interest in the Freudian methods of analysis, and interpretation. Apart from this, Freud himself was well educated in the classics. Among other honours, he received the Goethe Prize for literature. So, when he wanted to describe mental illnesses and their causes and cure, he found useful analogies in literary works. Using psychoanalysis as his tool, he interpreted works of literature known to him. His *The Interpretation of Dreams* (1900), and the essay 'The Uncanny' are among the best-known pieces of writing. He used psychoanalysis to interpret Shakespeare's characters, Hamlet, Macbeth and Lear.

Psychoanalytic criticism can be conveniently divided into three phases. The first two belong to the early or classical phase, and the third to the poststructuralist phase. In the first phase (classical Freudian criticism), the work of literature was likened to a dream or fantasy of the writer. The focus here is on the psychoanalysis of the author. Characters in literature were seen and treated as real living beings who belong to the created fantasy world. Freud's interpretation of symbols was applied in a rigid manner to the language of a work of literature. Such an application is referred to as 'vulgar Freudianism'. Since the psychoanalytic critics treated literary texts as analogous to dreams, they maintained that a diagnostic analysis of the text would tell us about the writer and his life, and knowledge of the workings of the creator's mind would help us in interpreting the text. Following Freud, quite a few critics wrote critical analyses of works, using the lives of the authors, and the themes of their works. Two of the best known works of literary criticism, employing classical Freudianism, are Ernest Jones's (his British colleague) book *Hamlet and Oedipus* (1949), the notes for which were made earlier by Freud himself; and Marie Bonaparte's *Life and Works of Edgar Allan Poe: A Psycho-analytic Interpretation* (1949) for which Freud wrote the introduction. Both of them were students of Freud, and he had endorsed their interpretations. These two studies are to be seen as landmarks in early psychoanalytic criticism. Later psychoanalysts have dismissed these studies on many counts. They are naive in their reading; they pay little attention to the language. Jones is not aware of Elizabethan dramatic conventions, while Bonaparte is repetitive and tedious in her examination of Poe's stories. Many other psychoanalytic studies do not gain acceptance in modern scholarship. They are dismissed as reductive, inflexible, one-sided and often tedious in their repeated use of psychoanalytic jargon. Classical Freudian psychoanalytic criticism still continues: there are journals exclusively devoted to such studies.

The second phase of classical psychoanalysis came about roughly in the 1960s and 1970s. The emphasis now is not upon the author, but upon the reader. Its ancestry can be traced to I. A. Richards who, in the 1920s, spoke of the impact of an art experience on the reader. Norman Holland takes up the lead, and examines the interaction between the reader and the text. He terms it 'transactive criticism'. The source of the pleasure (experience) we derive from a literary work lies in the transformation of our unconscious wishes, and fears into culturally acceptable meanings. Holland uses the acronym DEFT (Defences, Expectations, Frustrations, and Transformations) to define this process. Reading recreates the reader's identity.

Jacques Lacan (1901–81), called 'the French Freud', is a French psychoanalyst. He too started his career, like Freud, as a medical practitioner with a medical degree. From about 1930 onwards until his death, he was the most influential figure in psychoanalytic circles. He presented his famous paper called the 'Mirror Stage' in 1936. Later, he came to be influenced by the works of Saussure and Levi Strauss. He was something of a rebel. He was expelled from the International Psychoanalytic Association. When his research findings were published in 1966, under the title *Ecrits*, he became a prominent Parisian intellectual, and his fame as a 'structuralist psychoanalyst' spread far and wide. With Lacan is born modern psychoanalytic criticism and theory.

What Lacan is interested in is re-writing, re-interpreting classical Freudian psychoanalysis in the light of poststructuralist theories. He dismisses Freud's notion of the instinctual unconscious that precedes language. This is a pre-Saussurean view. His view is that the unconscious is structured like a language, and it is a product of language. The unconscious comes into being simultaneously along with language. It is the result of the structuring of desire by language. Since Lacan's focus is on language and the structuring of desire by language, he replaces Freud's concepts of condensation and displacement with Roman Jakobson's metaphor and metonymy. Lacan uses linguistic and literary traditions unlike Freud. Metonymy and displacement are both defined by contiguity, nearness in space and time as though existing in a chain. Metaphor and condensation are characterised by similarity and association. The unconscious consists of signifiers rather than instincts. The unconscious is structured like language, and the dream is structured like a sentence. For Lacan, the subject comes into being when it acquires its consciousness, the sense of being. It develops a concept of self and self-hood. This happens in every human being at a mythic moment for which Lacan's term is 'the mirror stage'. This occurs usually between six months and eighteen months, when the child begins to conceive of itself as a unified being, separate from the rest of the world. Before this, when the sense of the self is not acquired, the child exists in a realm which Lacan terms 'the Imaginary'. In this stage, there is no distinction between the self and the Other; but there is a kind of total identification with the mother. The mirror stage is a pre-linguistic stage towards the close of which the child enters into the language system. The new order into which the child enters is called by Lacan 'the symbolic'. According to Lacan, the unconscious is the 'kernel of our being'. The unconscious is structured like language, and language exists as a structure before the individual enters into the system of language.

Lacan's theory is influenced by poststructuralism, and his undermining of the stable self (the liberal humanist notion) has resulted in a change in the relation between psychoanalysis and literary criticism, which, in turn, has produced a transformation in the reading, and critical practice. Classical psychoanalysis was engaged in using the literary text as a clue to the psychology of the author or his characters. The Lacanian method of psychoanalysis would involve searching the text for uncovering contradictory suggestions of meaning, which, like the unconscious, lie beneath the overt text. Robert Con Davis beautifully sums up the method in his anthology *The Fictional Father: Lacanian Readings of the Text.* The ideal reader

> comes to Lacanian thought for an important perspective on how to dismantle standard presences in literature, such as father figures, mother substitutes, Christ figures, neurotics, and outsiders, and to find, instead, functions and transformations in fiction that can be examined critically in the context of their real environment—within the narrative structure. To that end, a Lacanian question regarding narrative . . . can be asked . . . of any text: what does it mean for the father to be the subject of the narrative? The answer is

> not a taxonomy of inferiority complexes, and mother attachments . . . but a sophisticated confrontation with narrative structure as a complex of (ultimately) indeterminate elements constituted on many levels of textuality (184–5).

Psychoanalytic criticism, whether Freudian or Lacanian, helps us in our critical assessment of literary works in many ways. This criticism is based upon the assumption that sexuality is the basic constituent element in the construction of the subject. Hence, any psychoanalytic reading involves explaining the presence of sexuality in a text. It can be author-based, text-based, or reader-based. The Oedipal dynamics, family dynamics, relationship to death, sexuality, the narrator's unconscious problems, etc., can be tackled with this persuasion. All these relate to the author of the work. Critics most often resort to psychoanalysing the behaviour of literary characters. Such a method of analysis is as legitimate as the analyses undertaken from a feminist or Marxist perspective. This relates to the content of the work. Psychoanalytic concepts are not just limited to one medium. Any human production involving narration, production of images, can be analysed and interpreted using psychoanalytic tools. These relate to the impact of the works on the audience. Psychoanalysis is also used in the writing of literary biographies which are called psycho-biographies. These trace the growth and development of the author's genius, drawing evidences from his life and writings—his mind and art. One final word: psychoanalytic criticism is neither verifiable, nor falsifiable.

Work Cited

Davis, Robert Con. *The Fictional Father: Lacanian Readings of the Text.* Amherst: University of Massachusetts Press, 1981.

Select Bibliography

Bloom, Harold. *The Anxiety of Influence: A Theory of Poetry.* Oxford: Oxford University Press, 1975.

Felman, Shoshna. *Jacques Lacan and the Adventure of Insight: Psychoanalysis in Contemporary Culture.* Cambridge, Mass: Harvard University Press, 1987.

Freud, Sigmund. *The Interpretation of Dreams.* 1900. Ed. George Stade. New York, NY: Barnes & Noble Classics, 2005.

Gilman, Sander, ed. *Introducing Psychoanalytic Theory.* New York: Brunner-Mazel, 1982.

Holland, Norman. *The Dynamics of Literary Response.* New York: Columbia University Press, 1969.

———. *5 Readers Reading.* New Haven: Yale University Press, 1975.

Klein, George. *Psychoanalytic Theory: An Exploration of Essentials.* New York: International University Press, 1976.

Lacan, Jacques.. *The Four Fundamental Concepts of Psychoanalysis.* Ed. Jacques-Alain. Tr. Alain Sheridan. London: Hogarth Press, 1977.

———. *Ecrits: A Selection.* 1977. Trans. Bruce Fink. New York: W.W. Norton, 2002.

Skura, Meredith. *The Literary Use of the Psychoanalytic Process.* New Haven: Yale University Press, 1981.

Trilling, Lionel. 'Freud and Literature'. *Liberal Imagination: Essays on Literature and Society.* Garden City, N.Y.: Doubleday, 1953.

Wilson, Edmund. *The Wound and the Bow: Seven Studies in Literature.* Boston: Houghton Mifflin Company, 1941.

Wright, Elizabeth. *Psychoanalytic Criticism: Theory in Practice.* London: Methuen, 1984.

———, ed. *Feminism and Psychoanalysis.* Oxford: Blackwell, 1992.

MARXIST CRITICISM

The German philosopher Karl Marx (1818–83), and the German sociologist Friedrich Engels (1820–95) are the founding fathers of this school of criticism. In 1848, they jointly wrote the communist manifesto, which is still in vogue. Marxist criticism is not interested in solving individual problems, or attaining individual salvation. Marx and Engels were basically concerned with political philosophy, and economic production and thought, in the context of European capitalistic society. They did not attempt a full-length study of art and literature. And they never advocated judging the merits of a piece of literature in terms of its political tendencies, or using some ready-made socioeconomic formula. They were not emotional boors, but two of the most deeply learned, and highly cultured German intellectuals of their time for whom art and literature, in any form, constituted the air they breathed. Only their interests lay in the direction of economics rather than literature. In course of time, the principles underlying Marxian thought came to be adapted and modified to create what has now come be known as Marxist criticism. Marx's famous maxims were, 'nothing human is alien to me', and 'one must doubt of everything'.

Marxism is a materialist philosophy. It supports a naturalist as opposed to a supernaturalist world view. It foregrounds economic realities of human culture. Economic power is behind all institutions. In other words, it attempts to explain things without assuming that there is a force beyond the natural world and the society we inhabit. In this sense, it stands in opposition to the idealist philosophy, which has faith in the existence of a spiritual world with reference to which explanations can be offered to our doubts and queries. Indian philosophic thought is based on such an assumption. Friedrich Hegel preached the philosophy of idealism which maintains that the world is governed by thought. Ideas, not men, rule the world. Material existence is the expression of an immaterial spiritual essence. Marx reverses—and thereby rejects—this Hegelian philosophy. Here is Marx in his *The German Ideology* (1845–6):

> The production of ideas, concepts and consciousness is first of all directly interwoven with the material intercourse of man, the language of real life. Conceiving, thinking and the real intercourse of men, appear here as the direct efflux of men's material behaviour. The same applies to mental production as expressed in the language of the politics, laws, morality, religion, and metaphysics, of a people. Men are the producers of their conceptions, ideas, etc.—real, active men, as they are conditioned by a definite development of their productive forces and of the intercourse corresponding to these, up to its furthest forms. Consciousness can never be anything else than conscious existence, and the existence of men is their actual life-process . . . Life is not determined by consciousness but consciousness by life. (197–8)

Foucault would call Marxism an author-function. Marxism is a very wide field comprising a theory of economics, history, society, and revolution. Marxist literary theories do not constitute a school. Marxists assign a structure to social reality. It is called a structured view of reality. Society is not a vague, indistinct background. It has a definite shape in history. There is always a series of struggles among antagonistic social classes, and the types of production they are engaged in. This is termed 'dialectical'. The struggle between opposed forces is dynamic. Marx posits methods by which history and society can be analysed. How literature fits into the structure is problematic. Literature reflects and/or distorts social reality. There is a lack of consensus with regard to this. Marx and Engels say that literature can only be properly understood within a larger framework of social reality. Any theory which treats literature in isolation divorcing it from society and history, will be deficient in its ability to explain what literature really is. The socioeconomic element (social relations created by the kind of economic production preponderant in a given society) in any society is the ultimate determinant of that society's character. Do we not classify societies in such general terms as agriculturist or industrialist, etc.?

Marx employs an architectural metaphor, which is most commonly used to explain the relationship between economic production, and other elements which depend on it. The basic economic structure ('base') engenders a number of social institutions and beliefs which act to regulate or dissipate the conflict and keep the mode of production in being. All elements which arise from the socioeconomic base form the 'superstructure' of society. From about 1870 to 1920, the view held was deterministic that the base caused the superstructure or the superstructure reflected the base, and that there was a direct correlation between the two. This view of economic determinism—now discarded—goes by the name of 'vulgar Marxism'. Later (after the decline of Lenin), there has been a revisionist and flexible view that the superstructure can influence the base, and that works of art can and do possess a relatively autonomous existence. How else can we account for the eternal beauty of a work of art, enshrined in 'monuments of unageing intellect'? There is no one-to-one correspondence between base and superstructure; and the causation between them is a complex and problematic phenomenon. Marx lodges literature in the superstructure of society.

Economics is the base on which the superstructure of social, political, and ideological realities are built. It includes political and social power. Economic conditions are the *material* circumstances and those generated by it are *historical* circumstances. Human affairs cannot be understood without reference to these circumstances, in a timeless abstraction. Marxist methodology maintains that theoretical ideas can be judged only by their concrete application with reference to the world we live in. People are divided primarily by their differences in socioeconomic conditions. There is an eternal struggle for power between the social classes. History is a class struggle. The proletariat, the working class, is always subjugated by the bourgeoisie—the rich who control the resources, and the wealth of a nation. The result of this exploitation is 'alienation'. It is a process by which a worker is 'deskilled' and made to perform tasks, the nature and purpose of which he cannot know. He relinquishes his labour power to the capitalist in exchange for wages, and becomes an appendage of a machine. This results in 'reification' in which the world of human relationships appears as a set of relationships between things. Workers form the labour force. They are thought of as hands. People become commodities. The power structures can only be altered by the coming together of the proletariat, forgetting its divisions.

Marx and Engels were the first to discuss the different ramifications of the much-misused term *ideology* in their book *The German Ideology*. This highly loaded term has come in for a lot of widely differing interpretations, positive and negative. The concept of *ideology* is central to an understanding of Marxism. It is not just a set of doctrines *per se*: it signifies a set of beliefs and values (which people cling to) that prevent them from a fuller and truer understanding of the world they inhabit. Hence *ideology* in Marxism means a system of beliefs, conditioned culturally: a system of beliefs using which human beings make sense of the world they live in. Louis Althusser describes ideology as a 'system (possessing its logic and proper rigour) of representations (images, myths, ideas or concepts according to the case) endowed with an existence and an historical role at the heart of a given society.' In *For Marx*, he defines the term, more accurately:

> In a class society ideology is the relay whereby, and the element in which, the relation between men and their conditions of existence is settled to the profit of the ruling class. In a classless society ideology is the relay whereby, and the element in which, the relation between men and their conditions of existence is lived to the profit of all men (235–6).

Every field has its ideological component, and not all ideologies are beneficial, or productive, or desirable for a society. Undesirable ideologies are repressive, but they make way, through appearances, as natural ones for the society. Repressive ideology, in the words of Engels, is 'false consciousness'. It is a distortion of the material, because the ideas are opposed to the material reality on which alone experience should be based. Repressive ideology is put in circulation by the ruling class to establish consensus in society. It is a set of beliefs in which people deceive themselves. For example, the belief that man is superior to woman is a sexist ideology. To own a big, cosy home, is a capitalist ideology. Repressive ideologies prevent us from seeing the material/historical conditions of our existence. What people are led to think is different from, and opposed to what they believe or should believe in. Hence, ideologies are never recognised as harmful, but thought of as natural and inevitable ways of living, and dealing with this world. The American dream is an ideology implanted in the middle class that success is the result of hard work and initiative, and poverty is the result of laziness. It is a power ideology meant for legitimising and perpetuating the interests of the privileged ruling class. Ideology promotes false class-consciousness. Patriotism, religion, individualism, consumerism are all the different manifestations of repressive bourgeois ideology. Cultural productions and literature, film, music, television—all these carry, and spread ideologies.

Having reviewed the basic concepts in Marxism, let us examine how Marxian literary theorists have applied these concepts in relation to literature. For the sake of convenience, they can be classified (according to David Forgacs in his essay, 'Marxist Literary Theories') under five headings, each bearing some relationship to the other.

The Reflection Model: This goes back to the Aristotelian tradition of mimesis. Literature is understood as reflecting the reality outside it. The material world of our being is reflected in the mind of man and then translated to forms of thought. The major exponent of this system is the Hungarian Marxist Georg Lukacs. He says that literature is knowledge of reality, and not just a mirroring of it. The form of the literary work reflects the form of reality. Literature creates a fictional world which is a reflection of the real world, with all its contradictions, rendered with utmost clarity and concreteness possible. He attacks the dogma of modernism which is reactionary and decadent: it represents individuals who are alienated from society. The personality of man is represented as disintegrated: he is shown to be solitary, asocial, and unable or unwilling to enter into a happy communion with fellow human beings. Solitariness and its consequent mental illnesses are the inescapable burden of modern man. Eliot's 'The Hollow Men' sums up this condition succinctly. 'Shape without form, shade without colour/ Paralysed force, gesture without motion'. Lukacs' theory is concerned mainly with the novel, and the realistic novel at that. For him, it is the novel that matters. He does not take into consideration the language of fiction. Language, for him, is just a vehicle for shaping the form.

The Production Model: The French Marxist Pierre Macherey developed this theory. Literary composition is seen as productive labour in which materials are turned into end products. The author is not a shaman who creates out of nothing, but one who beats into shape literary genres, literary conventions and practices already in existence, The text that is produced is in some sense incomplete, and is concerned primarily with the staging of ideology.

The Genetic Model: This approach is called 'genetic' because it is concerned with the origins of literary production. The Rumanian sociologist, Lucien Goldmann, developed this model. How did literature develop out of the social life and customs of the people? Literary works arise out of social consciousness. Some social groups possess a superior form of ideology, a superior form of 'world view', shall we say? These social groups may be reactionary, or revolutionary. The views of this group form the mental structure, which is shaped and given 'coherence' by great writers in their works. The literary work is not to be understood as the expression of the author's self, or his individual genius (as the romantics believed) but the expression of the social class. A literary work is the collective product of a social community. It is built on 'transindividual mental structures'. The mental structures of Goldmann are not linguistic structures, but interrelations of concepts. He calls them 'homologies'. World views are social facts. Artistic works represent the coherent and adequate expressions of the world views. The problem is one of finding out how the various parts of the superstructure (literature, philosophy, politics, religion) were related to one another, and to class relationships. Great writers discover these mental structures and transform, or better still, transmute them into lasting works of art. Goldmann's *The Hidden God* (1964) is a classic illustration of this theory. Such an accommodative view stands in clear contrast to the vulgar Marxian view that economics (base) causes literature (superstructure).

The Frankfurt School of Marxism promoted by Theodore Adorno rejects the earlier view (held by Lukacs) that art is a reflection of objective reality, but suggests that the world of art is different from the world of social reality. The two stand far apart from each other. Art has its own 'formal' laws. Art is the essence and image of reality, and not its photographic reproduction. Art exposes the contradictions of reality. 'Art is the negative knowledge of the actual world'. Negative knowledge is not negation, but a knowledge that can negate a false or reified condition. Hence, Adorno and his followers applaud modernism and experimental art. For them, modernism should be approached as a critique of late capitalism. Techniques, such as the use of fragmented form of narration, are meant to serve as formal features, which offer us a negative knowledge of the dehumanised society of capitalism. Modernism, as depicted by such able practitioners as Beckett, for instance, exposes the alienation of man from society which capitalism causes. Knowledge of reality is thus indirectly achieved. *Avant-garde* is that which resists conformity, never willing to submit to conventions. It is this autonomy, and antagonism to bourgeois norms that is supported as progressive. Adorno's followers are also sympathetic to the technological reproduction of art through films, TV, and other mass media. These have rendered elite and esoteric art accessible to the common man. The wall of distinction between 'high' art and 'low' art has broken down.

The Marxist theories we have discussed so far do not assign a central role to language. Language has never found a place in the Marxian dialectic. Mikhail Bakhtin and a few other Russian formalists developed a theory in the 1920s which maintains that ideology is made of language in the form of linguistic signs. 'Ideology is the material embodiment of social interaction'. Language is a social activity. Literature is itself an ideology, which reflects another ideology which reflects the social base. The language of a literary work does question authority and convention, and subverts stability. This can be seen in the 'polyphony' of the novel, which is characterised by the many voices present in it, none of which is controlled by the writer. The monologic novel is dominated by the authoritarian voice of the writer, while the dialogic novel has many voices. Literature is to be understood as a practice of language within reality. The language of the carnival and popular festivals carries this polyphony. The 'Menippean' tradition involves the use of different types of discourse in which the characters have a free play. This Bakhtinian view of Marxism treats literature as a social practice, rather than as a form of knowledge. This language-centred model has opened up several possibilities of rethinking Marxism in the light of the post-Saussurean view of the world. Concepts drawn from deconstruction and psychoanalysis are made use of in reading literary works, especially prose fiction.

Current Marxist theory is interested in examining the subtle ways by which society works. From the 1960s onwards, there is a departure from traditional Marxism, which always relied on a single source for examining social phenomena. It is seen, more and more, as a growing and evolving historical process. The power of the ideology is seen to be far greater than the power of the material. And so, literature has its own justification for existence. The base/superstructure model is being given up in preference to an examination of literature based on the post-structuralist view. This is termed revisionist Marxism. Louis Althusser, Raymond Williams, Terry Eagleton and Fredric Jameson have made significant contributions to it in the last two decades of the twentieth century. Althusser would treat literature as 'state apparatus', an ideological imposition on society. Raymond Williams was interested in presenting a cultural history of the Western world, deploying the Marxian matrix. His chief disciple, Terry Eagleton, views literature as not necessarily reflecting reality, but influencing an ideology that creates reality. Fredric Jameson contends that Marxist criticism alone can be an inclusive and foolproof method in bringing to light 'the political unconscious', subversive ideology which lies concealed in the sub-text of a work. He takes an uncompromising stand that the political perspective is the absolute horizon of all reading and all interpretation.

Marxist critics are interested in examining human behaviour as a product of ideological forces transmitted through arts, and other institutions. Literature does not exist in a vacuum, or as a timeless aesthetic artefact. It is a manifestation of the ideological condition of the time. A literary work might reinforce or critique the ideologies it represents or encloses. Both content and form are involved in this practice. Marxism has special affinities with the realistic mode of representation, because it presents the real world as it is, without any deliberate distortion. Marxian critics do not fancy much the experimental mode that keeps the common readers away from it. There is a woeful lack of a consistent view of human nature. Sometimes, experimental writings are seen in a positive light as reflecting the alienated world in which most of us are cast.

Works Cited

Althusser, Louis. *For Marx.* Paris: F. Maspero, 1965.

Marx, Karl. *The German Ideology. Marx's Concept of Man.* Ed. T.B. Bottomore. Rev. ed. New York: Frederick Ungar Publishing Co., 1969.

Select Bibliography

Althusser, Louis. *For Marx.* Paris: F. Maspero, 1965.

———. *Essays on Ideology.* 1976. London: Verso, 1984.

Bakhtin. *Rabelais and his World.* Cambridge, Mass: Harvard University Press, 1968.

———. *Dialogic Imagination.* Ed. Michael Holoquist. Austin: University of Texas Press, 1981.

Baxandall, Lee and Stefan Morowski, eds. *Marx and Engels on Literature and Art: A Selection of Writings.* New York: International General, 1973.

Bennet, Tony. *Formalism and Marxism,* London: Methuen, 1979.

Caudwell, Christopher. *Illusion and Reality: A Study of the Sources of Poetry.* Berlin: Seven Seas Publishers, 1973.

Eagleton, Terry. *Marxism and Literary Criticism.* Berkeley: University of California Press, 1976.

———. *Criticism and Ideology: A Study in Marxist Literary Theory.* London: Humanities Press, 1976.

———, ed. *Ideology.* London: Longman, 1994.

Goldmann, Lucien. *The Hidden God.* Trans. Philip Thody. New York: Humanities Press, 1964.

Jameson, Fredric. *Marxism and Form.* 1971. Princeton, N.J.: Princeton University Press, 1974.

———. *The Political Unconscious.* Ithaca, N.Y.: Cornell University Press, 1981.

———. *A Singular Modernity: Essay on the Ontology of the Present.* London: Verso, 2002.

Lukacs, George. *The Historical Novel.* Trans. Hannah and Stanley Mitchell. Harmondsworth: Penguin, 1969.

Trotsky, Leon. *Art and Revolution.* 1970. *Leon Trotsky on Literature and Art* (new title). New York: Pathfinder, 1992.

Williams, Raymond. *Marxism and Literature.* Oxford: Oxford University Press, 1977.

———. *Problems in Culture and Materialism.* London: Verso, 1980.

HERMENEUTICS

> Veil after veil may be drawn (from the poem), and the inmost naked beauty of the meaning never exposed. A great poem is a fountain forever overflowing with the waters of wisdom and delight; and after one person and one age has exhausted all its

> divine effluence which their particular relations enable them to share, another and yet another succeeds, and new relations are ever developed, the source of an unforeseen and an unconceived delight.
>
> P.B. Shelley, 'Defence of Poetry'

The word 'hermeneutics' comes from a Greek word which means 'to say' or 'to explain', and thus, also 'interpretation'. The term refers both to the theory, and the practice of interpretation. According to Greek mythology, it was derived from Hermes who was a messenger as well as an interpreter of the gods. The principal function of hermeneutics is to bring to light some work that is obscure and foreign to one's tongue. There is no hermeneutic school of criticism as such, nor does the term stand for any particular brand of interpretation. In the twentieth century, it has to do with ontology, the essence of being. The oldest tradition in hermeneutics involves Biblical exegesis, and there are different orientations in this. Then, there is the legal hermeneutics concerned with the understanding and interpretation of the law, and the philological hermeneutics which is concerned with the preservation of classical texts. In criminal law and in legal parlance, it is a concept that is used to distinguish between the various degrees of crimes, and their relative punishment. A crime that is the result of premeditation or intention deserves greater punishment than the one that is sudden and impulsive. In aesthetics and literary study, we quite often use the term to denote the intention of the author who composed a work. In interpreting scriptures or canonical texts, this is the basis. As a subject of philosophical enquiry, hermeneutics has occupied the best of minds from the period of Enlightenment onwards. Schleiermacher, Dilthey, Heidegger, Godamer, Habermas, Paul Ricoeur are some of the best thinkers associated with the epistemology of hermeneutics.

Wimsatt and Beardsley jointly wrote an article entitled 'Intention' for the *Dictionary of World Literature,* edited by Joseph T. Shipley (1942). The Indian aesthetician Ananda K. Coomaraswamy, an intentionalist and iconographer, wrote a rejoinder to this article, also entitled 'Intention' in *American Bookman* (1944). He raised two questions about a work: 1. whether the artist achieved his intentions; and 2. whether the work of art 'ought ever to have been undertaken at all' and so 'whether it is worth preserving'. With Wimsatt and Beardsley's

'The Intentional Fallacy' (1946), in which they take up the issue for a fuller treatment, this concept grew in importance. They reinforced their view that 'the design or the intention of the author is neither available nor desirable as a standard for judging the success of a work of literary art' (334). Their view is expressed in the following words:

> The poem is not the critic's own and not the author's (it is detached from the author at birth and goes about the world beyond his power to intend about it or control it). The poem belongs to the public. It is embodied in language, the peculiar possession of the public, and it is about the human being, an object of public knowledge. What is said about the poem is subject to the same scrutiny as any statement in linguistics or in the general science of psychology (335).

When once the poem is released into the public territory, it becomes the property of its reader, and hence is subject to any interpretation he deems fit. It is up to the reader to choose his interpretation: there cannot be any sort of authorial control.

This, in turn, was followed up by the article 'Intention' by R.W. Stallman for the *Princeton Encyclopedia of Poetry and Poetics* (1965) edited by Alex Preminger. Stallman, a confirmed New Critic, further strengthened the claims made by Wimsatt and Beardsley.

> Once a work is produced, it possesses objective status—it exists independently of the author and his declared intention. It contains, in so far as it is a work of art, why it is thus and not otherwise. The difference between art and its germinal event is absolute. The best artist constructs his work in such a way as to admit of no interpretation but the single intended one; its single intention being a single effect, one over-all meaning, one composite theme. All parts of the work of art are, *ideally,* relevant or functional to the whole. Irrelevant to the objective status of the work as art are criteria which dissolve the work back into the historical or psychological or creative process from which it came . . . No judgment of intention has relevancy unless corroborated by the work itself, in which case it is supererogatory (399).

With E.D. Hirsch, the focus shifted from the evaluative aspect of intention to the interpretative. And this is of greater concern to students of literature. Have we not wondered whether the authorial notes to *The Waste Land* are a necessary part of the poem, or an irrelevant appendage for the reader? E.D. Hirsch is associated with hermeneutics in our time. His *Validity in Interpretation* (1967) is concerned with a method for distinguishing between correct and incorrect interpretations. Hirsch's main problem is the quest for valid interpretation. Hirsch opposes two traditions in meaning, one that makes meaning relative, and the other that attaches meaning to words rather than consciousness. His aim is to establish the view that meaning is determinate, and that the original intention of the author bears the valid interpretation. The work, after all, is created by a particular author who lived at a particular period of time. This involves a recreation of the work by the person who seeks to understand it. And this again, involves the context in which the work was created and its relation to its historical origins. The first view is opposed on the ground that literary texts have always shown differing interpretations based on newer modes of enquiry and tools for discovery of newer meanings. Freudian and Marxian interpretations developed at a later point of time and have added to newer possibilities of interpretation.

Hirsch distinguishes between two kinds: the first of which is the meaning, and the second, the significance. The first is the verbal meaning, and the second is the variable level of significance. Verbal meaning is the willed type. The meaning is intended, and it is determinate and capable of being shared. Significance, on the other hand, is a relationship between verbal meaning and something outside of it. The range of significance is far and wide, and even limitless. Meaning can be related to an infinite number of things and their various manifestations. Here is Hirsch in his essay, 'Three Dimensions of Hermeneutics':

> The important feature of meaning as distinct from significance is that meaning is the determinate representation of a text for an interpreter . . . Significance is meaning-as-related-to-something-else . . . Thus, while meaning is a principle of stability in an interpretation, significance embraces a principle of change . . . Meaning is what an interpreter actualizes from a text; significance is that actual speaking as heard in a chosen or variable context of the interpreter's experiential world (190–1).

This distinction makes it possible for Hirsch to retain a determinate meaning, while permitting him to allow for a variety of interpretations. He does not subscribe to the New Critical view, at all. Rather, he argues that there is a connection between meaning and authorial intent. Structuralists contend that language itself conveys meaning independent of human agency. Meaning goes beyond the intention of the author. Hirsch reinstates the author at the centre because he is the one who is the basis for determining the validity of interpretation. Valid interpretation is the one that is represented by the text (by the author). Meaning is the outcome of consciousness. And this consciousness may belong to the reader or the author. If the reader's consciousness is taken as the standard, then we do not have any basis or yardstick to determine the valid interpretation. Hence the author's meaning is the only determining norm to compare different interpretations. There are many objections to determining this norm, such as the changes of meaning according to the conditions under which it is read, the inaccessibility to the author's meaning, and the irrelevance of the author's meaning. Hirsch defends all these charges. But all his defences are rather shaky. And his objectivist notion of interpretation appears outmoded in the present context. Caught up in a weird atmosphere, Hirsch developed interest in the area of cultural literacy. Hermeneutic thought gets into a blind alley, and it cannot enter into any productive dialogue with poststructuralist views on language. Deconstructive criticism maintains that it is impossible to unveil, or reach out to the meaning of a text: the text has no meaning at all.

Works Cited

Hirsch, E.D. 'Three Dimensions of Hermeneutics'. *Contemporary Criticism*. Ed. V.S. Seturaman. Madras: Macmillan India Ltd, 1989.

Stallman, R. W. 'Intention'. *Princeton Encyclopedia of Poetry and Poetics*. Ed. Alex Preminger. Princeton: Princeton University Press, 1965.

Wimsatt, William K and M. Beardsley. 'The Intentional Fallacy'. *Twentieth Century Literary Criticism*. Ed. David Lodge. London: Longman, 1972.

Select Bibliography

Godamer, Hans-Georg. *Philosophical Hermeneutics.* Trans. David E. Linge. Berkeley: University of California Press, 1976.

Habermas, Jurgen. *Knowledge and Human Interests.* Trans. Jeremy Shapiro. Boston: Beacon Press, 1971.

Heidegger, Martin. *Being and Time.* Trans. John Macquarrie and Edward Robinson. New York: Harper and Row, 1971.

Hirsch, E.D., Jr. *Validity in Interpretation.* New Haven: Yale University Press, 1967.

———. *The Aims of Interpretation.* Chicago: University of Chicago Press, 1976.

———. *The Philosophy of Composition.* Chicago: University of Chicago Press, 1977.

Ricoeur, Paul. *The Conflict of Interpretations: Essays on Language, Action, and Interpretation.* Trans. and ed. Don Ihde. Evanston, IL.: Northwestern University Press, 1974.

———. *The Course of Recognition.* Trans. David Pellauer: Cambridge, MA: Harvard University Press, 2005.

Schleiermacher, Friedrich. *Hermeneutics: The Handwritten Manuscripts.* Trans. Terence N. Tice. Atlanta: John Knox Press, 1966.

7

American, African-American and British Criticism: A Short Survey

American Criticism

ngland has had an uninterrupted critical tradition dating back to the Renaissance in the sixteenth century. Right from Sir Philip Sidney, there has been a succession of literary critics, discussing literature or setting standards for creative works. Such, of course, is not the case with the United States. It is said that the entire population of the US, at the turn of the nineteenth century, was just around five million, most of which was concentrated in the northeast. One can imagine the quantum of literary production in a country which was rural, wherein industry and printing technology, in particular, had just arrived. Little magazines, hand-printed, commanding small, regional readership began publishing articles supporting the creative efforts of the local gentry. This forms the genesis of the American critical tradition.

A new nation was coming up, trying to establish an identity of its own, and define the framework of its national literature. It neither possessed a history, nor a usable past with a cultivated literature to boast of. Hence, the little magazines pleaded for a greater integration of the writings with the life of the people. As the population grew with fresh arrivals of immigrants from different countries, the reading public widened, and magazines multiplied in numbers. Quest for a national identity was the foremost theme in much of the writings of this era. Necessity is the mother of invention. Two writers of this period who stand out prominently are also two of the greatest American writers: Ralph Waldo Emerson (1803–82), and Edgar Allan Poe (1809–49). Emerson's essay, 'The American Scholar', acclaimed as the inaugural address of the declaration of American literary independence, was published in *The Democratic Review* and Poe's 'The Philosophy of Composition' which recreates the method by which he composed the poem 'The Raven', and 'The Poetic Principle' which talks about the true subject for poetry were published in journals. While Emerson, the transcendentalist, busied himself with laying the foundations for the establishment of an American tradition free from the European influence, Poe took up the aesthetics of the form and content of poetry. A society which depended on derivative philosophy for its sustenance needed some force and effort to awaken it. Emerson and Poe were the two regenerative forces which gave direction and leadership to the writers of this period.

The second half of the nineteenth century witnessed changes in the social set-up consequent on spurts of industrial growth and urbanisation of the country. A gradual formation of a middle-class urban culture was the result of this change from the erstwhile rural structure. This is usually (sometimes even pejoratively) designated by the acronym WASP, meaning White Anglo-Saxon Protestant culture. Little magazines gave room to more learned and prestigious journals such as *Atlantic Monthly,* and *Century Magazine* which commanded a wider circulation. These helped in setting higher intellectual standards in creative art, resulting in literary movements such as idealism, which later gave birth to naturalism and realism. Among the most notable critics of this generation are Henry James (1843–1916), George Santayana (1863–1952) and Joel Spingarn (1875–1939).

Henry James, one of the most distinguished American novelists of all time, was the first to break away from the provincialism that marked the writings of his contemporaries. He was the first to introduce realism and the genre novel of manners in American fiction. He was more of an international writer. A novel, for him, should represent truth and beauty, and not just transcribe life like a photograph. Characters must have individual traits and life of their own. In his well-known essay, 'The Art of Fiction', published in *Longman's Magazine,* he emphasises two essential virtues of fiction: formal pattern and artistic sensibility. A superficial mind cannot produce a good work of art. On the nature of art experience, James points out in 'The Art of Fiction':

> Experience is never limited, and it is never complete; it is an immense sensibility, a kind of huge spider-web of the finest silken threads suspended in the chamber of consciousness, and catching every air-borne particle in its tissue. It is the very atmosphere of the mind; and when the mind is imaginative—much more when it happens to be that of a man of genius—it takes to itself the faintest hint of life, it converts the very pulses of the air to revelations (1396).

Of James, it is often said that he recovered the novel from the street, and brought it to the living room.

In a strict sense, literary criticism can be said to have come of age in the US only in the twentieth century. This is not to say that criticism of some sort was not in vogue in the earlier periods. George Santayana coined the phrase 'the genteel tradition'. He used it to describe the tendency that prevailed in criticism at the beginning of the twentieth century. In his famous lecture 'The Genteel Tradition in American Philosophy', delivered at the University of Berkeley in 1911, he said, 'The American Will inhabits the sky-scraper; the American intellect inhabits the colonial mansion. The one is the sphere of the American man: the other, at least predominantly, of the American woman. The one is an aggressive enterprise; the other is all *genteel tradition'* (40, italics added). This notoriously disparaging term has done a lot by way of altering the course of twentieth century American criticism. It summed up the malady of American intellectual life: a fen of stagnant waters, as Wordsworth once described England. A cultural revolution was the prime need of the day, and Santayana gave a clarion call. He had stirred the hornet's nest. The reaction came, as was expected, from several quarters, first from France in the form of naturalism, symbolism and impressionism.

The first major American voice to react vehemently against this mode was H.L. Mencken (1880–1956), linguist, critic, journalist and satirist. Well-known for his book *The American Language* (1919), he showed interest in criticism also, besides his many-sided interests. His criticism was shaped by three influences: the Age of Enlightenment which emphasised the importance of reason, faith in intellectual aristocracy embodied in the Nietzchean ideal of the Superman, and Darwinism with its belief not in a supernatural God but in evolution. His contemporary Joel Spingarn (1875–1939) was a crusader for what he called 'creative criticism', a criticism in which the creator and the critic became one. What Spingarn meant was that the critic's taste, his disciplined aesthetic enjoyment should be such as to reproduce the work of art in order to understand and judge it. At that moment aesthetic judgment becomes, more or less, creative art itself. Mencken, on the other hand, pleaded for 'catalytic criticism', in which the critic is concerned with provoking the reader to think about the work. The function of the critic is to provoke the reaction between the work of art and the spectator. He looked upon the critic as an artist who tries to express himself. Criticism need not be constructive, trying to win over anyone to any side. According to modern standards, Mencken's ideas were funny; he rated poetry lowly, he favoured only the novel and the drama of ideas. Shakespeare, according to him, was a second-rate philosopher, but a great musician who created music with words. Mencken had a poor opinion of most nineteenth century American writers. Conrad and Mark Twain were the two writers whom he most admired. As a stimulating iconoclast, he revelled in demolishing the reputations of established authors and in polemics. But, he performed a major function by liberating American writing from complacency and provincialism. And in this sense, he may be looked upon as a reformer. His writings were witty and pungent, but as a literary critic his contribution has only a limited value. His ideas have grown outdated. According to modern standards, his views are conservative and not liberal enough.

Van Wyck Brooks (1886–1963) also attacked much of American culture and literature by taking up arms against the complacencies of the Puritans. In his *America's Coming of Age* (1915), he charged that most American writers were idealistic without being attached to the people, and hence, remained unintegrated. Literature remained separated from the people. He expected critics to awaken the consciousness of people. Critics must be champions and crusaders, so to speak. He dubbed *Huckleberry Finn* (1884), a much admired American classic, 'a book of boys, for boys, by a boy'. He did not like the urbanisation of America. He brought to light many lesser-known American writers. His view of literature was that it should contribute to a richer life, and enhance the quality of life of the people. He pleaded for primary literature which would talk about progress and the goodness of man; he detested the secondary or 'coterie literature' that included French symbolists, Joyce, Pound and the New Critics. Quite unreasonably, he attacked modernism and Eliot. He donned the role of a preacher, and a moralist, repudiating the commercial nature of American society. His criticism is not much relevant these days, but he did something to rediscover the great American tradition, which was lost to the people for long. His approach to criticism was biographical. Two main reasons for which Van Wyck Brooks is still remembered are his attack on the isolation of the American artist from society, and his insistence on the need for discovering a 'usable past'.

The new humanists (also referred to as neohumanists, or simply humanists) were those who discussed American culture and literature seriously, but they are almost a forgotten lot now. Most of them were learned men of letters who opposed the American abhorrence of old values. They wanted to revive the forgotten past tradition with its respect for morality and moderation. The names of Irving Babbitt (1865–1933) and Paul Elmer More (1864–1937) stand out outstandingly as the two who were involved in the neohumanist movement. Babbitt was Professor of French at Harvard University for twenty years and More, his student, was a Thoreau to Babbitt's Emerson. The debate between the humanists and the antihumanists is a thing of the past, nearly forgotten by us now. The whole movement collapsed with the upsurge of Marxism, and the impact of Depression. But, the spirit still survives. One has only to read Eliot's essays on the subject to understand its survival. Babbitt may have many weaknesses as a critic, but he was a forceful historian of ideas, and very learned too of political and moral ideas. He was instrumental in pleading for comparatism in criticism, and quite rightly, the Harvard chair is named after him. To him should go the credit of asserting the function of criticism and defending open-mindedness in the pursuit of literary studies. More's *Shelburne Essays,* in eleven volumes, speak of his work as a critic. Norman Foerster called him 'the greatest of all American critics, better than a trans-Atlantic copy of a French critic. He stands with Coleridge, Sainte-Beuve, Samuel Johnson and three or four others in the first rank of critical art.' He was an ideal judicial critic. The new humanists believed in removing any historical barrier that stood between the reader and the work. They argued that while evaluating a work, its artistic beauty should be taken into consideration. Does the work contribute to the perfection of human nature? It is in the work of Norman Foerster that the criticism of new humanists can be seen at its best. Alfred Kazin sums up the contribution of the new humanists:

> The New Humanists had, if not an applicable standard, a *sense* of standards, a conviction of the necessity of order, a belief in some exterior authority and discipline; and it was the assurance with which they inveighed against naturalism in literature and impressionism in criticism, the deliberation with which they propounded the need of a literature based on human responsibility and aristocratic dignity, that gave them their importance (221).

For George Santayana (1863–1952), literary criticism was not a major preoccupation, but a minor activity. As a classicist in taste, he depended more on evaluating a literary work on moral grounds, than on analysing or explaining it. He is best known for his work *The Genteel Tradition in American Philosophy* (1911). His book *Sense of Beauty* (1896) is concerned with general aesthetics. He combines technical philosophy with literary criticism. And that is probably why his own contribution as a literary critic is not substantial.

In England, there was always a steady tug-of-war between the study of the classical languages and English, a new entrant in the field. For reasons such as pride in their nationality, English was defended as a subject worthy of study, if not for its own sake. It was only in the twentieth century that criticism began to raise its head, and Arnold was the name constantly invoked by Richards and Leavis, the twin custodians of criticism in England. In the US, rhetoric and oratory were taught. In Johns Hopkins, in 1876, English was introduced in the graduate curriculum, and the Modern Languages Association was founded in 1883. Antiquarian scholarship held the fort in the American universities up until the twentieth century. This might have been good in many ways, such as bringing up good and definitive editions of literary texts, studies in biography and history, but it did not further the cause of humanist learning. Specialised learning, for its own sake, is not good enough. Appreciation and enjoyment of the good and the beautiful are the true ends of criticism.

Joel Elias Spingarn (1875–1939) delivered a lecture in 1910 at Columbia University called 'The New Criticism' in which he rejected much of impressionism and dogmatic criticism, all of which shift our interest from art to something else. He said that criticism should raise questions such as, 'What has the poet tried to do and how has he fulfilled his intention? What is he striving to express and how has he expressed it?' He attacked insistence on moralistic criteria, deplored the neglect of the aesthetic concerns, and pleaded for responsibility and taste in judgment. His collection of essays was published under the title *The New Criticism* in 1917. He himself was a good student of the history of criticism. His *History of Criticism in the Renaissance* (1899) remains a standard work to this day. He was the founder of the prestigious *Journal of Comparative Literature.* According to Robert Spiller, he was the first critic to supply the rationale, the method and even the tools for analytical criticism. Ransom titled his book *The New Criticism* (1941), borrowing the title from Spingarn who used it in a different sense.

John Livingston Lowes of Harvard and the author of *The Road to Xanadu*(1926), in his presidential address of the MLA, said that 'the ultimate end of our research is criticism in the fullest sense of the often misused word' to which Howard Mumford Jones replied that literary scholarship should not be aesthetic but historical. The controversy between these two scholars was the main point of interest in the academic scene. R.S. Crane (1886–1967) of the University of Chicago took up the issue, and wrote an article in 1935 called 'History versus Criticism in the Study of Literature'. He said that history and criticism should be kept separate from each other. He strongly advocated the introduction of criticism in universities. Crane and his colleagues, called 'The Chicago Neo-Aristotelians', collected their critical essays in the volume *Critics and Criticism* (1952). The journal *Modern Philology,* one of the oldest in the US, of which Crane was the editor, helped in furthering their cause in the 1940s. They were committed to a plurality of critical methods, and their commitment to Aristotle was strictly pragmatic. Though they pleaded for tolerance, in their practice they severely attacked the New Critics, and condemned modern criticism. They appealed to commonsense apprehension. They worshipped Aristotle, refuted Plato, and any theory that adhered to the Platonic doctrine. Aristotle considered poems as concrete objects and artistic wholes, while Longinus and the others who came after him considered poems as modes of discourse. Criticism concerned itself with poetic qualities, instead. The Chicago critics recommended the use of the Aristotelian hierarchy in the structural composition of a work: mythos, ethos, dianoia, lexis, music and spectacle. In their poetics, the consideration of 'plot' and 'pleasure' was central. They were strong adherents to genre distinctions. They undervalued the importance of language in poetry, and hence they do not evince much interest in semantics or modern linguistics or factors such as paradox, ambiguity, etc. They were also very learned historians of criticism. Despite all their learning, the end product by way of practical criticism of works was, by no means, substantial. The school did not have much of an impact, but remained for the most part a local phenomenon with local adherents like Robert Marsh and Wayne C. Booth. New Criticism, which was slighted by the Chicago critics, triumphed over it; and as critical practice, it came to occupy the whole of the country, indeed most of the world. In such a context, the conflict between history and criticism went out of focus. And in the present day, it sounds wholly inappropriate, if not irrelevant.

There were also some conventional and traditional historians and scholars who practised criticism of a high calibre. John Livingstone Lowes (1867–1945), whom we referred to earlier, wrote a book, *Road to Xanadu* (1927) in which he hunted scrupulously—and speculatively—after the possible sources, which could have gone into the making of Coleridge's 'Kubla Khan'. He employed what goes by the name of associationist psychology: the work has ample evidence of extraordinary scholarship. Eliot did not consider it genuine literary criticism: it went beyond what he called the frontiers of criticism. Elmer Edgar Stoll (1874–1959) was a Shakespeare scholar of eminence, who rejected the motive hunting scholarship of the Bradleyan variety of criticism which equates the play to a transcript of life. He advocated a method that would rely on stage conventions and stagecraft. The problem was one of recreating Shakespeare's audience—a daunting task formidably impossible now. Also, works have meanings added on to them, and we cannot afford to give up four centuries of scholarship which help us to read and interpret Shakespeare. Joseph Warren Beach (1880–1957) anticipated much of modern narratology in fictional studies. He was perhaps the first American to write about the techniques employed in fiction. Morris W. Croll (1872–1947) practised stylistic analyses of texts, modelled after the Germans, Leo Spitzer and Eric Auerbach.

Arthur O. Lovejoy (1873–1962) was a philosopher and historian of philosophy. He developed a concept of the history of ideas, wherein 'unit ideas' could be discovered as operating in literature. His monumental work The *Great Chain of Being* (1936) broke the German *zeitgeist* and split it up into atomistic unit-ideas. These were Nature, God, Romanticism, etc. The greatest drawback in this vastly great intellectual system is its extreme reductionism in imposing standards drawn from philosophy on the world of literary imagination. *The Journal of the History of Ideas* is committed to publishing articles which interpret works on the basis of the 'unit ideas' recommended by Lovejoy. F.O. Matthiessen (1902–50) wrote two interesting studies, *American Renaissance* (1941), and *The Achievement of T.S. Eliot* (1935). The first one was a study in aesthetic evaluation of Emerson, Thoreau, Hawthorne, Melville, and Whitman. He also edited the *Oxford Anthology of American Verse* (1948). All in all, he was a scholar-critic par excellence. Alfred Kazin (1915–99) published his *On Native Grounds* (1942), which was a study in prose literature since the 1890s in three divisions, 1890–1914, 1918–29, and 1930–40. He rejects New Criticism, and sings in glorious terms of the past condemning the present. Stanley Edgar Hyman (1919–70) wrote an important book in criticism called *The Armed Vision: A Study in the Methods of Modern Literary Criticism* (1948). He studies modern criticism in the light of concepts derived from sociology, psychoanalysis, anthropology, and recent and related disciplines. These academic scholar-critics have done much by way of reassessing American literature for the later generations. And that, indeed, is a great contribution to literary scholarship.

Hippolyte Taine, the French critic, is perhaps the first to be associated with a sociological approach to literary study. His proclamation that literature is the product of race, moment and milieu has become the cornerstone for this extrinsic approach. Literature, as is so often said, is an institution first and last. Marx and Engels added another dimension, the economic factor to this threefold scheme, implying thereby that literature is also shaped by an ideology that seeks the protection and welfare of the masses. In the US, especially in the early years, Marxism is not to be strictly understood as an actual adherence to Marxist ideology, but a loose or general opposition to capitalism, and sympathy for the labouring and working classes. Max Eastman (1893–1967) edited The *Masses* (1912–17) and the *Liberator* (1918), took active interest in Russian communism, only to abandon it totally in later years. His *Literary Mind: Its Place in an Age of Science* (1932) is a valuable contribution to Marxist approach to criticism. Irwin Granich alias Michael Gold (1893–1967), Granville Hicks (1901–82), James T. Farrell who wrote *A Note on Literary Criticism* (1936) are other names in Marxist criticism. *Partisan Review* was founded in 1934 by Philip Rahv (1908–73) under the auspices of the Communist party. This periodical attempted to combine modernism with Marxism, and Rahv remained committed to this ideology till his end. Rahv is always remembered for his formula for two traditions in American literature—the red skin/ the plebian (Whitmanesque), and the pale face/ the patrician (Jamesian). Rahv never took up writing about poetry. His best efforts are seen in his criticism of Russian literature. The best these Marxist critics could do was to bring attention to social and non-literary sources behind works of literature—a thing not known to generations before them.

Edmund Wilson (1895–1972) is one among the renowned American critics who are known outside the US. He wrote novels, poetry and drama besides practising criticism. His essays, 'Marxism and Literature' (1937), and 'Historical Interpretation of Literature' (1941) are among his best-known works. His works precede the era of New Criticism and he never accepts any evaluation of the New Critics. He charges Leavis with dogmatism. He dismisses Eliot as a literary dictator and a reincarnated Dr Johnson: he does not approve of either his religion or his politics. Early in life he was influenced by Taine's view of literature, and later he adopted the Marxian approach. As a practical critic, he aired his views on a wide variety of authors. He disliked historical romances and detective fiction. He did not possess the skills necessary for poetic or narrative analysis. He had too deep an interest in sex, and writings about it, and he never cultivated any interest in the fine arts. Religion was anathema to him. His world view was rather narrow; his authoritative tone often crude and insolent. Nevertheless, as a critic and man of letters whose interests were wide, he had but few equals in magisterial proclamations. V.L. Parrington (1871–1929), a progressive liberal intellectual, is another important sociological critic of this era. His *Main Currents in American Thought* (1927), in three volumes, is the only literary history written on the basis of the social, economic and political development in the US. It is undoubtedly a trend-setting work; but strictly speaking, it is a history of American political thought, written from the perspective of American liberalism. As literary history, it suffers from economic determinism. It gets into a social track which is concerned mainly with political ideology. Like Edmund Wilson, Lionel Trilling (1905–75) was also a critic of American culture and a man with wide interests such as psychology, politics and teaching. In his book of essays *The Liberal Imagination* (1950), *The Opposing Self* (1959), and *Sincerity and Authenticity* (1972), he attempted to reconcile radicalism in politics with modernism, since the two appeared rather irreconcilable. He wished for a modified tradition of liberalism. Trilling was shaped by the beliefs of New Criticism. He was part of the establishment that goes by the name 'English Institute' which was a forum for New Criticism. He encouraged the reaction against the positivism and scientism in studies. He said that literary study must be a study of language. He took New Criticism to task for ignoring the historicity of works. His excellent essay 'Sense of the Past' illustrates this. We can feel that a work is alive, only if we know the historicity of its past. This was a salutary corrective to the unbridled excesses of New Criticism. He insisted on the moral and intellectual values of a work besides the merely aesthetic ones. His interests were given more to the novel and he, with all his broad-based catholicity interests, preferred the European to the American.

Towards the middle of the twentieth century, two major voices dominated the circuit of criticism in England and America: F.R. Leavis and T.S. Eliot. Nineteenth century beliefs grew outmoded; content and form in poetry were accepted to be inseparable. Literary works were understood to be wholes. Literature was considered and treated as an art. Critics realised their fiduciary responsibility that they must differentiate between works of art and non-art, establish criteria for such a separation and evaluation and, thereby, build up a tradition of literary canons. Sheer irresponsible impressionism and literary chitchat must be given up to be replaced by a close analysis of works and serious critical attention. This led to a consideration of the language of literature with greater attention to metaphors, images, and figurative language as a whole. Some differing views were held with regard to poetry and its function. It was felt that poetry presented an ideal world, and it was thought that it conveyed occult meanings. Some focussed on the 'extrinsic' methods and some on the 'intrinsic'. Literature began to be related to some basic myths of mankind. Wilson Knight, Richard Chase, and Northrop Frye were some who practised this criticism. Philip Wheelwright and Francis Fergusson were the others. Frank Kermode reacted against Frye's methodology of alienating the artist in preference to the seer with whom he came to be associated. Frye's impact was perceived by Abrams, Hartman, and Bloom as a revival of interest in the US in romantic poetry.

The whole outlook on criticism underwent a sea change in the US after the conference on 'The Languages of Criticism and the Sciences of Man', held at Johns Hopkins University, Baltimore in 1966. French-inspired structuralism, under the influence of Saussure and Claude Levi-Strauss, spread in the US through Robert Scholes and Jonathan Culler. Gerard Genette and Tzvetan Todorov in France did far better work. In the US, however, poststructuralism has had a strong influence and a good backing. Jacques Derrida, its founder, and Paul de Man and Hillis Miller, the practitioners, have contributed to its growth and publicity. New ideas and methods of reading, generated by European theories, challenged the complacency of the past. Deconstruction (one form of poststructuralism) enlarges upon structuralism using its hypothesis that language is a closed system without any reference to reality outside. We are caught, as it were, in a web called language, where one word leads to another and yet another, *ad infinitum*. Nothing exists outside the text and even the author, the producer of the work, is declared dead! There is no difference between literature as imaginative writing and any other writing (*ecriture*). All writing is one, even as mankind is one. There is no such thing as an aesthetic experience in itself. It does not differ from other experiences. Life emotion and art emotion get equated to one another. Such notions are at variance with ideas on literary study held for centuries. There is no separate category called art: nor is there any criterion of judgement about its value. There are no commonly held norms to evaluate writing. Value judgments are a thing of the past. Every text is polysemic, and meaning is indeterminate. Bloom says, 'All reading is misreading'. Hillis Miller feels that all texts are 'unreadable'. His view is that nihilism is an inalienable presence in Western thought. Paul de Man echoes the same sentiment when he says that poetry asserts itself as pure nothingness. Every text allows for mutually self-destructive points of view. All said and done, deconstructionist criticism has encouraged a healthy scepticism of the time-honoured view that meanings of literary works are always unitary and all contradictions in a work are resolvable into a majestic synthesis.

England, on the other hand, had always resisted some of the European-biased theories. Leavis was opposed to theory. With the growth and proliferation of these theories, especially in metropolitan universities, there is also in existence conventional systems of scholarship in reviewing books, editing texts, interpreting them, searching for sources in literary works and building up historical facts about them. Paradoxically, these two go hand in hand. After all the major function of criticism remains, as always, preserving the past and making it available to the ages that follow. A great deal of the traditional practice still survives, and happily so. Established methods need to be defended as often as possible. Otherwise literary education cannot go on. Equally important is theory. Theory is the result of an unending discussion on the arts, often intimidating though. In the interest of literary study and literary scholarship, this discussion on the old and the new, the traditional and the contemporary, must go on:

> But there is no competition . . . .
> There is only the fight to recover what has been lost
> And found and lost again and again . . .
>
> T.S. Eliot, 'Little Gidding'

Works Cited

James, Henry. 'The Art of Fiction'. *Concise Anthology of American Literature.* Ed. George McMichael. New York: Macmillan Publishing Company, 1985.

Kazin, Alfred. *On Native Grounds: An Interpretation of Modern American Prose Literature.* 1942. San Diego, Calif.: Harcourt Brace & Co., 1995.

Santayana, George. *The Genteel Tradition.* Ed. Douglas L. Wilson. Cambridge, MA: Harvard University Press, 1967.

Select Bibliography

Glicksberg, Charles Irving. *American Literary Criticism, 1900–1950.* New York: Hendricks House, 1952.

Leitch, Vincent B. *American Literary Criticism from the Thirties to the Eighties.* New York: Columbia University Press, 1988.

AFRICAN-AMERICAN CRITICISM

> I have a dream that my children will one day live in a nation where they will not be judged by the colour of their skin but by the content of their character.
>
> Martin Luther King Jr.

Martin Luther King's (1929–68) memorable speech 'I have a dream' delivered in 1963 needs to be understood in the context in which it was delivered. African-American history and culture had been deliberately and consistently excluded from American education and literary history. Great events such as the antislavery movement, and the Harlem Renaissance had been repressed and obscured from public view. There was a felt need to awaken the blacks to this stark reality. The time for redressal of the wrongs had come in the 1960s.

African-American criticism is as old as American criticism itself. Its genesis can be located in the earliest writings which seek to contest the prevailing belief that the writings of the African Americans are inferior in quality to those of the others. The first official organ of the African Americans, *Freedom Journal,* was founded in 1827 with the editorial policy which openly declared, 'We wish to plead our own cause.' The motif of discussion that ran through their occasional verses was slavery. In course of time, they found publication channels in high-powered journals such as *Atlantic*. Defining the attributes that would make up African-American literature, and creating an identity for their literature were the main points in the agenda of their discussion. Literature should be the weapon to fight against institutionalised racism, and segregation. Literary societies began cropping up and 'Bibliography of Negro Literature' was published and circulated to people to widen the reading public. Just around the same time, in 1900, *Woman's Era,* a newspaper for African women was founded. The first major work, *The Souls of the Black Folk* by W.E.B. Du Bois came out in 1903. It argued that they (African-Americans) have a heritage of their own—uncontaminated by the white culture—and it derives from the folk tradition that prevails in Africa. In his articles in the journal he edited, *Crisis,* and in his essay 'Criteria of Negro Art', Du Bois called upon black artists to effect a social change. He re-emphasised the twin functions of art: beauty and utility. Black art should be a repository of beauty, goodness and truth and it had an obligation to fight for social justice.

In the second and third decades of the twentieth century, after World War I, there was a marked migration of the blacks from the rural to the urban and to the metropolitan areas in search of jobs. New jobs were available in a society that was getting industrialised fast. This signalled a spurt in literary activity. Langston Hughes, Zora Neil Hurston, Richard Wright, Ralph Ellison, James Baldwin, to name a few major writers, represent this sudden spurt. Writers began to feel that they should not depend on the patronage of the whites; they should strike their own path, and use their black culture to their advantage. The white writers had stereotyped them, and had not represented them in three dimensions. It was, therefore, their duty to portray the blacks as human, with all foibles a human possesses. Langston Hughes's essay, 'The Negro Artist and the Racial Mountain', published in 1926, exhorted fellow artists, in no uncertain terms, to draw out their vast cultural black heritage, and create works that would establish an identity of their own. All this was part of the literary movement that later came to be called the Harlem

Renaissance. Protest literature grew strong with the publication of Richard Wright's *Native Son.* Poets, like Gwendolyn Brooks, voiced forth their protest in strong verse. Journals, such as *New Digest,* carried voices of protest directed against the unjust educational and judicial systems that denied blacks equal rights.

Protest literature happily came to an end during the 1960s with the growth of 'black aesthetics' (the slogan being 'Black is beautiful'). Major writers, Ralph Ellison and James Baldwin, argued that protest would lead only to hatred. The best thing would be to assert their art and join the mainstream of literature by showing to the world what black writers are made of. Black aesthetics was growing alongside of modernism. As could be expected, there was a reaction to the accommodationist stance of Ellison and Baldwin. They were charged with wooing western white audiences, who were racists. The controversy was fuelled by journals like *Black World* spearheaded by diehard black nationalists like Amiri Baraka (Le Roi Jones). A new era in interpretation of black literature was ushered in with the publication of *Afro-American Literature: A Reconstruction of Instruction* (1978). Using the methods of rhetorical analysis and intertextuality, advocated by poststructuralism, the reconstructionist critics re-interpreted African-American classics. A semiotic study of literature was made by Henry Louis Gates, Jr. which approached African-American works based upon purely artistic considerations, eschewing politics and social considerations. *Black Literature and Literary Theory* (1985) and *The Signifying Monkey: A Theory of Afro-American Literary Criticism* (1988) are such studies that emphasise a semiotic approach. This again found disfavour with those antagonists whose view was that the function of criticism was to aid writers in developing their art. Criticism should aid creation.

Black women's writings have now emerged full-scale as diasporic feminist literature. There is a growing tradition in their writings which underscores their experiences which is far different from the experiences of the white. They have now come forward to portray, avoiding all cultural stereotypes, their women as real people, who have to face many complex problems. Their relationships, aspirations, and their creativity are examined in depth. They are engaged in a mission of revisionism, so to speak. African-American feminist criticism analyses their problems.

'Suspended woman', 'assimilated woman', 'emergent woman', and 'liberated woman' are some categories of their representation. Feminist critics bring out several strategies employed by writers like Alice Walker and Toni Morrison, who bring home the black experience most convincingly by foregrounding it. African-American criticism also engages in a revisionary reading of white American writers. The white text constructs the African presence in American history in its own terms and for its own benefit. Toni Morrison's *Playing in the Dark: Whiteness and the Literary Imagination* (1993) is one such study. Africanism is a white conception of the African people.

There are some concepts in the African-American experience which are used in discussions. The term 'racialism' is a belief that moral and intellectual characteristics are biologically determined. 'Racism' believes in unequal power relations. It is a discriminatory practice. 'Institutionalised racism' refers to those social practices that do not treat all people as equals in the matter of education, jobs, etc. While framing the syllabi for college courses of study, for example, the Western literary canon is dominated by Eurocentric writers. 'Internalised racism' refers to an indoctrination of racist beliefs into coloured people. The problem of 'double consciousness' refers to the predicament of the black writers: whether to write for the white or the black audience or both. On the one hand, there is the social responsibility they have to bear in mind, and on the other they do not wish to be excluded from mainstream writing.

The common sub-text of all their writings is the economics of slavery, bondage and centuries old oppression. With the proliferation of black literature in diverse forms, African-American canon is getting well established. All these have helped in a free discussion of their literature without any need to defend it as a subject suitable for academic study and research. And that is the bottomline!

Select Bibliography

Arnett, Ervin Hazel, ed. *African American Literary Criticism, 1773 to 2000.* New York: Twayne, 1999.

BRITISH CRITICISM

For most of us, English criticism always meant British criticism. Since English is the language of the British, these two were used synonymously. In the twentieth century, British criticism may be said to start roughly from the second decade of the century, when modernism in arts emerged in many countries of Europe. In England, the year 1922 represents the *annus mirabilis* of modernism with the publication of *The Waste Land* and *Ulysses.* In the Victorian period, only general aesthetic or romantic views, mostly inspirational in character, were aired and no critical thought of any prominence came into question. The symbolist movement of French origin did have an impact on England. Arthur Symons (1865–1945) publicised the ideas of French symbolism in his trailblazing book *The Symbolist Movement in Literature* (1900), which won the admiration of Eliot, and which affected his course of life and literary career. The Irish Yeats had his own brand of theory built around his private, esoteric symbols, which he discusses at length in his complex and puzzling work *Vision* (1925).

Criticism came to occupy its place in the universities in the beginning of the twentieth century. Until then, men of letters combined criticism and scholarship and articulated their views in learned journals. The situation now is different: criticism does not—indeed cannot—exist outside the academia. How criticism entered the portals of the university is interesting, indeed. Hugh Blair was the first Professor of Rhetoric and Belles Lettres at the University of Edinburgh in 1762, and Thomas Wharton, the author of *The History of English Poetry* (1774–81), Fellow of Trinity College, Oxford, was a critic of some reputation. All other important critics remained outside the university fold. Coleridge, Hazlitt, Macaulay, Carlyle and De Quincey were rank outsiders. The second half of the nineteenth century saw some change. Arnold became the Professor of Poetry at Oxford in 1857, and was the first to lecture in English at the Chair established in 1704. He lectured almost every year for ten years in total. But his main studies in criticism were published in learned magazines outside the university. Swinburne, Bagehot and Leslie Stephen had nothing to do with the universities. Walter Pater was a fellow of Brasenose College, Oxford. Though English literature as a subject came to be taught in the colleges from the nineteenth century, criticism was not a part of it. Rev Thomas Dale taught in University College, London, from 1828 and Henry Morley from 1865 to 1885, but they were not worthy of note for their interest in criticism. They were biographers or moralisers. F.J. Furnivall (1837–1934) taught in Manchester from 1866. A.W. Ward (1837–1934) also taught there from 1866. Teaching, for these scholarly men, meant doling out factual history, or supplying biographical facts. George Saintsbury was the first to effect some reforms, when he became Professor of Rhetoric and Belles Lettres at Edinburgh in 1895. Edward Dowden (1842–1913) of Trinity College, Dublin, and the author of *Shakespeare: His Mind and Art*, A.C. Bradley who became Professor of Modern Literature and History in University College, Liverpool, W.P. Ker of University College, London were the other critics of prominence entering the university for the spread of their critical enterprise.

The School of English was established in Oxford in 1894, where the Merton Professorship was instituted in 1885. By and large, those who taught in the universities upheld classical education, and did not do much to encourage modern literature. English was taught along the lines of classical philology. Editing and commentaries were carried on as research. These had their own use. In 1904, the Merton Professorship was held by Walter Raleigh and Sir Arthur Quiller-Couch became the King Edward VII Professor at Cambridge. Neither of them took criticism seriously, and neither of them had any taste for it. Quiller-Couch's edition of the *Oxford Book of English Verse* created a taste for poetry. Scholarship meant some degree of learning and some enjoyment of literature as an amateur. Gradually this lost its appeal to the student generation. When I.A. Richards appeared on the scene, literary studies took a different shape altogether.

A.C. Bradley (1851–1935): At the time Walter Raleigh and Sir Arthur Quiller-Couch were occupying positions of prominence in the two citadels of learning, criticism came into its own in the universities at the beginning of the twentieth century. There were some scholar-critics elsewhere also. Of them, the most distinguished and widely known to Indian students of literature was the redoubtable A.C. Bradley. His *Shakespearean Tragedy* (1904) was so much as a Bible for Indian students. It used to be a wisecrack in any undergraduate class that Shakespeare failed in the 'Shakespeare' paper because he had not read his Bradley. Middleton Murry thought that it was the greatest single work of criticism in English, while Leavis and the *Scrutiny* scholars forcibly pushed Bradley off the pedestal. Bradley was a committed student of Hegel, whom he read at the feet of the Oxford scholar, Green. No wonder then that his aesthetic theory was based on Hegel's philosophy of tragedy. He had read the German critics of Shakespeare, and was most at home in German metaphysics. The English had known of the meaning of tragedy from the Aristotelian tradition, and its effect on the audience by arousing the twin emotions of pity and fear. The Germans had enquired into the phenomenon as something inward arising out of what is to be done out of necessity and as freedom.

For him (Bradley), reality is one and the same. All things which exist are only imperfect manifestations of the real one, the infinite. Evil is that which alienates the part from the whole. Finite is imperfect while the infinite is perfect. Finally moral order is restored and harmony prevails. Tragedy as an art is the very image of this human drama. Tragedy defends and confirms this order of the world. The tragic hero goes against this order and succumbs and submits. 'We feel that this spirit, even in the error and defeat, rises by its greatness into ideal union with the power that overwhelms it' (Bradley, 292). Passive suffering cannot lead to the tragic. A tragic hero is one who is responsible for his actions. There is no element of chance in tragedy. The concept of poetic justice, that virtue is rewarded and evil punished, is again alien to the tragic spirit. To understand tragedy, Bradley has to look at the characters, because actions issue through character. It is this insistence on character that has come in for much criticism. There is some justification for such a charge, for he is not always clear to himself about the distinction between art and life, fiction and reality, art-emotion and life-emotion. L.C. Knights made a scathing attack on him in his famous essay, 'How many children had Lady Macbeth?' Leavis seems to have suggested this title, which Knights seems to have regretted later.

The rejection of Bradley came from different quarters: from those who maintained that Shakespeare's plays should be discussed as effective stage drama, from those who thought that he was unhistorical in his concept of tragedy, from those who wanted to interpret Shakespeare's plays as poems in terms of imagery and themes. Bradley relied on his personal emotional reactions to Shakespeare. He had his notion of tragedy, he analysed characters and their motives for action and recorded his personal responses to emotional situations. By following these ideas, he has succeeded in inculcating in us something about the profundities of Shakespeare's plays. At least, he did not veer away from the essential Shakespeare by proposing strange, whimsical interpretations, as most of those who came after him have done. The fact remains that Bradley laid the foundations for a philosophic criticism of Shakespeare practised later by such well-known critics such as Middleton Murry and Wilson Knight. In this way he led all the rest. He still goes strong, read quite often by students, discussed freely and disagreed with equally freely.

A few other critics merit our consideration. Oliver Elton (1866–1960) produced a large body of writing, but is remembered mostly for his *Survey of English Literature* (1928), in two volumes, covering a period from 1730 to 1880. It contains a series of direct and personal judgments on literary works. For him, it is the primary work of the critic to redefine the classic and this he performs adequately. The others are Walton Paton Ker (1855–1923), Herbert Grierson (1866–1960) and H.W. Garrod (1878–1960). A few intelligent Cambridge undergraduates formed a group in 1899, and met regularly to discuss matters relating to art and literature in Gordon Square, Bloomsbury. It later came to be called the Bloomsbury group. It included the two daughters of Leslie Stephen, Vanessa who later married Clive Bell, and Virginia who married Leonard Woolf, John Maynard Keynes the economist, Lytton Strachey, Roger Fry, Desmond MacCarthy, and E.M. Forster. The group had some common beliefs: it repudiated conventional manners, morals and wisdom. It asserted that the most valuable things in the world are the pleasures of human interaction, and enjoyment of beautiful objects. 'Nothing mattered except states of mind, our own and other people's, of course, but chiefly our own. These states of mind were not associated with action or achievement or with consequences. They consisted in timeless, passionate states of contemplation and communion, largely unattached to the "before" and the "after".' They did not claim that the aesthetic experience was mystical, as did Middleton Murry. They had nothing in common with the prevailing notions on art. They were Bohemians—quite different from others in their ideas on life and art.

It is true that the changes in the outlook on theory and criticism took place under the benign influence of T.S. Eliot, I.A. Richards, and their disciples. But there were several factors that helped in the change of outlook. Even in the realm of arts and poetry, the climate became most conducive to these changes. Georgian poetry yielded place to a new kind of poetry. Imagism and vorticism was the norm. Evoking visual image without the need of the rhetoric, writing free verse and adding dynamism to the movement of the image were the motives for new poetry. The terms 'modernism' and 'modernist' were later appended to the movement. The term is derived from the Latin *modo* which means 'today'. In this sense, it was opposed to the *antique.* Swift's well-known *Battle of the Books* enacted the drama of the polarisation between the two. Classical-romantic is another instance. The term attained currency only in the nineteen fifties, and then, it has now come to be contrasted with postmodernism.

F.R. Leavis (1895–1978): In 1962, at the age of sixty-seven, Leavis retired from Downing College, Cambridge. George Steiner referred to it as the close of an age, the end of an era in English sensibility. Just about the same time, Leavis delivered—what was later to become a famous controversy—the Rede lecture at Cambridge (1959) in which he attacked Sir C. P. Snow for his book *The Two Cultures and the Scientific Revolution* (1959). It was a sensational event, this clash between the two titans. Leavis maintained that literature affords us examples of writers like Arnold, Ruskin, Conrad and Lawrence, who showed what it is to lead an ideal life, a life not accessible to the one promoted by science and technology. Leavis was aware of the likely danger that the spread of science education might cause. It would certainly spell ruin to all that he had so carefully built in his career as a critic and teacher. It was his way of showing his resistance.

Leavis was always a maverick, opposing the entrenched academicians at Cambridge, which refused him a lectureship. He was sidelined and marginalised, but he carried on his tirade against the establishment with which his relationship was always charged with conflict, and created a ginger group at Downing College promoting English studies. He became the *bete noire* of the British academia. The official organ that spread Leavisian views on the profession and purpose of English studies was, of course, *Scrutiny*, a journal that ran for twenty-one years, from 1932 to 1953. He, along with his wife, founded this quarterly journal of literary and social criticism which, perhaps, is his best contribution to English letters. These volumes are the voice of the master. Selections from *Scrutiny*, in two volumes, were issued by the Cambridge University Press. Boris Ford, one of Leavis's disciples, edited *The Pelican Guide to English Literature* in eight volumes, and these sold extremely well. Now many of Leavis's works are available in paperback editions, which speak volumes for the large-scale impact he has had on the academic world at large. He was a charismatic and undisputed leader of the critical world of England. Many of his friends and followers have now grown into celebrities. L.C. Knights and Derek Traversi are some names to contend with in the world of Shakespeare scholarship. It can be argued that much of his isolation was of his own making. He fell foul on the elders in his field, he had no sympathy for Marxism, and he willingly alienated himself from such widely read journals as the *TLS*. He was unfriendly to Bateson and despised his journal, *Essays in Criticism*. It used to be said that he was discourteous to others, and even ill-mannered on occasions. However, despite his lack of manners and courtesy to others, he did succeed, and succeed enormously, in creating a following which has no equal in recent history.

Leavis not merely inherited, but took upon himself the role of the torchbearer of the humanistic tradition earlier initiated by his spiritual predecessor Arnold in the nineteenth century. Under the influence of Eliot, he wrote his first book *New Bearings in English Poetry* (1932) in which he strongly laments the plight of poetry at the very end of the Victorian era, when it became cheap Sunday picnic stuff. He was the first to approach Eliot sympathetically, and his judgement that Hopkins would be the most influential poet for future generations has proved true since. His second book, *Revaluations* (1936), better realised though less ambitiously conceived, re-examines British poetry from the twentieth century perspective. *The Great Tradition* (1948) is a work in fictional poetics discussing the merits of Jane Austen, George Eliot, Henry James and Joseph Conrad. He declared boldly that D. H. Lawrence belonged to the great tradition of novelists. *The*

Common Pursuit (1952)—with the title derived from Eliot's 'The Function of Criticism'—is a collection of essays which follow the essential Leavisian approach to textual criticism. Leavis made a clear distinction between philosophy and literary criticism in his *Scrutiny* essay 'Literary Criticism and Philosophy' in which he made a frontal assault on Réné Wellek for his review of *Revaluations.* Wellek charged Leavis with a lack of philosophic bearing in his critical assessments. Leavis maintained that a good reader is a good critic whose objective should be to realise in full measure—and with coherence—the complex experience embedded in a poem. He was concerned with the concrete particulars. He writes, 'everything worth saying in criticism of verse and prose can be related to judgments concerning particular arrangements of words on the page' (120). This insistence on the particulars on the page, and a purely personal response to it led him on, willy-nilly, to the dismissal of scholarship or literary history.

Leavis did not hold any of the critics who had preceded him in high esteem, Aristotle not exempted. His only concession was given to Matthew Arnold. Leavis favoured preserving a literary tradition in Arnold's sense: but he did not relate it to religion, as Eliot did, or to social problems, as the Marxists are prone to do. Literary criticism must be humanistic for him. He valued that art which ministers to life, serves and enhances it. And here he had a restricted sense of art by which he meant only realist art. Modernism and avant-gardism had no value for him. Again he was fond of equating good life with rural life, with its own charms. It is no wonder he rated high those writers who shared this outlook. His knowledge of literature was restricted to England and America. The charge that he was insular and provincial has some justification to it. Another of Leavis's limitations is his distrust of theory and principles of criticism. But, in defining accurately what taste means—and in creating such a taste—Leavis has always been the right side. In the history of criticism he has a firm place, a place as firm as that of his preceptor, Matthew Arnold.

Leavis's post-retirement period (from official duties) was more productive in terms of the number of publications. He published seven books, two of which were co-authored with his wife Q.D. Leavis, a specialist in British fiction, besides other writings in the forms of essays and letters. Much of these reaffirm his position that he so carefully built up and maintained, during his stormy career at Cambridge. Leavis was staunchly against the industrial revolution, which resulted in a mechanical machine civilisation. His hobby horse was the same old theme of the pre-industrial organic communal and rural civilisation. It would be hard to think of Leavis's reaction to the cyberspace civilisation, were he alive now. Pre-industrial civilisation had its own advantages. These were available to Shakespeare and others, and not available to the metropolitan writers. He regretted that literary culture too had become diluted. Hence, he wished for a revival of the English school he had entertained in his thoughts. Leavis was a die-hard, always maintaining obstinately and with unyielding forthrightness that he was always right. For him, criticism is a common pursuit that has an appeal to the enlightened public. His authority was constantly imposed on his followers and students. He brainwashed them with his likes, dislikes, and prejudices. He was never able to shake off his early enthusiasm. Lawrence remained his favourite novelist and critic, even greater than Eliot. Those who emerged as great and prominent writers in the fifties were totally ignored by him.

F.W. Bateson (1901–78), a scholar-critic and bibliographer who edited *Essays in Criticism,* and William Empson (1906–84) whom Frank Kermode called 'the chief English literary critic of the century' are two other well-known British literary critics. Empson is justly famous for his *Seven Types of Ambiguity, Some Versions of Pastoral,* and *The Structure of Complex Words.* His *Seven Types* was one of the most influential studies in the analysis of poetry in the first half of the twentieth century. It is not possible, regretfully, to give extended treatment to them as well as to many other British critics. With the arrival of New Criticism, the distinction between British and American criticism ceases to exist. And now, all get subsumed into what goes by the grandiose name 'Theory'.

Works Cited

Bradley, A.C. *Oxford Lectures on Poetry.* London: St Martin's Press, 1965.

Leavis, F.R. *Education and the University. A Sketch for an 'English School'.* 1943. Cambridge: Cambridge University Press, 1979.

Appendix

Speech-Act Theory

> The reason for concentrating on the study of speech acts is simply this: all linguistic communication involves linguistic acts . . . The production or issuance of a sentence token under certain conditions is a speech act, and speech acts are the basic or minimal units of linguistic communication.
>
> Searle, *Speech Acts*

In the section on structuralism, we argued that structuralist criticism grew out of linguistics, a broader name for which would be linguistic philosophy. Linguistic philosophy is concerned with the elements of actual natural languages. It employs a method that describes the actual structures—semantic, phonological or syntactic—of the languages of the world. There is the philosophy of the language, on the other hand, which is a subject of enquiry into the general features of language, such as truth, meaning, reference, etc. that language conveys. The philosophy of language is not concerned with the elements of any particular language.

This subject, the philosophy of language, acquired importance in the mid-twentieth century with the work of the British philosopher, J.L. Austin (1911–60), whose 'The Williams Lectures' delivered in Harvard in 1955, were published posthumously as *How to Do Things With Words* (1962). Further explorations on this subject by philosophers like John R. Searle (*Speech Acts,* 1969) and others have led to an expansion of the scope of this subject that, in turn, has affected literary studies and our conceptions about it. Austin examines two tendencies in language: 1. There are sentences which are 'statements' that describe an action or some state of affairs which are either true or false. They are verifiable. Such a statement is named 'constative'. 2. There are also utterances that do not 'describe' or 'report' and which cannot be verified as either true or false, but the uttering of it is part of the doing or accomplishing of an action. Let us take two examples: 1. The bridegroom in a church marriage ceremony utters the words 'I do take this woman to be my lawful wedded wife', 2. 'I herewith bequeath my property to my younger brother.' An utterance of this type is named 'performative'. The performative is not to be judged as true, or false, but as 'felicitous' or 'infelicitous', depending on whether the action is performed or not, appropriate or not. Whereas 'constatives' report on actions, 'performatives' accomplish them. This aspect of language as performance had not been given sufficient attention by earlier philosophers. Research on speech acts has led to further discoveries. Some of them have influenced literary criticism, which is our concern here.

All that we designate as literature is performative. Literary criticism always believes that what is important in a work of literature is what language *does*. A poem does not mean, but *is*. Poetry is not expression but action. Language, says Kenneth Burke, is symbolic action. Performatives are felicitous or infelicitous. In literary works too, utterances are not to be deemed true or false. An utterance that fits in with the totality of the fictional world conveyed is felicitous. For D.H. Lawrence, the morality of the novel is to be judged by its being felicitous or infelicitous, in this sense. In narratology, we have unreliable narrators who are infelicitous. Do the parts of a work cohere to make it a whole? If not, those are infelicitous. Speech-act theorists claim that literature is 'mimetic discourse' in that it imitates, in a verbal medium, human action. In recent feminist theory too, one can notice the 'performative' theory as applied to gender and sexuality. Feminists have come to argue that gender itself is 'performative'. Woman's identity is created. Right from the time of her birth, the female child is directed to perform repeatedly such of those actions which are expected of a woman. Actions determine gender. One becomes a woman by performing actions which turn out to be habitual, or which are socially or conventionally sanctioned. These repetitive acts are like Austin's 'performatives'.

In the Indian view of life, with its rich oral tradition, there are many actions in which language takes on the role of performance. In classical music, in devotional songs and dance, folk traditions, rituals connected with marriage, worship, and even in our concept of poetry as *mantra*, language performs. Words in the language *act* and *do*. There are many more dimensions to speech acts worth exploring. After all, more than anything else, words and languages shape our life, our destiny, 'rough hew them how we will.'

Select Bibliography

Austin, J.L. *How to Do Things with Words.* Cambridge, Mass: Harvard University Press, 1962.

Felman, Shoshana. *The Literary Speech Act.* Ithaca, NY: Cornell University Press, 1983.

Petrey, Sandy. *Speech Acts and Literary Theory.* New York: Routledge, 1990.

Pratt, Mary Louis. *Toward a Speech Act Theory of Literary Discourse.* Bloomington: Indiana University Press, 1977.

Searle, John, R. *Speech Acts: An Essay in the Philosophy of Language.* Cambridge: Cambridge University Press, 1969.

———. *The Philosophy of Language.* Oxford: Oxford University Press, 1971.

———. *Expression and Meaning: Study in the Theory of Speech Acts.* Cambridge: Cambridge University Press, 1979.

———. *Rationality in Action.* Cambridge, Mass.: MIT Press, 2001.

———. *Consciousness and Language.* New York: Cambridge University Press, 2002.

A Glossary of Critical Terms

addresser/addressee: In critical parlance, addresser means author/writer, and addressee means audience/reader. Roman Jakobson, in his essay, 'Linguistics and Poetics', made a diagrammatic representation of the network of literary communication.

There are six elements in this network, and each element performs a distinct function. Each critical theory places its emphasis on one of these elements to the exclusion of the others. For example, New Critics emphasise the function of the 'message', and reader-response critics fix their attention upon the 'addressee'.

affective: It stands for the psychological impact a work has upon a reader. I.A. Richards in his *Principles of Literary Criticism,* Wimsatt and Beardley, in their essay, 'The Affective Fallacy', and Stanley Fish in his *Affective Stylistics,* have employed this term to mean different things.

alienation: It is a process by which a worker gives up his/her labour power to the capitalist in return for wages, and in course of time, becomes an appendage of a machine. The labourer is thus estranged from the products of labour.

alienation effect: The German dramatist, Bertolt Brecht, employs this dramatic technique in his 'epic' theatre. The purpose is to overcome dramatic illusion and thwart empathy of the audience with what is performed on the stage.

ambiguity: The *OED* defines it as 'a double meaning which is caused by inexactness of expression'. William Empson, in *Seven Types of Ambiguity*, uses the term in a special sense to mean 'any verbal nuance however slight which however gives room for alternative reactions to the same piece of language'. The presence of ambiguity, which is deemed a defect in ordinary language, enriches poetry.

androgyny: Possessing the characteristics of both the male and the female. It is said that Coleridge believed that the human mind is androgynous. Feminists do not accept this view.

anxiety of influence: Harold Bloom developed this concept. Major or great poets exert a strong influence on the poets of the later generation who have to struggle hard to overcome their indebtedness.

aporia: The term is derived from the Greek for 'impasse'. It means an inherent contradiction or paradox which cannot be resolved. Derrida uses the term to refer to the unresolvable difficulties a text may open up.

archaeology: Foucault uses this term in a technical sense It is a method of investigating and analysing dimensions of knowledge (discursive formations) which lie buried in human consciousness. Since these are not available for direct observation, they have to be dug out and reconstructed from available social practices/discourses.

arbitrary: The relationship between a word and its meaning is arbitrary. The oral or the written form of a word, and the concept it represents, have no inherent relationship. It is convention or social practice that establishes a link between the two sides of a linguistic sign—the phonetic and the conceptual.

author: Conventionally the term refers to the creator of a work of literature. In the poststructuralist context, it has assumed several meanings. Preferring the term 'scriptor', Roland Barthes declares in 'The Death of the Author' that a text is a space in which all writings clash and the scriptor is born simultaneously with the text. 'The birth of the reader must be at the cost of the death of the author.' For Foucault, the author is not a timeless, irreducible category but a 'function' of discourse which has changed in the course of history. Literary theorists subscribe to the notion of social and cultural forces that shape textual production.

base and superstructure: These two concepts are derived from Karl Marx's *A Contribution to the Critique of Political Economy.* In Marxian dialectics, 'base'refers to the socioeconomic structures in a society and superstructure, the legal, political, religious, intellectual beliefs and cultural practices. Marx situates literature in superstructure. It is reductive and simplistic to hold the view that the base generates and determines the superstructure. The relationship between the two is complex. The two influence each other and are mutually dependent.

biological determinism: It is the view that cultural differences are to be attributed to biological characteristics. For example, the male is superior to the female.

bricoleur: One who uses instruments at hand for multiple purposes. In criticism, *bricolage* refers to the act of borrowing concepts from different sources and redesigning them to suit one's needs. According to Derrida, critical language partakes of the characteristics of *bricolage*.

canon: The word's origin is the Greek word *kanon*, meaning a straight rod or standard. In theology, the word means chosen, sacred texts. In literary studies, canon has come to mean texts which are necessary for a sound education. It is associated, rather loosely, with the curriculum or the syllabus. For Harold Bloom canon is 'achieved anxiety'.

carnival: A festival that is associated with merry-making and revelry. Mikhail Bakhtin employs this term to mean a form of counter-culture which was popular during the Middle Ages. It stood in opposition to the ruling, aristocratic, official culture prevalent at that time. Bakhtin notices an interplay of many voices (polyphony) in fiction for which he suggests the term carnivalesque. Hence, the novel is richer in its plenitude and abundance than the single-voiced epic.

code: Literary communication involves using a set of shared conventions which link the writer and the reader. A work is not meaningful to those who do not possess the competence to make meaning out of the codes. Structuralists maintain that literature is a code without a message. The aim of literary education is to equip a student with knowledge about codes.

condensation and displacement: Freud uses these terms to show us how our dreams work. Our desires are transformed into dream images. Condensation is the process by which a number of events are represented by a single image in a dream. In displacement, one event is represented by another. It is a case of symbolic substitution. Like literary works, dreams communicate indirectly and obliquely.

connotation and denotation: The language of science is denotative, while the language of poetry is connotative. In scientific (and conversational) language, the function of a word stops after it conveys its meaning. This usage is denotative. In poetic language, besides conveying meanings, words do arouse emotions. This usage is connotative.

defamiliarisation: The Russian formalists brought this term to circulation. It is a device to obliterate automatic or habitual perception. Victor Shklovsky, in his essay, 'Art as Technique', develops this notion. He says that the technique of art is to make things unfamiliar. 'Art is a way of experiencing the artfulness of an object: the object is not important.'

diachronic and synchronic: These terms are used with reference to language study. Whereas diachronic study involves a study of the language as it has evolved over a period of time, synchronic study would limit itself to an analysis of the structure of language at a given point of time. Ferdinand Saussure places emphasis on the synchronic in his revolutionary theory on language which he expounds in *Course in General Linguistics.*

dialectic: Systematic analysis, debate or argument. The Hegelian dialectic is defined as an argument in three parts: thesis, antithesis and synthesis.

dialogic: The word 'dialogue', in ordinary usage, refers to a verbal exchange between two persons. Bakhtin develops the concept that, in novelistic discourse, utterances carry many meanings which have been used before. Words are never neutral, but are always contaminated with meanings as used by others.

differance: It is a neologism. Derrida coined the portmanteau term 'differance', got by a telescoping of *differ* (be different from) and *defer* (delay or postpone). Saussure said that the linguistic sign is arbitrary owing to the differential character of language. 'In language, there are only differences without positive terms.' Derrida goes a step further. Meaning is endlessly put off, since each word leads us on to another word in a system of signification.

discourse: In common speech, discourse means 'communication of thought by speech'. Discourses are cultural/social practices embodied in 'psychic and physical reality'. Foucault defines discourses as 'the material manifestations of a thought that is preserved, transmitted and still affects our present-day thinking'.

ecriture feminine: In broad terms, it means the feminine practice of writing. It is not possible to theorise this practice. It is a form of writing that is oriented towards the female: a writing that facilitates a free play of meanings, and celebrates the female physiology.

episteme: Foucault coined this term, retaining partially the Greek sense of knowledge. At any given point of time in a society, it is possible to investigate a dimension of knowledge (*episteme*) which regulates the functioning of the thought of the people.

epistemology: The theory/science of the method/grounds of knowledge.

erasure: Derrida uses this term which means undoing/preserving. In thought, elements are never fully present. The elements always refer to something other than themselves. Each element refers to something other than itself. A linguistic sign is always already inhabited by the trace of another sign which never appears as such.

essentialism: Often used in a pejorative sense that certain attributes are inherent in the objects that we examine. For example, the belief that biology is more significant than culture in 'subject' formation is essentialist.

Eurocentric: The belief that Europe is the centre and source of all knowledge, and the philosophic traditions of the European world are superior to the traditions of the rest of the world: all branches of knowledge originate from Europe. Postcolonial theory uses this term to show how Eurocentrism has subordinated and marginalised all other countries of the world.

fabula* and *sjuzet: These two terms are employed by Russian formalists. Loosely they may be rendered in English as story and plot. *Fabula* refers to the externals, the sequence of events which are rendered chronologically. It is a temporal causal sequence. *Sjuzet* is the informing principle that gives shape to the incidents and the story proper. It is the artistically ordered narrative structure. If *fabula* strings together incidents, *sjuzet* organises the narrative and gives it shape.

foregrounding: The act of giving prominence to some features in a work. Russian formalists and stylistic critics put the term in circulation. The opposite term is backgrounding, which, as the name implies, is relegating features of a work to the back.

gaze: A term used by feminist and postcolonial critics, borrowed from film criticism. Gaze is in possession of men, often directed at the female figure. Gaze is said to involve anxiety and desire for possession.

gender: One has to make a distinction between gender and sex differences. Sex is biologically determined: hence, we have the male and the female sex. Gender, on the other hand, is a psychological concept, and is socially/culturally constructed: hence, we have the masculine and feminine gender. The difference between sex and gender is the difference between natural and social functions. Feminist critics argue that the inequality between the sexes is produced by cultural constructions of gender differences.

grammatology: Grammatology is a science of writing. It is defined as 'a treatise upon letters, upon the alphabet, syllabation, reading and writing'. Derrida uses a broader concept, grammatology, in preference to the material concept of writing, since the word 'grammatology' keeps alive the unresolved contradictions.

genealogy: Foucault uses the term to mean an analysis of modalities of power. Knowledge and power are not to be separately understood. Knowledge is power. Genealogy is a method of understanding the mutual relations between systems of truth and modalities of power. It is a method for searching hidden structures and associations.

grand and little narratives: This term gained wide currency with Francois Lyotard's book *The Postmodern Condition.* 'Grand narratives' maintain the sense of order or stability in society. A grand narrative is to be understood as an all-encompassing world view, such as God, man, etc. It uses a totalising framework for explaining the world. Postmodernism rejects global or world views, which are held to be true once and for all. Instead, it favours little or mini-narratives which are provisional and contingent with no claim to universality.

gynocriticism: Feminist criticism which studies women as writers. It concentrates on the specificity of women's writings by recuperating the lost tradition of women authors.

gynesis: It is the French version of gynocriticism. It emphasises, not the gender of the writer, but the writing effect (*ecriture feminine*). It textualises woman, so to speak.

hegemony: A term used in Marxist criticism to refer to the potential possession of power and social control though it may not be directly used. The term may be contrasted with 'rule', which uses force, if and when necessary.

hermeneutics: In Greek mythology, Hermes was a messenger of the gods. The term 'hermeneutics' comes from a Greek word which means 'to say'. Originally, it meant interpreting scriptures. It has now come to denote the art or science of interpretation, distinguished from exegesis or practical exposition.

homosocial: Social bonding (as distinguished from homosexual) between persons of the same sex.

hybridity: Also known as syncreticism, hybridity is an intermingling of different cultural artefacts. The term stands in opposition to decolonisation, which believes in asserting the tradition of native cultures. Hybridity encourages cultural transplantation; it believes in cross-pollination.

ideology: In a general sense, it can be understood to mean a system of ideas or beliefs collectively held. In Marxian criticism, this key term signifies a set of beliefs and values which people hold on to which prevent them from a fuller and truer understanding of the world they live in. It is 'false consciousness', and a distortion of material reality on which alone experience should be based.

illocutionary act: Speech is not just utterance but also an act. An illocutionary act in 'speech act theory' refers to utterances which perform, warn, assert, promise, command, etc. A good example would be Gandhiji's famous utterance, 'Quit India'. They cannot be checked to be true or false. These come under the category *performatives* in John Austin's book *How to do Things with Words.*

intention: This term gained prominence with the publication of Wimsatt and Beardsley's article, 'The Intentional Fallacy', in which they maintain that 'the design or the intention of the author is neither available nor desirable as a standard for judging the success of a literary work of art'. This concept of the authorial intention has lost its authority with the onset of poststructuralist views about the death of the author.

interpretive/interpretative communities: A group of people who share the same or similar strategies while writing, or reading texts. An interpretive community stabilises and validates interpretation by weeding out unlikely ones.

intertextuality: A term coined by Julia Kristeva. Every literary work is a field which contains within it bits and pieces of other works. A text is a web of complex, interwoven interrelationships which contains codes, fragments, drawn from other works; it also echoes other texts in terms of literary conventions. Every text has a tentacular hold on other texts.

intrinsic criticism: Literary study that concentrates on the work itself: a study that could be called centrally literary or 'ergocentric'. It is opposed to extrinsic criticism (literature and biography, for example) that applies deterministic causal methods to literary study.

jouissance: It is a French word which means delight, joy, and especially, sexual pleasure. Roland Barthes employs this term in *The Pleasure of the Text* to bring out the orgasmic experience and the gratification of the senses involved in the activity of reading. The pleasures of the text are likened to the pleasures of the body.

langue* and *parole: The Swiss linguist, Ferdinand de Saussure in his *Course in General Linguistics* (1915), introduced these two terms. *Langue* is the supra-personal system. It is a grammatical system that has a potential existence in every mind. It is likened to the reservoir of language available to a community. *Parole* is the utterance of an individual in actual instances. One may compare these terms with Noam Chomsky's 'competence', and 'performance'.

lisible* and *scriptible: Roland Barthes in his *S/Z* coined these terms. The English rendering is 'readerly'and 'writerly'. The readerlv texts are those in which the writer and reader share conventions. Such texts do all the work for the reader. The reader passively consumes the meaning/message of the text. The writerly texts, on the other hand, activate the reader to produce the text. The reader and writer are co-participants in the joint enterprise of constructing the text.

logocentrism: Systems of thought which claim justification by referring them to some external proposition (metaphysics of presence). Jacques Derrida coined this term to refer to the belief in Western philosophy in a centre which controls a structure, though it is not part of the structure. Deconstruction dismantles logocentrism.

marginality: Centre and margin stand opposed to each other in power structures. Postcolonialism affirms that imperial expansion, and the supposed cultural hegemony of the Empire have marginalised colonies, relegating them to the background. Feminists charge patriarchy with marginalising female experience.

meaning and significance: E.D. Hirsch employs these two terms in his hermeneutical theory. Meaning is the 'determinate representation of a text for an interpreter', and significance is 'meaning-as-related-to-something-else'. In interpretation, meaning is a 'principle of stability', while significance embraces a 'principle of change'.

metalanguage: 'Meta' is used in the formation of compound words. It may mean 'after', 'beyond', 'of a higher or second-order', etc. In this sense, metalanguage is 'language about language'. If we regard literary work as language, then literary criticism is metalanguage. Thus, we have metafiction which is self-referential in character; metanarrative which refers to its own narrative procedure; metadrama which refers to a play within a play; metacriticism which is 'criticism of criticism', the modern name for which is 'theory'.

mimicry: Homi K. Bhabha employs this concept to mean the slavish acceptance of the colonialist ideology (cultural cringe) which consists in behaving in a way the coloniser had planned and intended, thereby reinforcing his authority willingly. It is a form of colonial control of the subject. The term may also be used in the opposite sense of the colonial subject making fun of the coloniser.

mirror stage: Jacques Lacan introduced this concept in his essay, 'The Mirror Stage as Formative of the Function of the I as revealed in Psychoanalytic Experience'(1949). It is the stage in life, between six and eighteen months, when the child acquires its identity. At birth, the child is in the 'imaginary'stage: it cannot distinguish between its self and the other. It is at the mirror stage, the child can recognise its reflection in a mirror and is able to conceive of itself as an autonomous being. Thus the 'ideal-I' is fixed. Lacan adds that it is at this stage the child enters the language system.

myth: Myth may be understood as a complex of story elements which contain aspects of human existence which lie deeply buried in our psyche. It can also mean some basic way of envisaging and organising human experience. It is a synthesising activity of human consciousness which offers a perspective to understand reality.

narratology: A theory of narrative (poetics of fiction) that attempts to understand the components of the narrative as well as how particular narratives achieve their effect. Tzvetan Todorov popularised the term in 1969. Now it has come to mean an analysis of the narrative aspects of even non-literary discourses, such as films. A narrator is the person (or agent) who narrates. The narrator as *teller* and the author as *creator* are two separate entities. The author has two selves: 1. the historical author, and 2. the implied author (the intelligence that superintends the fictional world). There are privileged and effaced narrators as well as reliable and unreliable narrators.

nativism: Recuperating and empowering pre-colonial culture and language, and asserting one's own native culture. Third World countries advocate this practice in order to salvage, preserve, and valorise their age-old traditions which face the danger of being wiped off by dominant power groups.

negritude: The term is of French origin. It was coined out of the necessity for creating a separate identity for the blacks. It is a term of honour that asserts the distinctive characteristics of black culture and expresses the racial pride of the blacks. African American writers began using the term to glorify black culture, black aesthetics, black art, all of which is enshrined in the slogan 'Black is beautiful'.

ontology: The study of 'being'. It belongs to that branch of metaphysics which relates to the essence of things.

oppositional reading: It is reading against the grain, as it were. It is a reading that goes against normally held interpretations.

orature: Works which have an oral tradition. These are stored in memory and passed on from one generation to another by word of mouth. Rev Fr Walter Ong's *Orality and Literacy* (1982) is the most valuable work on orature and studies relating to it.

orientalism: In the conventional sense of the word, orientalism stands for a humanistic study/scholarship of matters pertaining to the countries of the Eastern hemisphere (orient, as distinct from the occident). Scholars like Max Muller and G.U. Pope are orientalists in this positive sense. Edward Said redefines the term in his most influential book, *Orientalism* (1978), by investing new meanings in it. Orientalism, for him, is a Western style for dominating and having authority over the East. It is a huge body of texts which are meant to establish the superiority of the Caucasian culture over the Asiatic and the African.

other: This term has many connotations in psychoanalytic and postcolonial theories: but the one that is common and frequently invoked is to treat a person/subject as outside the purview of consideration. The coloniser treats the colonised as the other. The voice of the other is stifled.

phallocentrism: Feminists have appropriated this term to indicate the avowed superiority of the masculine over the feminine. The absence of the phallus renders the woman as the 'other'. By extension, phallocentrism has other suggestive connotations as well.

phenomenology: The science of 'phenomena', as distinct from the science of 'being'. The term is usually associated with the German philosopher, Edmund Husserl. It is our consciousness that creates the world. The saying goes, 'beauty lies in the eye of the beholder'. Reader-response criticism is based on phenomenology.

phonocentrism: Also used synonymously with logocentrism. Phonocentrism is the privileging of 'speech' over 'writing'. It is the result of the view that speech is closer to meaning than writing. Derrida dismantles phonocentrism.

queer theory: It is a term that asserts the identity of homosexuals. It includes all 'non-straight'people. Gays and lesbians are proud to call themselves 'queer'. Sexuality, for the queer, is socially constructed: it is not controlled either by biological needs or gender roles.

reification: A Marxian term to describe the process by which a world of human relationships appears as a set of relationships between things. Human labour is equated to a commodity that is being bought or sold.

repression: A term associated with Freudian psychoanalysis. Undesirable events of the past, unpleasant memories, conflicts, etc., are put under hold, as it were, by our conscious mind. They get lodged in the unconscious mind and emerge later without our knowledge.

resonance: Resonance, wonder, circulation, and social energy are terms associated with new historicism. A text/artefact arouses in us kindred feelings with other cultural artefacts, and by this process, it is rendered eternally alive. Resonance circulates social energy and sustains in us a feeling of wonder.

semiology/semiotics: Ferdinand de Saussure coined the term semiology in his *Course in General Linguistics* (1915). The two terms are used synonymously: the British prefer semiology and the Americans, semiotics. There might be sharp divisions between the terms but, in a general sense, they stand for the science of signs.

sexism: A term that degrades women in the relationship between men and women. In this sense, it is close to patriarchy in meaning.

Feminism aims at liberating women from the tyranny of sexism that stereotypes them.

simulacrum: Jean Baudrillard used this term to explain the reality effect: the ways by which reality is established through hyper-real media such as the film or photography. The real is replaced by its shadow.

stereotype: Usually used in a pejorative sense to describe things which are rigid, inflexible, static and fixed.

structure: In the simplest sense, a structure may be defined as the internal relationship among elements which constitute a whole. A structural analysis discovers these elements and their relationships.

style and stylistics: The term 'style' stands for the mode of expressing thought in writing or speech that is characteristic of a person or a group. Stylistics is an academic discipline that examines the style of a work or an author. It is a study of a work in terms of its aesthetic function and meaning. It defines the specific characteristics of a work.

subaltern: It is a military term which means 'of lower rank'. Initially used by the Italian communist Antonio Gramsci to refer to the plebeians (the working class), the term is appropriated by postcolonial theorists and put in wide circulation. Gayatri Spivak's influential article, 'Can the subaltern speak?' shows how the elitist political historiography has stifled the voice of the subaltern groups.

subject/subjectivity: According to common sense humanist notions, we are the authors of what we think and do, and we are the authors of ourselves. Man is the centre: human nature determines human identity. Contemporary theory rejects this view. Language, history, culture, etc., construct the identity of an individual. The human subject, therefore, is created by the forces of power which are inbuilt in a social formation. Derrida, Lacan, Foucault, and feminist critics have further widened this basic concept of subjectivity.

text and work: In his essay, 'The Theory of the Text', Roland Barthes erects a distinction between these two. A work is a completed piece, a finished object which can be envisaged as a physical entity. A text is an ever wide-open 'methodological field'. In contemporary theory, the term 'text' is preferred to the term 'work', since the term frees itself from the notion of the author's control over writing.

unconscious: In psychoanalytic theory, the unconscious is that part of the mind which lies beyond the conscious mind. The unconscious occupies six-sevenths of the mind and exerts a very strong control over our thinking and actions.

universalism: The practice of making assumptions concerning humanity as though it is valid for all human beings.

utterance: A sentence is a unit of language, and an utterance is a unit of communication.

vraisemblance: A word of French origin. It is equivalent to recuperating or naturalising a text: to define the ways by which it can be brought into contact with other texts. It is to make the text at once legible and intelligible.

Select Bibliography

This bibliography lists only some significant works, mostly books. It does not undertake to offer a complete or comprehensive coverage of the ever-growing, massive material on the subject of literary theory and criticism.

Abrams, M.H. *The Mirror and the Lamp: Romantic Theory and the Critical Tradition.* New York: Oxford University Press, 1977.

———. *Doing Things with Texts: Essays in Criticism and Critical Theory.* New York: W.W. Worton, 1989.

Adams, Hazard, ed. *Critical Theory since Plato.* New York: Harcourt Brace Jovanovich, 1971.

———. *Critical Theory since 1965.* Tallahassee: Florida State University Press, 1986.

Althusser, Louis. *For Marx.* London: Allen Lane, 1969.

———. *Lenin and Philosophy.* New York: Monthly Review Press, 1970.

Appiah, Anthony. *In My Father's House: Africa in the Philosophy of Culture.* London: Methuen, 1992.

———. *The Ethics of Identity.* Princeton, NJ: Princeton University Press, 2005.

Arac, Jonathan, and Barbara Johnson, eds. *The Consequences of Theory.* Baltimore: Johns Hopkins University Press, 1991.

Ashcroft, Bill. *Postcolonial Transformation.* New York: Routledge, 2001.

Ashcroft, Bill, Gareth Griffiths, and Helen Tiffin. *Key Concepts in Post-colonial Studies.* London: Routledge, 1988.

———. *The Empire Writes Back: Theory and Practice in Postcolonial Literatures.* London: Routledge, 1989.

———, eds. *The Postcolonial Studies Reader.* London: Routledge, 1995.

Atkins, J.W.H. *Literary Criticism in Antiquity: A Sketch of its Developments.* 1934. 2 vols. Cambridge, 1952.

———. *English Literary Criticism: The Medieval Phase.* 1943. London: Methuen & Co. Ltd., 1952.

———. *English Literary Criticism: The Renascence.* London: Methuen & Co. Ltd., 1947.

———. *English Literary Criticism: 17th and 18th Centuries.* 1951. New York: Barnes and Noble, 1966.

Atkins, G. Douglas, and Laura Morrow, eds. *Contemporary Literary Theory.* London: Macmillan, 1969.

Attridge, Derek, Geoff Bennington, and Robert Young, eds. *Post-Structuralism and the Question of History.* Cambridge: Cambridge University Press, 1987.

Attridge, Derek, ed. *Acts of Literature/Jacques Derrida.* New York: Routledge, 1992.

Auerbach, Eric. *Mimesis: The Representation of Reality in Western Literature.* Trans. Willard Trask. Princeton: Princeton University Press, 1953.

Austin, J.L. *How to Do Things with Words.* Cambridge: Oxford University Press, 1962.

Bakhtin, Mikhail. *Rabelais and His World.* Trans. Helene Iswolsky. Cambridge: MIT Press, 1968.

———. *The Dialogic Imagination.* Trans. Caryl Emerson. Ed. Michael Holquist. Austin: University of Texas Press, 1981.

———. *Problems of Dostoevsky's Poetics.* Trans and ed. Caryl Emerson. Minneapolis: University of Minnesota Press, 1984.

Bal, Mieke. *Narratology: Introduction to the Theory of Narrative.* Toronto: University of Toronto Press, 1985.

———, ed. *Narrrative Theory: Critical Concepts in Literary and Cultural Studies.* London: Routledge, 2004.

Barry, Peter. *Beginning Theory: An Introduction to Literary and Cultural Theory.* Manchester: Manchester University Press, 1995.

———. *English in Practice: In Pursuit of English Studies.* London: Oxford University Press, 2003.

Barthes, Roland. *Mythologies.* New York: Hill and Wang, 1973.

———. *S/Z.* Trans. Richard Miller. London: Jonathan Cape, 1974.

———. *Writing Degree Zero.* Trans. Annette Lavers and Colin Smith. New York: Hill and Wang. 1975.

———. *The Pleasure of the Text.* Trans. Richard Miller. New York: Hill and Wang, 1975.

———. *Image, Music, Text.* Trans. Stephen Heath. New York: Hill and Wang, 1977.

Beardsley, Monroe. *Aesthetics: Problems in the Philosophy of Criticism.* New York: Harcourt, Brace and World, 1958.

Belsey, Catherine. *Critical Practice.* London: Methuen, 1980.

———. *Post-Sructuralism: A Very Short Introduction.* Oxford: Oxford University Press, 2002.

———. *Culture and the Real.* New York: Routledge, 2005.

Belsey, Catherine, and Jane Moore, eds. *The Feminist Reader.* London: Macmillan, 1989.

Benjamin, Andrew, ed. *Post-Structuralist Classics.* London: Routledge, 1989.

Bhabha, Homi, ed. *Nation and Narration.* London: Routledge, 1990.

———. *The Location of Culture.* New York: Routledge, 1994.

Blakmur, R.P. *Language as Gesture.* New York: Harcourt Brace, 1952.

Blamires, Harry. *A History of Literary Criticism.* New York: St Martin's Press, 1991.

Bloom, Harold. *The Anxiety of Influence.* New York: Oxford University Press, 1973.

———. *Kabbalah and Criticism.* New York: Seabury Press, 1975.

———. *A Map of Misreading.* New York: Oxford University Press, 1975.

———. *The Western Canon: The Books and School of the Ages.* New York: Harcourt Brace, 1994.

———. *How to Read and Why?* New York: Scribner, 2000.

———, et. al. *Deconstruction and Criticism.* 1979. New York: Continuum, 1987.

Booth, Wayne, C. *The Rhetoric of Fiction.* Chicago: University of Chicago Press, 1961.

———. *A Rhetoric of Irony.* Chicago: University of Chicago Press, 1974.

———. *Critical Understanding: The Powers and Limits of Pluralism.* Chicago: University of Chicago Press, 1979.

Brooks, Cleanth. *Modern Poetry and Tradition.* Chapel Hill: University of North Carolina Press, 1939.

———. *The Well-Wrought Urn: Studies in the Structure of Poetry.* New York: Reynal and Hitchcock, 1947.

———. *A Shaping Joy: Studies in the Writer's Craft.* London: Methuen, 1971.

Brooks, Cleanth, and William K. Wimsatt, Jr. *Literary Criticism: A Short History.* New York: Alfred Knopf, 1957.

Brooks, Peter. *Reading for the Plot.* New York: Alfred A. Knopf, 1984.

Burke, Kenneth. *Language as Symbolic Action: Essays on Life, Literature, and Method.* Berkeley: University of California Press, 1966.

Chatman, Seymour. *Literary Style: A Symposium.* New York: Oxford University Press, 1971.

———. *Approaches to Poetics.* New York: Columbia University Press, 1973.

———. *Story and Discourse.* Ithaca, N.Y.: Cornell University Press, 1978.

———, ed. *New Perspectives on Narrative Perspective.* Albany; State University of New York Press, 2001.

Chomsky, Noam. *Syntactic Structures.* The Hague, Mouton, 1965.

———. *Cartesian Linguistics.* New York: Harper & Row, 1966.

Cohen, Ralph, ed. *New Directions in Literary History.* Baltimore: The Johns Hopkins University Press, 1974.

———, ed. *The Future of Literary Theory.* London: Routledge, 1989.

Coyle, Martin, Malcolm Kelsall, and John Peck, eds. *Encyclopaedia of Literature and Criticism.* London: Routledge, 1990.

Coward, Harold. *Derrida and Indian Philosophy.* Albany, NY: State University of New York Press, 1990.

Chase, Richard. *Quest for Myth.* Baton Rouge: Louisiana State University Press, 1949.

Crane, Ronald S. *The Languages of Criticism and the Structure of Poetry.* Toronto: University of Toronto Press, 1953.

———, ed. *Critics and Criticism: Ancient and Modern.* Chicago: University of Chicago Press, 1952.

———. *The Idea of Humanities and other Essays.* 2 vols. Chicago: University of Chicago Press, 1967.

Culler, Jonathan. *Structuralist Poetics: Structuralism, Linguistics, and the Study of Literature.* Ithaca: Cornell University Press, 1975.

———. *Literary Theory: A Very Short Introduction.* Oxford: Oxford University Press, 1977.

———. *The Pursuit of Signs: Semiotics, Literature, Deconstruction.* Ithaca: Cornell University Press, 1981.

———. *On Deconstruction: Theory and Criticism after Structuralism.* Ithaca, N.Y.: Cornell University Press, 1982.

———. *Framing the Sign: Criticism and its Institutions.* Oxford: Blackwell, 1988.

———, ed. *Deconstruction: Critical Concepts in Literary and Cultural Studies.* London: Routledge, 2003.

Davis, R.C., ed. *The Fictional Father: Lacanian Readings of the Text.* Amherst: University of Massachusetts University Press, 1981.

———, ed. *Contemporary Literary Theory: Modernism through Post-Modernism.* London: Longman, 1986.

De Beauvoir, S. *The Second Sex.* 1949. Harmondsworth: Penguin, 1972.

De George, Richard, and Fernande De George, eds. *The Structuralists.* New York: Doubleday, 1972.

De Man, Paul. *Allegories of Reading: Figural Language in Rousseau, Nietzche, Rilke, and Proust.* New Haven: Yale University Press, 1979.

———. *Blindness and Insight: Essays in the Rhetoric of Contemporary Criticism.* Minneapolis: University of Minnesota Press, 1983.

———. *The Resistance to Theory.* Minneapolis: University of Minnesota Press, 1986.

———. *Aesthetics of Ideology.* Minneapolis: University of Minnesota Press, 1996.

Derrida, Jacques. *Of Grammatology.* Trans. Gayatri Spivak. Baltimore: Johns Hopkins University Press, 1967.

———. *Speech and Phenomena—and other Essays on Husserl's Theory of Signs.* Trans. David B. Allison. Evanston: Northwestern University Press, 1973.

———. *Writing and Difference.* Trans. Alan Bass. Chicago: University of Chicago Press, 1978.

———. *Positions.* Trans. Alan Boss.Chicago: University of Chicago Press, 1981.

———. *Acts of Literature.* Ed. Derek Attridge. New York: Routledge, 1992.

Dollimore, Jonathan. *Radical Tragedy.* Chicago: University of Chicago Press, 1984.

———. *Sex, Literature and Censorship.* Cambridge: Blackwell, 2001.

Dollimore, Jonathan, and Alan Sinfield, eds. *Political Shakespeare: New Essays in Cultural Materialism.* Ithaca, N.Y.: Cornell University Press, 1985.

Donoghue, Denis. *Ferocious Alphabets.* New York: Columbia University Press, 1984.

———. *The Pure Good of Theory.* Oxford: Blackwell, 1992.

Dorsch, T.S., trans. *Classical Literary Criticism.* Harmondsworth: Middlesex, England: Penguin. 1965.

During, Simon, ed. *The Cultural Studies Reader.* London: Routledge, 1993.

Eagleton, Mary, ed. *Feminist Literary Theory: A Reader.* Oxford: Blackwell, 1986.

———. *Working with Feminist Criticism.* Oxford: Blackwell Publishers, 1996.

———, ed. *A Concise Companion to Feminist Theory.* Oxford: Blackwell, 2003.

Eagleton, Terry. *Criticism and Ideology.* London: New Left Books, 1976.

———. *Marxism and Literary Criticism.* Berkeley and Los Angeles: University of California Press, 1976.

———. *Literary Theory: An Introduction.* Minneapolis: University of Minnesota Press, 1983.

———. *The Significance of Theory.* Oxford: Basil Blackwell, 1989.

———. *The Idea of Culture.* Malden, MA: Blackwell, 2000.

———. *After Theory.* New York: Basic Books, 2003.

Easthope, Antony. *British Post-structuralism since 1968.* New York: Routledge, 1988.

———. *Privileging Difference.* Ed. Catherine Belsey. New York: Palgrave, 2002.

Eco, Umberto. *A Theory of Semiotics.* Bloomington: Indiana University Press, 1976.

———. *The Role of the Reader: Explorations in the Semiotics of Texts.* Bloomington: Indiana University Press, 1979.

———. *Limits of Interpretation.* Bloomington: Indiana University Press, 1990.

Ehrmann, Jacques, ed. *Structuralism.* Garden City, New York: Anchor, 1971.

Ellis, John M. *Against Deconstruction.* Princeton: Princeton University Press, 1989.

———. *Language, Thought, and Logic.* Evanston, Ill.: Northwestern University Press, 1933.

Ellman, Mary. *Thinking about Women.* New York: Harcourt Brace and World, 1968.

Empson, William. *Seven Types of Ambiguity.* New York: New Directions, 1947.

———. *The Structure of Complex Words.* Norfolk: New Directions, 1951.

———. *Using Biography*. London: Hogarth Press, 1984.

Felperin, Howard. *Beyond Deconstruction: The Uses and Abuses of Theory*. Oxford: Oxford University Press, 1985.

———. *The Uses of the Canon: Elizabethan Literature and Contemporary Theory*. Oxford: Clarendon Press, 1992.

Fetterley, Judith. *The Resisting Reader: A Feminist Approach to American Fiction*. Bloomington: Indiana University Press, 1978.

Fetterley, Judith, and Marjorie Pryse. *Writing out of Place: Regionalism, Women and American Literary Culture*. Urbana: University of Illinois Press, 2003.

Fish, Stanley. *Surprised by Sin: The Reader in 'Paradise Lost'*. London: St Martin's Press, 1967.

———. *Self-Consuming Artifacts: The Experience of Seventeenth Century Literature*. Berkeley: University of California Press, 1972.

———. *Is There a Text in Class? The Authority of Interpretative Communities*. Cambridge, Massachusetts: Harvard University Press, 1980.

———. *How Milton Works*. Cambridge, Mass.: Harvard University Press, 2001.

Fiske, John. *Understanding Popular Culture*. Boston: Unwin, 1989.

Forster, E.M. *Aspects of the Novel*. New York: Harcourt, 1927.

Foucault, Michel. *The Order of Things: An Archaeology of Human Sciences*. London: Tavistock, 1970.

———. *The Archeology of Knowledge and the Discourse on Knowledge*. Trans. A.M. Sheridan Smith. New York: Harper and Row, 1972.

———. *Discipline and Punish: The Birth of the Prison*. Trans. Alan Sheridan. New York: Pantheon, 1977.

———. *The History of Sexuality*. Trans. Robert Hurley. New York: Pantheon Books, 1978.

———. *Power/Knowledge: Selected Interviews and other Writings*. Ed. Colin Gordon. New York: Pantheon, 1980.

Fowler, Roger, ed. *Style and Structure in Literature: Essays in the New Stylistics*. London: Oxford University Press, 1975.

———. *Linguistic Criticism.* Oxford: Oxford University Press, 1996.

Freud, Sigmund. *The Standard Edition of the Complete Psychological Works of Sigmund Freud.* Ed. and trans. James Strachey. London: Hogarth Press and the Institute of Psychoanalysis, 1957.

———. *The Interpretation of Dreams.* 1900. London: Hogarth Press and the Institute of Psychoanalysis, 1957.

Frye, Northrop. *Anatomy of Criticism: Four Essays.* New York: Atheneum, 1957.

———. *Fables of Identity: Studies in Poetic Mythology.* New York: Harcourt, Brace and World, 1963.

———. *The Critical Path: An Essay on the Social Context of Literary Criticism.* Bloomington: Indiana University Press, 1971.

———. *Myth and Metaphor: Selected Essays.* Ed. Robert Denham. Charlottesville: University Press of Virginia, 1990.

Frye, Northrop, and Jay Macpherson. *Biblical and Classical Myths: The Mythological Framework of Western Culture.* Toronto: University of Toronto Press, 2004.

Gates, Henry Louis, Jr., ed. *Black Literature and Literary Theory.* New York: Methuen, 1984.

———, ed. *'Race', Writing and Difference.* Chicago: University of Chicago Press, 1986.

———. *The Signifying Monkey: A Theory of Afro-American Literary Culture.* New York: Oxford University Press, 1988.

———. *America Behind the Color Lines: Dialogues with African Americans.* New York: Warner Books, 2004.

Gayle, Addison, Jr. *The Black Aesthetic.* Garden City: Doubleday, Anchor Books, 1971.

Genette, Gerard. *Narrative Discourse: An Essay in Method.* Ithaca, NY: Cornell University Press, 1980.

———. *Essays in Aesthetics.* Trans. Dorrit Cohn. Lincoln: University of Nebraska Press, 2005.

Glucksman, Miriam. *Structuralist Analysis in Contemporary Social Thought.* London: Routledge & Kegan Paul, 1974.

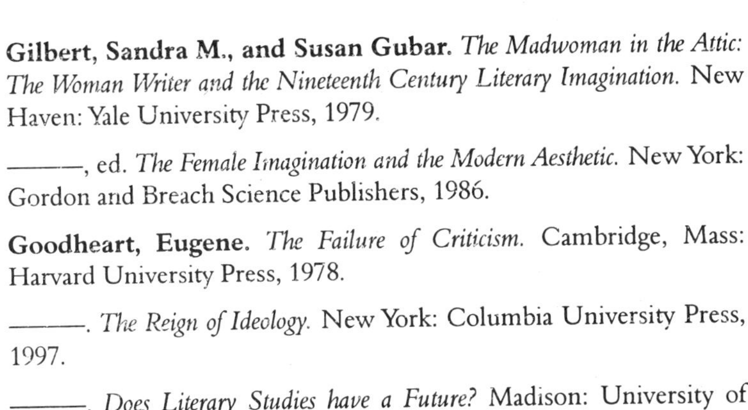

Gilbert, Sandra M., and Susan Gubar. *The Madwoman in the Attic: The Woman Writer and the Nineteenth Century Literary Imagination.* New Haven: Yale University Press, 1979.

———, ed. *The Female Imagination and the Modern Aesthetic.* New York: Gordon and Breach Science Publishers, 1986.

Goodheart, Eugene. *The Failure of Criticism.* Cambridge, Mass: Harvard University Press, 1978.

———. *The Reign of Ideology.* New York: Columbia University Press, 1997.

———. *Does Literary Studies have a Future?* Madison: University of Wisconsin Press, 1999.

Graff, Gerald. *Literature against Itself: Literary Ideas in Modern Society.* Chicago: University of Chicago Press, 1979.

———. *Professing Literature: An Institutional History.* Chicago: University of Chicago Press, 1987.

Gras, Vernon, ed. *European Literary Theory and Practice.* New York: Dell, 1973.

Greenblatt, Stephen J. *Renaissance Self-Fashioning: From More to Shakespeare.* Chicago: University of Chicago Press, 1980.

———. *Shakespearean Negotiations.* Oxford: Clarendon Press, 1988.

———. *Marvellous Possessions: The Wonder of the New World.* Oxford: Clarendon Press, 1991.

———. *Will in the World: How Shakespeare became Shakespeare.* New York: W.W. Norton, 2004.

Greenblatt, Stephen, and Catherine Gallagher. *Practicing New Historicism.* Chicago: University of Chicago Press, 2000.

Harari, Josue V. ed. *Textual Strategies: Perspectives in Post-Structuralist Criticism.* Ithaca, N.Y.: Cornell University Press, 1979.

Harland, Richard. *Superstructuralism: The Philosophy of Structuralism and Poststructuralism.* London: Methuen, 1987.

———. *Literary Theory from Plato to Barthes: An Introductory History.* New York: St Martin's Press, 1999.

Halberg, Robert Van. *Canons.* Chicago: University of Chicago Press, 1984.

Halliday, M.A.K. *Explorations in the Function of Language.* London: Arnold, 1973.

Hartman, Geoffrey. *Beyond Formalism.* New Haven: Yale University Press, 1970.

———. *The Fate of Reading and Other Essays.* Chicago: University of Chicago Press, 1975.

———. *Criticism in the Wilderness: The Study of Literature Today.* New Haven: Yale University Press, 1980.

———. *Scars of the Spirit: The Struggle against Inauthenticity.* New York: Palgrave Macmillan, 2002.

Hawkes, Terence. *Structuralism and Semiotics.* Berkeley: University of California Press, 1977.

Hawthorn, Jeremy. *Unlocking the Text: Fundamental Issues in Literary Theory.* London: Edward Arnold, 1987.

———. *A Concise Glossary of Contemporary Literary Theory.* London: Routledge, 1992.

Hernadi, Paul. *Beyond Genre: New Directions in Literary Classification.* Ithaca: Cornell University Press, 1972.

———. *Cultural Transactions: Nature, Self, Society.* Ithaca: Cornell University Press, 1995.

Hirsch, E.D. *Validity in Interpretation.* New Haven: Yale University Press, 1967.

———. *The Aims of Interpretation.* Chicago: University of Chicago Press, 1976.

———. *The Philosophy of Composition.* Chicago: University of Chicago Press, 1977.

Holland, Norman. *Dynamics of Literary Response.* New York: Oxford University Press, 1968.

———. *5 Readers Reading.* New Haven: Yale University Press, 1975.

Hulme, T.E. *Speculations.* New York: Harcourt, Brace, 1924.

Hyman, Stanley Edgar. *The Armed Vision: A Study in the Methods of Modern Literary Criticism.* 1948. New York: Alfred A. Knopf, Inc., 1955.

Ingarden, Roman. *The Literary Work of Art.* Evanston, IL: Northwestern University Press, 1973.

Iser, Wolfgang. *The Implied Reader.* Baltimore: The John Hopkins University Press, 1974.

———. *The Act of Reading: A Theory of Aesthetic Response.* Baltimore: The Johns Hopkins University Press, 1978.

———. *Prospecting: From Reader Response to Literary Anthroplogy.* Baltimore: Johns Hopkins University Press, 1989.

———. *Range of Interpretation.* New York: Columbia University Press, 2000.

Jacobus, Mary. *Reading Woman: Essays in Feminist Criticism.* London: Methuen, 1986.

———, ed. *Women Writing and Writing About Women.* London: Croom Helm, 1979.

Jakobson, Roman. *Fundamentals of Language.* The Hague: Mouton, 1956.

———. *Selected Writings.* The Hague: Mouton, 1971.

———. *Main Trends in the Science of Language.* New York: Harper & Row, 1974.

———. *Language in Literature.* Cambridge, Mass: Harvard University Press, 1987.

Jameson, Fredric. *The Prison-House of Language: A Critical Account of Structuralism and Russian Formalism.* Princeton: Princeton University Press, 1972.

———. *The Political Unconscious: Narrative as a Socially Symbolic Act.* Ithaca: Cornell University Press, 1981.

———. *Marxism and Form.* Princeton: Princeton University Press, 1971.

———. *Postmodernism or the Cultural Logic of Late Capitalism.* Durham: Duke University Press, 1990.

———. *Singular Modernity: Essay on the Ontology of the Present.* London: Verso, 2002.

JanMohamed, Abdul. *Manichean Aesthetics: The Politics of Literature in Colonial Africa.* Amherst: University of Massachusetts Press, 1983.

JanMohamed, Abdul, and David Lloyd. *The Nature and Context of Minority Discourse.* New York: Oxford University Press, 1990.

Jauss, Hans-Robert. *Toward an Aesthetic of Reception.* Minneapolis: University of Minnesota Press, 1982.

Johnson, Barbara. *The Critical Difference: Essays in the Contemporary Rhetoric of Reading.* Baltimore: The Johns Hopkins University Press, 1980.

———. *A World of Difference.* Baltimore: The Johns Hopkins University Press, 1987.

———. *The Wake of Deconstruction.* Oxford: Blackwell, 1994.

———. *Feminist Difference: Literature, Psychoanalysis, Race and Gender.* Cambridge, Mass.: Harvard University Press, 1998.

Jones, Ernest. *Hamlet and Oedipus: A Classic Study in the Psychoanalysis of Literature.* New York: Anchor Books, 1954.

Juhl, P.D. *Interpretation: An Essay on the Philosophy of Literary Criticism.* Princeton: Princeton University Press, 1980.

Kavanagh, James H. *Alternative Shakespeares.* London: Methuen, 1985.

Kermode, Frank. *The Sense of an Ending.* Oxford: Oxford University Press, 1967.

———. *The Sense of an Ending.* Oxford: Oxford University Press, 1967.

———. *The Genesis of Secrecy.* Cambridge, Mass.: Harvard University Press, 1979.

———. *The Art of Telling: Essays on Fiction.* Cambridge: Harvard University Press, 1983.

———. *Pleasure and Change: The Aesthetics of Canon.* Ed. Robert Alter. New York: Oxford University Press, 2004.

Krieger, Murray. *The New Apologists for Poetry.* Minneapolis: University of Minnesota Press, 1956.

———. *Theory of Criticism: A Tradition and its System.* Baltimore: The Johns Hopkins University Press, 1976.

———, ed. *Directions for Criticism: Structuralism and its Alternatives.* Madison: Wisconsin University Press, 1977.

———, ed. *The Aims of Interpretation: Subject/Text/History.* New York: Columbia University Press, 1987.

———. *Words about Words about Words: Theory, Criticism and Literary Text.* Baltimore: The Johns Hopkins University Press, 1988.

———. *The Institution of Theory.* Baltimore: Johns Hopkins University Press, 1994.

Kristeva, Julia, et.al. *Essays in Semiotics.* The Hague: Mouton, 1971.

———. *Desire in Language: A Semiotic Approach to Literature and Art.* New York: Columbia University Press, 1980.

———. *The Powers and Limits of Psychoanalysis.* Trans. Jeanine Herman. New York: Columbia University Press, 2002.

Lacan, Jacques. *Ecrits: A Selection.* Trans. Alan Sheridan. New York: W.W. Norton, 1977.

———. *The Four Fundamental Concepts of Psychoanalysis.* Trans. Alan Sheridan. New York: W.W. Norton, 1978.

———. *On Feminine Sexuality: The Limits of Love and Knowledge.* Trans. Bruce Fink. New York: Norton, 1998.

Lane, Michael, ed. *Structuralism: A Reader.* London: Cape, 1970.

———. *Introduction to Structuralism.* New York: Harper Torchbooks, 1972.

Langbaum, Robert. *The Poetry of Experience: The Dramatic Monologue of Experience in Modern Literary Tradition.* Chicago: University of Chicago Press, 1972.

Lanser, Susan. *The Narrative Act: Point of View in Fiction.* Princeton: Princeton University Press, 1981.

———. *Fictions of Authority: Women Writers and Narrative Voice.* Ithaca: Cornell University Press, 1992.

Laplanche, J. and J.B. Pontalis. *The Language of Psychoanalysis.* London: Hogarth Press, 1973.

Leavis, F.R. *Education and the University: A Sketch for an "English School."* London: Chatto and Windus, 1943.

———. *The Common Pursuit.* London: Peregrine Books, 1962.

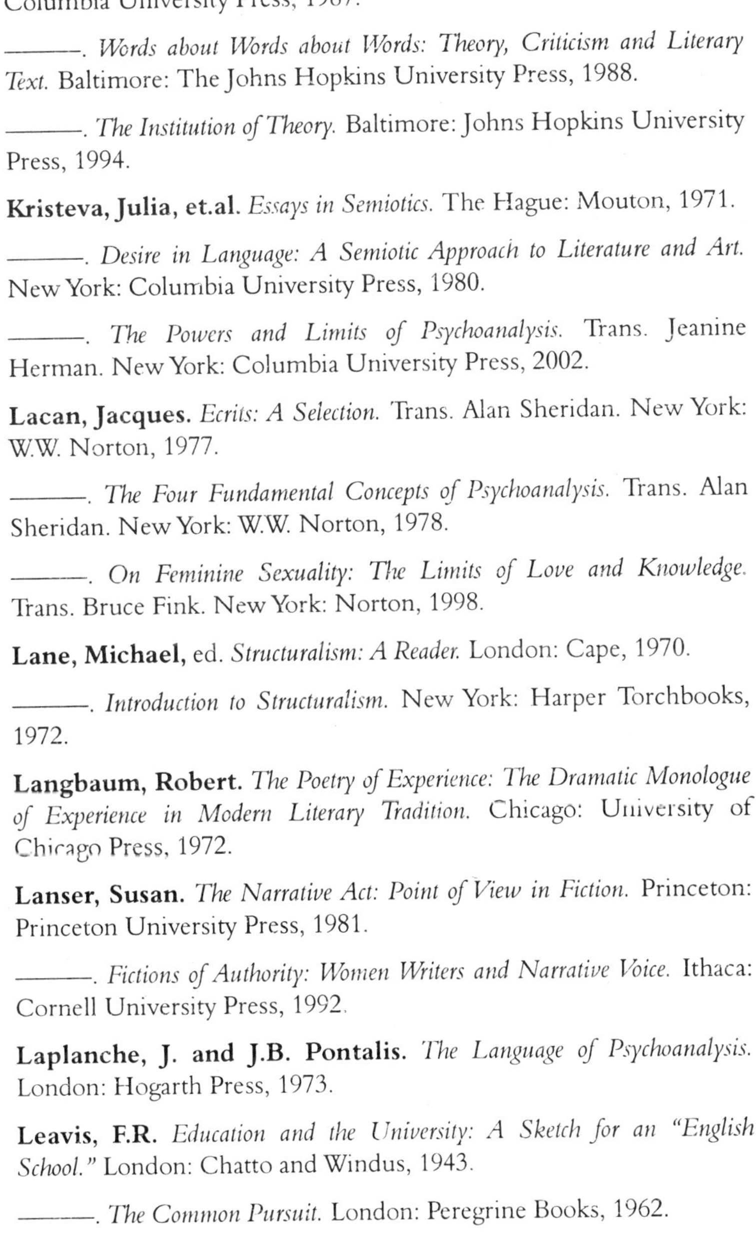

———, ed. *A Selection from Scrutiny*. 2 vols. Cambridge: Cambridge University Press, 1968.

———. *The Living Principle: English as a Discipline of Thought*. London: Chatto and Windus, 1975.

Leitch, Vincent B. *Deconstructive Criticism: An Advanced Introduction.* New York: Columbia University Press, 1983.

———. *American Literary Criticism: From the Thirties to the Eighties.* New York: Columbia University Press, 1987.

———. *Cultural Criticism, Literary Theory, Poststructuralism.* New York: Columbia University Press, 1992.

Lemon, Lee. T., and Marion J. Reis, eds. *Russian Formalist Criticism: Four Essays.* Lincoln: University of Nebraska Press, 1965.

Lentricchia, Frank. *After the New Criticism.* Chicago: University of Chicago Press, 1980.

Lentricchia, Frank, and Thomas McLaughlin, eds. *Critical Terms for Literary Study.* Chicago: University of Chicago Press, 1990.

Lentricchia, Frank, and Andrew DuBois, eds. *Close Reading: The Reader.* Durham, NC.: Duke University Press, 2003.

Lesser, Simon. *Fiction and the Unconscious.* Chicago: University of Chicago Press, 1957.

Levi-Strauss, Claude. *Structural Anthropology.* Tr. C. Jacobson and B.G. Shoepf. London: Allen Lane, 1968.

———. *Myth and Meaning.* New York: Schocken Books, 1977.

———. *The Savage Mind.* Chicago: University of Chicago Press, 1966.

Lodge, David. *Working with Structuralism* Boston: Routledge & Kegan Paul, 1981.

———, ed. *Modern Criticism and Theory: A Reader.* London: Longman, 1988.

———. *After Bakhtin: Essays on Fiction and Criticism.* London: Routledge, 1990.

———. *Author, Author.* New York: Viking, 2004.

Lovejoy, A.O. *The Great Chain of Being: A Study in the History of an Idea.* Cambridge, Mass: Harvard University Press, 1936.

———. *Essays in the History of Ideas.* Baltimore: Johns Hopkins University Press, 1948.

Lucas, F.L. *Tragedy: Serious Drama in Relation to Aristotle's Poetics.* London; Virginia Woolf, 1927.

Lukacs, George. *History and Class Consciousness: Studies in Marxist Dialectics.* Trans. Rodney Livingstone. Cambridge: MIT Press, 1971.

Lyotard, Jean-Francois. *The Postmodern Condition: A Report on Knowledge.* Minneapolis: University of Minnesota Press, 1984.

———. *Toward the Postmodern.* Ed. Robert Harvey. Atlantic Highlands, N.J.: Humanities Press, 1993.

———. *The Confession of Augustine.* Stanford, Calif.: Stanford University Press, 2000.

Macherey, Pierre. *A Theory of Literary Production.* Trans. Geoffrey Wall. London: Routledge and Kegan Paul, 1978.

Macksey, R., and Eugene Donato, eds. *The Structuralist Controversy.* Baltimore: The Johns Hopkins University Press, 1970.

Macksey, Richard, ed. *Velocities of Change: Critical Essays from MLN.* Baltimore: The Johns Hopkins University Press, 1974.

McLuhan, Marshall. *The Gutenberg Galaxy: The Making of the Technocratic Man.* Toronto: University of Toronto Press, 1962.

———. *Understanding Media: The Extensions of Man.* New York: McGraw-Hill, 1964.

Martin, Wallace. *Recent Theories of Narrative.* Ithaca, NY: Cornell University Press, 1986.

Marx, Karl, and Friedrich Engels. *The German Ideology.* New York: International Publications, 1970.

Medvedev, P.N. and Bakhtin, M.M. 1928. *The Formal Method in Literary Scholarship.* London: The Johns Hopkins University Press, 1978.

Miller, Hillis J, ed. *Aspects of Narrative: English Institute Essays.* New York: Columbia University Press, 1971.

———. *The Ethics of Reading.* New York: Columbia University Press, 1987.

Miller, Nancy. *The Poetics of Gender.* New York: Columbia University Press, 1987.

Millett, Kate. *Sexual Politics.* Garden City, N.Y.: Doubleday, 1970.

Mitchell, W.J.T., ed. *Against Theory: Literary Studies and the New Pragmatism.* Chicago: University of Chicago Press, 1985.

———. *Iconology: Image, Text, Ideology.* Chicago: University of Chicago Press, 1986.

Morrison, Toni. *Playing in the Dark: Whiteness and the American Literary Imagination.* Cambridge, Massachusetts: Harvard University Press, 1992.

Mohanty, Satya P. *Literary Theory and Claims of History.* Oxford: Basil Blackwell, 1989.

Murdoch, Iris. *The Fire and the Sun: Why Plato Banished the Artists.* Oxford: Clarendon Press, 1977.

Nelson, Cary, ed. *Theory in the Classroom.* Urbana-Champaign, Ill.: University of Illinois Press, 1986.

Newton, Judith. *From Panthers to Promise Keepers: Rethinking the Men's Movement.* Lanham, MD: Rowman & Littlefield, 2005.

Newton, Judith, and Deborah Rosenfelt, eds. *Feminist Criticism and Social Change.* New York: Methuen, 1985.

Newton, K.M., ed. *Twentieth Century Literary Theory: A Reader.* London: Macmillan, 1987.

———, ed. *Theory into Practice: A Reader in Modern Literary Criticism.* New York: St Martin's Press, 1992.

Norris, Christopher. *Deconstruction: Theory and Practice.* London: Routledge, 1982.

———. *Derrida.* London: Fontana, 1987.

———. *Epistemology.* London: Continuum, 2005.

O'Connor, William Van. *An Age of Criticism: 1900–1950.* Chicago: H. Regnery Co., 1952.

Olson, Elder. *Aristotle's 'Poetics' and English Literature: A Collection of Critical Essays.* Chicago: University of Chicago Press, 1965.

Ong, Walter J. *The Presence of the Word.* New Haven: Yale University Press, 1967.

———. *Orality and Literacy.* Cambridge: Harvard University Press, 1982.

Parrington, Vernon L. *Main Currents in American Thought: An Interpretation of American Literature from the Beginnings to 1920.* 3 vols. New York: Harcourt, Brace and Co., 1927–1930.

Paz, Octavio. *Claude Levi-Strauss.* Ithaca: Cornell University Press, 1970.

Petrey, Sandy. *Speech Acts and Literary Theory.* London: Routledge, 1990.

Pettit, Philip. *The Concept of Structuralism: A Critical Analysis.* Berkeley: University of California Press, 1975.

Pratt, A. *Archetypal Patterns in Women's Fiction.* Brighton: Harvester Press, 1982.

Pratt, Mary Louise. *Toward a Speech Act Theory of Literary Discourse.* Bloomington: Indiana University Press, 1977.

Preminger, Alex, Frank K. Warnke and O.B. Hardison, eds. *Princeton Encyclopaedia of Poetry and Poetics.* Princeton: Princeton University Press, 1965.

Prince, Gerald. *A Grammar of Stories.* The Hague: Mouton, 1973.

———. *Narratology: The Form and Functioning of Narrative.* New York: Mouton, 1982.

———. *A Dictionary of Narratology.* Lincoln: University of Nebraska Press, 2003.

Propp, Vladimir. *Morphology of the Folktale.* Tr. Laurence Scott. Austin: University of Texas Press, 1970.

Rajnath, ed. *Deconstruction: A Critique.* London: Macmillan, 1989.

Ray, William. *Literary Meaning: From Phenomenology to Deconstruction.* Oxford: Blackwell, 1984.

———. *Logic of Culture: Authority and Identity in the Modern Era.* Malden, MA: Blackwell Publishers, 2001.

Rice, Philip, and Patricia Waugh, eds. *Modern Literary Theory: A Reader.* London: Edward Arnold, 1989.

Rich, Adrienne. *Of Woman Born: Motherhood as Experience and Institution.* New York: Norton, 1976.

Ricoeur, Paul. *The Conflict of Interpretations: Essays in Hermeneutics.* Evanston, IL.: Northwestern University Press, 1974.

———. *The Course of Recognition.* Trans. David Pellaver. Cambridge: Harvard University Press, 2005.

Riffaterre, Michael. *Semiotics of Poetry.* Bloomington: Indiana University Press, 1978.

———. *Text Production.* Trans. Terese Lyons. New York: Columbia University Press, 1983.

Robinson, Lillian. *Sex, Class, and Culture.* Bloomington: Indiana University Press, 1986.

Robey, David, ed. *Structuralism: An Introduction.* London: Oxford University Press, 1973.

Robey, David, and Ann Jefferson. *Modern Literary Theory, a Comparative Introduction.* London: Betsfield, 1982.

Ray, William. *Literary Meaning.* Oxford: Oxford University Press, 1984.

Rorty, Richard. *The Consequences of Pragmatism.* Minneapolis: University of Minnesota Press, 1982.

Rosenblatt, Louise. *The Reader, the Text, the Poem: The Transactional Theory of the Literary Work.* Carbondale: Southern Illinois University Press, 1978.

Ruthven, K.K. *Feminist Literary Studies.* Cambridge: Cambridge University Press, 1984.

———. *Critical Assumptions.* Cambridge: Cambridge University Press, 1979.

Sacks, Sheldon, ed. *On Metaphor.* Chicago: University of Chicago Press, 1979.

Said, Edward. *Beginnings.* New York: Basic Books, 1975.

———. *Orientalism.* New York: Pantheon, 1978.

———. *The World, the Text and the Critic.* Cambridge: Harvard University Press, 1983.

———. *Culture and Imperialism.* New York: Knopf, 1993.

———. *Edward Said: Continuing the Conversation.* Ed. Homi Bhabha. Chicago: University of Chicago Press, 2005.

Saussure, Ferdinand De. *Course in General Linguistics.* Tr. Wade Baskin. New York: The Philosophical Library, 1959. Originally published in French in 1916, this, the most important of Saussure's works, was compiled and edited from students' notes from his course in general linguistics given at Geneva in 1906–7, 1908–9 and 1910–11. Saussure left no text of his lectures.

Scholes, Robert. *Structuralism in Literature: An Introduction.* New Haven: Yale University Press, 1974.

———. *Semiotics and Interpretation.* New Haven: Yale University Press, 1982.

———. *Textual Power: Literary Theory and the Teaching of English.* New Haven: Yale University Press, 1985.

———. *Protocols of Reading.* New Haven: Yale University Press, 1990.

———. *The Crafty Reader.* New Haven: Yale University Press, 2001.

Scholes, Robert, and Robert Kellog. *The Nature of Narrative.* New York: Oxford University Press, 1966.

Schorer, Mark, Josephine Miles and Gordon McKenzie, eds. 1948. *Criticism: The Foundations of Modern Literary Judgment.* New York: Harcourt, Brace and Co., 1958.

Searle, John. *Speech Acts: An Essay in the Philosophy of Language.* Cambridge: Cambridge University Press, 1969.

———. *The Philosophy of Language.* Oxford: Oxford University Press, 1971.

———. *Expression and Meaning: Study in the Theory of Speech Acts.* Cambridge: Cambridge University Press, 1979.

———. *Consciousness and Language.* New York: Cambridge University Press, 2002.

Sebok, Thomas. *Approaches to Semiotics.* The Hague: Mouton, 1964.

———. *The Sign and its Masters.* Austin: University of Texas Press, 1979.

Seldon, Raman, ed. *The Cambridge History of Literary Criticism: From Formalism to Poststructuralism.* Vol. viii. Cambridge: Cambridge University Press, 1995.

Shapiro, Gary, and Alan Sica, eds. *Hermeneutics: Questions and Prospects.* Amherst: University of Massachusetts Press, 1984.

Showalter, Elaine. *Women's Liberation and Literature.* New York: Harcourt Brace Jovanovich, 1971.

———. *A Literature of their Own: British Women Novelists from Bronte to Lessing.* Princeton, N.J.: Princeton University Press, 1977.

———, ed. *Feminist Criticism: Essays on Women, Literature, Theory.* New York: Pantheon, 1985.

———. *Faculty Towers: The Academic Novel and its Discontents.* Philadelphia: University of Philadelphia Press, 2005.

Singleton, Charles. ed. *Interpretation: Theory and Practice.* Baltimore: The Johns Hopkins University Press, 1969.

Skura, Meredith. *The Literary Use of the Psychoanalytic Process.* New Haven: Yale University Press, 1981.

Spacks, P.M. *The Female Imagination.* New York: Knopf, 1975.

Spingarn, Joel. *The New Criticism.* New York: Columbia University Press, 1911.

Spivak, Gayatri. *In Other Worlds.* New York: Routledge, Kegan and Paul, 1987.

———. *The Post-Colonial Critic: Interviews, Strategies, Dialogues.* Ed. Sarah Harasym. London: Routledge, 1990.

———. *Outside in the Teaching Machine.* New York: Routledge, 1993.

———. *Death of a Discipline.* New York: Columbia University Press, 2003.

Stallman, Robert Wooster, ed. *Critiques and Essays in Criticism: 1920–1948.* New York: The Ronald Press Co., 1949.

Steiner, George. *The Death of Tragedy.* London: Faber and Faber, 1961.

———. *Language of Silence: Essays on Language, Literature and the Inhuman.* New York: Athenaeum, 1967.

———. *After Babel: Aspects of Language and Translation.* London: Oxford University Press, 1975.

———. *What is Comparative Literature?* Oxford: Oxford University Press, 1995.

Strurrock, John, ed. *Structuralism and Since: From Levi Strauss to Derrida.* New York: Oxford University Press, 1979.

Sutton, Walter. *Modern American Criticism.* Englewood Cliffs, New Jersey: Prentice Hall, Inc., 1963.

Suleiman, Susan Rubin, ed. *The Female Body in Western Culture: Contemporary Perspectives.* Cambridge, Mass.: Harvard University Press, 1986.

Suleiman, Susan, and Inge Crosman, eds. *The Reader in the Text: Essays on Audience and Interpretation.* Princeton, N.J.: Princeton University Press, 1980.

Tillyard, E.M.W. *The Elizabethan World Picture.* New York: Macmillan, 1944.

Todorov, Tzvetan. *The Poetics of Prose.* Ithaca, N.Y.: Cornell University Press, 1977.

———. *Introduction to Poetics.* Minneapolis: University of Minnesota Press, 1981.

———. *Literature and Its Theorists: A Personal View of Twentieth-Century Criticism.* Trans. Catherine Porter. Ithaca: Cornell University Press, 1988

———. *Imperfect Garden: The Legacy of Humanism.* Trans. Carol Cosman. Princeton, N.J.: Princeton University Press, 2002.

———. *Hope and Memory: Lessons from Twentieth Century.* Trans. David Belos. Princeton, N.J.: Princeton University Press, 2003.

Tompkins, Jane P, ed. *Reader-Response Criticism: From Formalism to Post-Structuralism.* Baltimore: The Johns Hopkins University Press, 1980.

Veeser, H. Aram, ed. *The New Historicism.* New York: Routledge, 1989.

———, ed. *The New Historicism Reader.* New York: Routledge, 1994.

Webster, Roger. *Studying Literary Theory: An Introduction.* London: Edward Arnold, 1990.

Weeden, Chris. *Feminist Practice and Post-Structuralist Theory.* Oxford: Basil Blackwell, 1987.

Wellek, René. *Concepts of Criticism.* New Haven: Yale University Press, 1963.

———. *The Attack on Literature and other Essays.* Chapel Hill: University of North Carolina Press, 1982.

———. *A History of Modern Criticism: 1750–1950* in 8 vols. Vol. I: *The Later Eighteenth Century* (1955); Vol. II: *The Romantic Age* (1955); Vol. III: *The Age of Transition* (1966); Vol. IV: *The Later Nineteenth Century* (1966); Vol. V: *English Criticism, 1900–1950* (1986); Vol. VI: *American Criticism, 1900–1950* (1986); Vol. VII: *German, Russian and East European Criticism, 1900–1950* (1991); and Vol. VIII: *French, Italian and Spanish Criticism, 1900–1950.* (1992).

Wellek, René, and Austin Warren. *Theory of Literature.* New York: Harcourt, Brace and Co., 1949.

Wells, Susan. *The Dialectics of Representation.* Baltimore: The Johns Hopkins University Press, 1985.

White, Hayden. *The Content of the Form: Narrative Discourse and Historical Representation.* Baltimore: The Johns Hopkins University Press, 1973.

———. *Tropics of Discourse: Essays in Cultural Criticism.* Baltimore: The Johns Hopkins University Press, 1978.

Widdowson, H.G. *Stylistics and the Teaching of Literature.* London: Longman, 1975.

———. *Text, Context and Pretext: Critical Issues in Discourse Analysis.* Malden, MA: Blackwell Publishers, 2004.

Williams, Raymond. *Culture and Society, 1780–1950.* London: Chatto and Windus, 1958.

———. *Marxism and Literature.* Oxford: Oxford University Press, 1977.

Wilson, Edmund. *The Wound and the Bow.* Cambridge, Mass: Houghton Mifflin Co., 1941.

Wimsatt, William K. *The Verbal Icon: Studies in the Meaning of Poetry.* Lexington, Ky: University of Kentucky Press, 1954.

Winters, Yvor. *The Function of Criticism: Problems and Exercises.* Denver: A. Swallow, 1957.

Woolf, Virginia. *A Room of One's Own.* Harmondsworth: Penguin, 1985.

———. *Women and Writing*. London: The Women's Press, 1979.

Wright, Elizabeth. *Psychoanalytic Criticism: Theory in Practice.* London: Methuen, 1984.

———, ed. *Coming out of Feminism.* Oxford: Blackwell Publishers, 1998.

Young, Robert, ed. *Untying the Text: A Poststructuralist Reader.* Boston: Routledge and Kegan Paul, 1981.

———. *White Mythologies: Writing, History and the West.* London: Routledge, 1990.

———. *Colonial Desire: Hybridity in Theory, Culture and Race.* London: Routledge, 1995.

———. *Postcolonialism.* Oxford: Oxford University Press, 2003.

Zabel, Morton D, ed. *Literary Opinion in America.* 1937. 2 vols. New York: Harper and Brothers, 1937.

Periodicals

Critical Inquiry. Published by the University of Chicago Press.

Critique. Published by Minuit.

Diacritics. Published by the Johns Hopkins University Press, edited by the Department of Romance Studies, Cornell University, instrumental in promoting continental criticism in the English-speaking world.

New Literary History. Published by the Johns Hopkins University Press, edited by the Department of English, University of Virginia. Brings together some of the best essays in criticism in Europe and in the US and England.

Yale French Studies. Published by the Department of French at Yale. Discusses issues and problems in criticism.

Index